Middle School 2-2

기말고사 완벽대비

KB087545

적중100

영어 기출 문제집

중2

금성 | 최인철

Best Collection

구성과 특징

교과서의 주요 학습 내용을 중심으로 학습 영역별 특성에 맞춰 단계별로 다양한 학습 기회를 제공하여 단원별 학습능력 평가는 물론 중간 및 기말고사 시험 등에 완벽하게 대비할 수 있도록 내용을 구성

Words & Expressions

Step1 Key Words 단원별 핵심 단어 설명 및 풀이
Key Expression 단원별 핵심 숙어 및 관용어 설명
Word Power 반대 또는 비슷한 뜻 단어 배우기
English Dictionary 영어로 배우는 영어 단어

Step2 실력평가 단원별 수시평가 대비 주관식, 객관식 문제풀이

Step3 서술형 대비 학업성취도 및 수행능력평가 대비 서술형 문제풀이

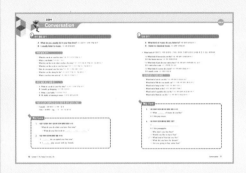

Conversation

Step1 핵심 의사소통 의사소통에 필요한 주요 표현 방법 요약
핵심 Check 기본적인 표현 방법 및 활용능력 확인

Step2 대화문 익히기 상황에 따른 대화문 활용 및 연습

Step3 기본평가 시험대비 기초 학습 능력 평가

Step4 실력평가 단원별 수시평가 대비 주관식, 객관식 문제풀이

Step5 서술형 대비 학업성취도 및 수행능력평가 대비 서술형 문제풀이

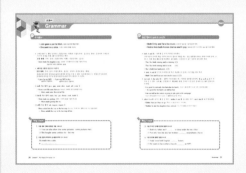

Grammar

Step1 주요 문법 단원별 주요 문법 사항과 예문을 알기 쉽게 설명
핵심 Check 기본 문법사항에 대한 이해 여부 확인

Step2 기본평가 시험대비 기초 학습 능력 평가

Step3 실력평가 단원별 수시평가 대비 주관식, 객관식 문제풀이

Step4 서술형 대비 학업성취도 및 수행능력평가 대비 서술형 문제풀이

Reading

Step1 구문 분석 단원별로 제시된 문장에 대한 구문별 분석과 내용 설명
확인문제 문장에 대한 기본적인 이해와 인지능력 확인

Step2 확인학습A 빈칸 채우기를 통한 문장 완성 능력 확인

Step3 확인학습B 제시된 우리말을 영어로 완성하여 작문 능력 키우기

Step4 실력평가 단원별 수시평가 대비 주관식, 객관식 문제풀이

Step5 서술형 대비 학업성취도 및 수행능력평가 대비 서술형 문제풀이
교과서 구석구석 교과서에 나오는 기타 문장까지 완벽 학습

Composition

|영역별 핵심문제|

단어 및 어휘, 대화문, 문법, 독해 등 각 영역별 기출문제의 출제 유형을 분석하여 실전에 대비하고 연습할 수 있도록 문제를 배열

|서술형 실전 및 창의사고력 문제|

학교 시험에서 점차 늘어나는 서술형 시험에 집중 대비하고 고득점을 취득하는데 만전을 기하기 위한 학습 코너

|단원별 예상문제|

기출문제를 분석한 후 새로운 시험 출제 경향을 더하여 새롭게 출제될 수 있는 문제를 포함하여 시험에 완벽하게 대비할 수 있도록 준비

|단원별 모의고사|

영역별, 단계별 학습을 모두 마친 후 실전 연습을 위한 모의고사

INSIGHT
on the textbook

교과서 파헤치기

- 단어Test1~2 영어 단어 우리말 쓰기와 우리말을 영어 단어로 쓰기
- 대화문Test1~2 대화문 빈칸 완성 및 전체 대화문 쓰기
- 본문Test1~5 빈칸 완성, 우리말 쓰기, 문장 배열연습, 영어 작문하기 복습 등 단계별 반복 학습을 통해 교과서 지문에 대한 완벽한 습득
- 구석구석지문Test1~2 지문 빈칸 완성 및 전문 영어로 쓰기

Contents

Lesson 7

Understanding Differences Makes a Difference

🎤 의사소통 기능

- 알고 있음 표현하기
  I heard that it will rain tomorrow.
- 주제 소개하기
  I'd like to tell you about a website called "Culture Shock."

🎤 언어 형식

- 목적격 관계대명사
  This is the website (**that**) you are looking for.
- 관계대명사 what
  I'm sure **what** she really meant was "yes."

Words & Expressions

교과서

Key Words

- □ **advice**[ədváis] 명 충고, 조언
- □ **age**[eidʒ] 명 나이
- □ **appointment**[əpɔ́intmənt] 명 약속
- □ **bow**[bau] 동 (고개를) 숙이다, 인사하다
- □ **calm**[kɑ:m] 형 침착한 동 진정시키다
- □ **capital**[kǽpətl] 명 수도
- □ **carve**[kɑ:rv] 동 새기다, 조각하다
- □ **clothing**[klóuðiŋ] 명 옷, 의복
- □ **complain**[kəmpléin] 동 불평하다
- □ **confident**[kɑ́nfədənt] 형 자신감 있는
- □ **confuse**[kənfjú:z] 동 혼동하다
- □ **costume**[kɑ́stju:m] 명 의상
- □ **country**[kʌ́ntri] 명 나라, 국가, 시골
- □ **difference**[dífərəns] 명 차이, 다름
- □ **German**[dʒə́:rmən] 형 독일의 명 독일어, 독일인
- □ **greet**[gri:t] 동 인사하다
- □ **guest**[gest] 명 손님, 하객
- □ **host**[houst] 명 주인, 주최자
- □ **invite**[inváit] 동 초대하다
- □ **Kenyan**[kénjən] 형 케냐의
- □ **language**[lǽŋgwidʒ] 명 언어
- □ **manner**[mǽnər] 명 예의, 예절
- □ **nod**[nɑd] 동 고개를 끄덕이다

- □ **perfect**[pə́:rfikt] 형 완벽한, 완전한
- □ **plate**[pleit] 명 접시
- □ **prepare**[pripέər] 동 준비하다
- □ **prize**[praiz] 명 상
- □ **promise**[prɑ́mis] 동 약속하다 명 약속
- □ **pumpkin**[pʌ́mpkin] 명 호박
- □ **punctual**[pʌ́ŋktʃuəl] 형 시간을 지키는
- □ **recommend**[rèkəménd] 동 추천하다
- □ **respect**[rispékt] 동 존중하다 명 존중
- □ **rude**[ru:d] 형 무례한, 예의 없는
- □ **scary**[skέəri] 형 무서운
- □ **set**[set] 동 정하다, 맞추다
- □ **shock**[ʃɑk] 명 충격(적인 일)
- □ **social studies** 사회(과목)
- □ **stick**[stik] 동 붙이다
- □ **thankful**[θǽŋkfəl] 형 감사하는, 고마워하는
- □ **thin**[θin] 형 마른, 얇은
- □ **tower**[táuər] 명 탑
- □ **traditional**[trədíʃənl] 형 전통의
- □ **turkey**[tə́:rki] 명 칠면조
- □ **unbelievable**[ənbilívəbəl] 형 믿기 어려운
- □ **upset**[ʌ́pset] 형 속상한, 화난
- □ **wave**[weiv] 명 파도 동 손을 흔들다

Key Expressions

- □ **be interested in** ~에 관심을 갖다
- □ **call upon** ~을 요청하다, ~을 부탁하다
- □ **for free** 무료로
- □ **get rid of** ~을 제거하다, ~을 없애다
- □ **have trouble -ing** ~하는 데 어려움을 겪다
- □ **I'd like to** ~ ~하고 싶다

- □ **make a difference** 변화를 일으키다
- □ **on time** 정시에
- □ **shake hands** 악수하다
- □ **sign up** 등록하다, 신청하다
- □ **take a look at** ~을 보다
- □ **take part in** ~에 참가하다

Word Power

※ 서로 반대되는 뜻을 가진 어휘

□ **thin** 얇은 ↔ **thick** 두꺼운

□ **different** 다른 ↔ **same** 같은

□ **host** 주인, 주최자 ↔ **guest** 손님

□ **ancient** 고대의 ↔ **modern** 현대의

□ **rude** 무례한 ↔ **polite** 예의바른

□ **punctual** 시간을 지키는 ↔ **unpunctual** 시간을 지키지 않는

□ **believable** 믿을 수 있는 ↔ **unbelievable** 믿을 수 없는

□ **perfect** 완벽한 ↔ **imperfect** 불완전한

English Dictionary

□ **advice** 조언, 충고
→ an opinion or a suggestion about what somebody should do in a particular situation
누군가가 특정한 상황에서 해야 하는 것에 대한 의견이나 제안

□ **appointment** 약속
→ a formal arrangement to meet or visit somebody at a particular time, especially for a reason connected with their work
특히 그들의 일과 관련한 이유로 누군가를 특정한 시간에 만나거나 방문하기로 한 공식적인 합의

□ **bow** 고개를 숙이다
→ to move your head or the top half of your body forwards and downwards as a sign of respect or to say hello or goodbye
존경의 표시로서 당신의 머리나 신체의 윗부분을 앞으로 그리고 아래로 움직이거나 인사를 하다

□ **capital** 수도
→ the most important town or city of a country, usually where the central government operates from
보통 중앙 정부가 운영되는 한 국가의 가장 중요한 마을이나 도시

□ **carve** 조각하다
→ to make objects, patterns, etc. by cutting away material from wood or stone
나무나 돌에서 재료를 깎아 내어 물건이나 양식을 만들다

□ **complain** 불평하다
→ to say that you are annoyed, unhappy or not satisfied about somebody/something
당신이 누군가나 무언가에 화나거나 불행하거나 만족하지 못하다고 말하다

□ **guest** 손님
→ a person that you have invited to your house or to a particular event that you are paying for
당신이 당신의 집이나 당신이 돈을 지불하는 특정한 행사에 초대하는 사람

□ **host** 주인, 주최자
→ a person who invites guests to a meal, a party, etc. or who has people staying at their house
식사나 파티 등에 손님을 초대하거나 사람들을 집에 머물게 하는 사람

□ **prize** 상
→ an award that is given to a person who wins a competition, race, etc. or who does very good work
대회, 경주 등에서 우승하거나 매우 좋은 일을 하는 사람에게 주어지는 상

□ **respect** 존중
→ a feeling of admiration for somebody/something because of their good qualities or achievements
그들의 좋은 자질들 또는 성취들로 인한 누군가나 무언가에 대한 존경의 감정

□ **rude** 예의 없는
→ having or showing a lack of respect for other people and their feelings
다른 사람들과 그들의 감정에 대한 존경의 부족함을 갖거나 보여주는

□ **shock** 충격
→ a strong feeling of surprise as a result of something happening, especially something unpleasant; the event that causes this feeling
특히 불쾌한 어떤 것으로, 일어나는 것에 대한 결과로서 놀람의 강한 감성; 이러한 감성을 야기하는 사건

□ **recommend** 추천하다
→ to tell somebody that something is good or useful, or that somebody would be suitable for a particular job, etc.
누군가에게 무언가가 좋거나 유용하다고, 또는 누군가가 특정한 직업 등에 알맞다고 말하다

□ **traditional** 전통적인
→ being part of the beliefs, customs or way of life of a particular group of people, that have not changed for a long time
오랫동안 바뀌지 않은 특정한 집단의 사람들의 믿음, 관습 또는 생활방식의 일부가 되는

서답형

01 다음 짝지어진 단어의 관계가 같도록 빈칸에 알맞은 말을 쓰시오.

teacher : student = _____ : guest

02 다음 영영풀이가 가리키는 것을 고르시오.

to say that you are annoyed, unhappy or not satisfied about somebody/something

① recommend ② complain
③ invite ④ nod
⑤ carve

중요

03 다음 중 밑줄 친 부분의 뜻풀이가 바르지 <u>않은</u> 것은?

① Would you give me some <u>advice</u> to solve the problem? 조언
② In art class, we carved the <u>pumpkins</u> for the Halloween. 호박
③ I have the greatest <u>respect</u> for your father. 존경
④ We should not be <u>rude</u> to each other. 예의 바른
⑤ I want to introduce Korean <u>traditional</u> food to the world. 전통적인

04 다음 우리말과 같은 뜻이 되도록 빈칸에 알맞은 말을 쓰시오. (주어진 철자로 시작할 것.)

(1) 나는 네 결정을 존중한다.
➡ I r_____ your decision.
(2) 영화 보러 갈 날짜를 정하자.
➡ Let's s_____ a date to go to the movies.
(3) 그는 벽에 사진들을 붙였다.
➡ He s_____ the photos on the wall.

서답형

05 다음 문장의 빈칸에 들어갈 말을 〈보기〉에서 골라 쓰시오.

┤ 보기 ├
Kenyan / manners / languages / perfect / recommend

(1) How many _____ can you speak?
(2) My mother told me to have good _____.
(3) I have a nice _____ friend.
(4) She got a _____ score on the test.
(5) Can you _____ a good book?

06 다음 주어진 문장의 밑줄 친 wave와 같은 의미로 쓰인 것은?

Why did you <u>wave</u> your hands at Jimin?

① Huge <u>waves</u> were breaking onto the shore.
② I went to the beach to ride the <u>waves</u>.
③ The <u>waves</u> are too high for swimming.
④ The <u>waves</u> were driving the ship to the shore.
⑤ Mina <u>waved</u> her handkerchief at her parents.

서답형

07 다음 주어진 우리말과 일치하도록 주어진 단어를 모두 배열하여 영작하시오.

너는 정시에 학교에 도착해야 한다.
(at / on / you / arrive / time / should / school

➡ _____

01 다음 짝지어진 단어의 관계가 같도록 빈칸에 알맞은 말을 쓰시오.

> thin : thick = polite : _____

02 다음 문장의 빈칸에 들어갈 말을 〈보기〉에서 골라 쓰시오.

┌─ 보기 ┐
unbelievable / traditional / invite /
upset / waved
└──────────────────────┘

(1) Gimchi is a _____ Korean food.

(2) His story was _____.

(3) Tell me why you're so _____.

(4) He _____ his hand at me.

(5) Who did you _____ to your birthday party?

03 다음 우리말에 맞게 빈칸에 알맞은 말을 쓰시오.

(1) 그녀는 우리에게 미소 지으며 인사했다.
➡ She _____ us with a smile.

(2) 그는 오늘밤 파티의 주최자이다.
➡ He is the _____ of the party tonight.

(3) 그녀는 대답을 들었을 때, 고개를 끄덕였다.
➡ When she heard the answer, she _____ her head.

04 다음 우리말을 주어진 단어를 이용하여 영작하시오.

(1) 서울은 한국의 수도이다. (of, city)
➡ _____

(2) Tom은 나무에 그의 이름을 새겼다. (on, carve)
➡ _____

(3) 그녀는 훌륭한 의상 디자이너이다. (great, dress)
➡ _____

(4) 그는 자기 나이보다 젊어 보인다. (younger)
➡ _____

05 우리말과 일치하도록 주어진 어구를 모두 배열하여 영작하시오.

(1) 한국 사람들은 종종 머리를 숙이며 악수를 한다.
(often / bowing / hands / Koreans / shake / their head)
➡ _____

(2) 마을 사람들은 마을의 문제를 해결하기 위해 그에게 부탁하였다.
(to / the villagers / him / called / problem / the town's / upon / solve)
➡ _____
_____

(3) 나는 요통 때문에 걷는 데 어려움을 겪어요.
(walking / backache / of / I / have / my / trouble / because)
➡ _____

(4) 한국에 있는 전통 석탑들을 소개해 줄래?
(you / towers / Korea / would / the / stone / traditional / introduce / in)
➡ _____
_____

Conversation

1 알고 있음 표현하기

I heard that it will rain tomorrow. (나는 내일 비가 올 것이라고 들었다.)

■ 알고 있는지 물을 때는 'Do you hear about ~?' 등의 표현을 이용하여 질문할 수 있으며 자신이 알고 있음을 나타내기 위해 'I heard (about / that) ~' 등의 표현을 사용하여 대답할 수 있다.

알고 있음 표현하기

- I heard that Christmas is in the summer in Australia. (나는 호주에서는 크리스마스가 여름이라고 들었다.)
- I have heard that drinking water is good for your health. (나는 물을 마시는 것이 건강에 좋다고 들었다.)
- I know about the English speaking contest. (나는 영어 말하기 대회에 대해 알고 있다.)
- I learned that Jane will leave tomorrow. (나는 Jane이 내일 떠날 것이라는 것을 알았다.)
- I've been told that "8" is a lucky number in China. (나는 8이 중국에서 행운의 숫자라는 것을 들었다.)

알고 있는지 묻기

- Did you hear about the weather? (일기예보를 들었니?)
- Have you heard about the new teacher? (새로 오신 선생님에 대해 들어 봤니?)
- Do you know how to make a paper bird? (너는 종이 새를 어떻게 만드는지 아니?)
- You know what I'm saying, don't you? (너는 내가 말하는 것을 알지, 그렇지?)
- Are you aware of the dangers of caffeine? (카페인의 위험에 대해 알고 있니?)

핵심 Check

1. 다음 주어진 우리말과 일치하도록 괄호 안에서 알맞은 말을 고르시오.

   A: I (heard / told) that Leonardo Da Vinci was once a cook.

   (나는 레오나르도 다빈치가 한 때 요리사였다고 들었어.)

   B: Really? That's interesting. (정말? 그거 흥미롭구나.)

2. 다음 주어진 우리말과 일치하도록 괄호 안에서 알맞은 말을 고르시오.

   A: I've been (heard / told) that Jimin is going to take part in the math contest.

   (나는 지민이가 수학 대회에 참가할 것이라고 들었어.)

   B: Great! I (know / aware) he is good at math. (잘됐다! 나는 그가 수학을 잘한다는 것을 알아.)

② 주제 소개하기

I'd like to tell you about a website called "Culture Shock."
("Culture Shock."이라고 불리는 웹 사이트에 대해 말해 주고 싶어.)

■ 'I'd like to tell you about ~' 등의 표현을 사용하여 주제를 소개할 수 있다.

주제 소개하기

- Let me tell you about *hanbok*. (한복에 대해 이야기할게.)
- I'd like to tell you about the Eiffel Tower. (에펠탑에 대해 이야기하고 싶어.)
- I want to tell you about the Statue of Liberty. (자유의 여신상에 대해 이야기하고 싶어.)
- I'd like to tell you something important. (중요한 무언가를 이야기해 줄게.)
- Now, let's talk about traditional Korean food. (이제, 전통적인 한국 음식에 대해 이야기하자.)
- I'd like to say something about this place. (이곳에 대해 이야기할 게 있어요.)
- I'd like to tell you what happened to me yesterday. (어제 내게 무슨 일이 일어났는지 말하고 싶어.)

핵심 Check

3. 다음 주어진 우리말과 일치하도록 빈칸에 알맞은 말을 쓰시오.

   A: I'd like to _____ _____ _____ about the Taj Mahal.
   (나는 타지마할에 대해 네게 무언가 말해 주고 싶어.)

   B: _____ is it? (무엇인데?)

   A: A king built it for his dead wife. (어떤 왕이 죽은 아내를 위해 그것을 지었대.)

4. 다음 주어진 우리말과 일치하도록 빈칸에 알맞은 말을 쓰시오.

   A: Let _____ _____ _____ about a great musical that I saw last weekend.
   (지난 주말에 내가 본 대단한 뮤지컬에 대해 이야기해 줄게.)

   B: What is the title of the musical? (뮤지컬 제목이 뭐야?)

Everyday English 1 B Listening Activity

Mina: Alex, do you have some time?

Alex: Yes, Mina, what is it?

Mina: ❶I heard that you went to Spain this summer!

Alex: Yes, I ❷went on a family trip.

Mina: Can you tell me more about your trip? I'm thinking of visiting Spain this winter.

Alex: I see. I think Spain is a really nice country to visit. ❸There are many interesting places.

Mina: Where do you recommend that I go?

Alex: I recommend ❹visiting the Prado Museum in Madrid. It's one of the most famous museums in the world.

Mina: Thanks for the help!

Mina: Alex, 너 시간 좀 있니?
Alex: 응, 미나야. 무슨 일인데?
Mina: 네가 이번 여름에 스페인에 갔다는 얘기를 들었어!
Alex: 응, 가족 여행을 갔었어.
Mina: 너의 여행에 대해 더 말해 줄 수 있니? 나도 이번 겨울에 스페인을 방문해 보려고 생각 중이야.
Alex: 알겠어. 나는 스페인이 방문하기에 정말 좋은 나라라고 생각해. 흥미로운 장소들이 많아.
Mina: 내가 갈 만한 장소로 어디를 추천하니?
Alex: 나는 Madrid에 있는 Prado 박물관을 추천해. 세계에서 가장 유명한 박물관 중 하나야.
Mina: 도와줘서 고마워.

❶ 알고 있음을 나타내는 표현으로 'I've been told that you went to Spain this summer.'로 바꾸어 쓸 수 있다.
❷ go on a trip: 여행을 가다
❸ There are 다음에는 복수 명사가 이어진다.
❹ recommend는 '추천하다'를 뜻하며 명사절 또는 동명사구를 목적어로 취한다.

Check(√) True or False

(1) Alex visited the Prado Museum in Madrid.   T ☐ F ☐

(2) Mina went on a family trip to Spain.   T ☐ F ☐

Everyday English 2 B Listening Activity

Tina: Hello, everyone. My name is Tina and I'm a travel writer. Today, ❶I'd like to tell you an important lesson that I learned ❷while traveling. When I first visited Korea, I thought Koreans were ❸rude ❹because many people asked me my age. However, I later found out that this was ❹because of their culture. Koreans use language differently to people who are older than them, so they need to know the other person's age. This experience has taught me the importance of learning and understanding other cultures.

Tina: 안녕, 모두들. 내 이름은 Tina이고 나는 여행 작가야. 오늘 나는 너희들에게 내가 여행에서 배운 중요한 교훈에 대해 말해 주고 싶어. 내가 처음 한국에 방문했을 때, 나는 많은 한국인들이 내 나이를 물었기 때문에 무례하다고 생각했어. 그런데 나중에 나는 이것이 그들의 문화 때문이라는 것을 알았어. 한국인들은 그들보다 나이가 많은 사람들에게는 언어를 다르게 쓰는데, 그래서 다른 사람들의 나이를 알 필요가 있는 거였어. 이 경험은 나에게 다른 문화를 배우고 이해하는 것의 중요성을 알게 해 주었어.

❶ 'I'd like to tell you 〜'는 주제를 소개하는 표현으로 'Let me tell you about 〜' 등으로 바꾸어 쓸 수 있다.
❷ while+〜ing: 〜하는 동안
❸ rude: 무례한
❹ because는 '주어+동사'가 이어지지만 'because of'는 명사(구)가 이어진다.

Check(√) True or False

(3) Koreans use language differently according to the age.   T ☐ F ☐

(4) Tina learned the importance of language in Korea.   T ☐ F ☐

Everyday English 1 A. Function Practice 2-(1)

G: I'm going camping with my family tomorrow!

B: Hmm.... ❶I heard that it will rain tomorrow.

G: What? ❷It can't be true.

B: I'm sorry, but it was on the news.

❶ 알고 있음을 나타내는 표현으로 'I learned that it will rain tomorrow.' 등으로 바꾸어 표현할 수 있다.
❷ '그럴 리 없다.'는 의미로 놀라거나 믿을 수 없음을 표현한다.

Everyday English 1 A. Function Practice 2-(2)

G: I heard that there is a science contest next week.

B: Really? ❶I'm interested in science.

G: Then you should ❷sign up. There is a big ❸ prize for the winner.

B: Great! Thanks for telling me.

❶ be interested in ～: ～에 관심이[흥미가] 있다
❷ sign up: 등록하다 ❸ prize: 상

Everyday English 1 A. Function Practice 2-(3)

G: It will be Halloween soon!

B: I heard that people ❶carve ❷pumpkins on Halloween. What else do people do?

G: Children wear ❸scary ❹costumes and visit houses to get ❺sweets.

B: That sounds interesting.

❶ carve: 조각하다 ❷ pumpkin: 호박
❸ scary: 무서운 ❹ costume: 의상 ❺ sweets: 사탕

Everyday English 2 A. Function Practice 2-(1)

G: ❶I'd like to tell you something about love.

B: What is it?

G: I think the most important thing in love is ❷ respect.

B: ❸I agree with you. ❹Respecting each other's differences is very important.

❶ 주제를 소개하는 표현으로 'Let me tell you about something about love.' 로 바꾸어 말할 수 있다.
❷ respect: 존경
❸ 'I agree with you.'는 상대방의 의견에 동의하는 표현으로 'I can't agree with you more.' 등으로 바꾸어 쓸 수 있다.
❹ 동명사가 주어로 사용되어 동사는 is가 왔다.

Everyday English 2 A. Function Practice 2-(2)

B: ❶Look at the Eiffel Tower.

G: It's really tall and pretty!

B: I'd like to tell you something about the Eiffel Tower. People didn't like ❷it at first.

G: Really? But ❸it has become one of the most popular places in Paris ❹these days!

❶ look at: ～을 보다
❷ it은 the Eiffel Tower를 가리킨다.
❸ these days: 요즘에는

In Real Life

(Phone rings.)

Suji: Hello, Suji speaking.

Diego: Hi, it's me, Diego. Do you have time to talk?

Suji: Yes, what's up?

Diego: I'm doing my ❶social studies homework on cultural differences, but I'm ❷having trouble finding the right information.

Suji: I'd like to tell you about a website called "Culture Shock." I heard that people ask and answer questions about other cultures on ❸ that website.

Diego: That sounds perfect. Thank you for your help.

Suji: You're welcome. Good luck with the homework.

❶ social studies: 사회
❷ have trouble ～ing: ～하는 데 어려움을 겪다
❸ that website는 "Culture Shock"을 가리킨다.

● 다음 우리말과 일치하도록 빈칸에 알맞은 말을 쓰시오.

Everyday English 1 A. Function Practice

1. G: I'm _____ _____ with my family tomorrow!

   B: Hmm…. I _____ that it will rain tomorrow.

   G: What? It can't be _____.

   B: I'm _____, but it was on the news.

2. G: I _____ _____ there is a _____ _____ next week.

   B: Really? I'm _____ _____ science.

   G: Then you should _____ _____. There is a big _____ for the _____.

   B: Great! _____ _____ telling me.

3. G: It will be Halloween soon!

   B: I heard that people _____ _____ on Halloween. _____ _____ do people do?

   G: Children wear _____ _____ and visit houses to get sweets.

   B: That _____ interesting.

1. G: 나는 내일 가족들과 캠핑을 갈 거야.
   B: 흠…. 나는 내일 비가 온다고 들었어.
   G: 뭐? 그럴 리 없어.
   B: 미안하지만, 뉴스에 나왔어.
2. G: 나는 다음 주에 과학 대회가 있다고 들었어.
   B: 정말? 나는 과학에 관심이 있어.
   G: 그럼 너는 신청해야 해. 우승자에게는 큰 상이 있어.
   B: 잘됐다! 내게 말해 줘서 고마워.
3. G: 곧 핼러윈이야!
   B: 사람들은 핼러윈에 호박에 조각을 한다고 들었어. 사람들은 또 어떤 것들을 하니?
   G: 어린 아이들은 무서운 의상을 차려 입고 사탕을 얻기 위해 여러 집들을 방문해.
   B: 그것 참 흥미롭게 들린다.

Everyday English 1 B

Mina: Alex, do you have _____ _____?

Alex: Yes, Mina, _____ is it?

Mina: _____ _____ _____ _____ you went to Spain this summer!

Alex: Yes, I _____ _____ a family trip.

Mina: Can you tell me _____ _____ _____ _____? I'm _____ _____ visiting Spain this winter.

Alex: I _____. I think Spain is a really nice country _____ _____. There are many _____ _____.

Mina: Where do you _____ that I _____?

Alex: I recommend _____ the Prado Museum in Madrid. It's _____ _____ _____ _____ _____ in the world.

Mina: _____ _____ the help!

Mina: Alex, 너 시간 있니?
Alex: 응, 미나야. 무슨 일인데?
Mina: 네가 이번 여름에 스페인에 갔다는 얘기를 들었어!
Alex: 응, 가족 여행을 갔었어.
Mina: 너의 여행에 대해 더 말해 줄 수 있니? 나도 이번 겨울에 스페인을 방문해 보려고 생각 중이야.
Alex: 알겠어. 나는 스페인이 방문하기에 정말 좋은 나라라고 생각해. 흥미로운 장소들이 많아.
Mina: 내가 갈 만한 장소로 어디를 추천하니?
Alex: 나는 Madrid에 있는 Prado 박물관을 추천해. 세계에서 가장 유명한 박물관 중 하나야.
Mina: 도와줘서 고마워.

Everyday English 2 A. Function Practice

1. **G:** I'd like to tell you _____ _____ _____.
   B: What is it?
   G: I think _____ _____ _____ thing in love is _____.
   B: I _____ with you. _____ each other's differences is very important.

2. **B:** _____ _____ the Eiffel Tower.
   G: It's really _____ and _____!
   B: I'd like to tell you _____ _____ the Eiffel Tower. People didn't like it _____ _____.
   G: Really? But it has become one of _____ _____ _____ _____ in Paris these days!

Everyday English 2 B

Tina: Hello, everyone. My name is Tina and I'm a _____ _____. Today, I'd like to tell you an _____ _____ that I learned _____ _____. When I first visited Korea, I thought Koreans were _____ because many people asked me my _____. However, I later _____ _____ that this was because of their _____. Koreans use language _____ to people who are _____ than them, so they need to know the other person's age. This _____ has taught me the importance of _____ and _____ other cultures.

In Real Life

(Phone rings.)

Suji: Hello, Suji _____.
Diego: Hi, it's me, Diego. Do you have time to talk?
Suji: Yes, what's _____?
Diego: I'm doing my _____ _____ homework on _____ _____, but I'm _____ _____ _____ the right information.
Suji: I'd like to tell you about a website _____ "Culture Shock." I heard that people ask and answer questions about _____ _____ on that website.
Diego: That sounds _____. Thank you for your help.
Suji: You're _____. _____ luck with the homework.

1. **G:** 사랑에 대해 너에게 해 주고 싶은 이야기가 있어.
   B: 무엇인데?
   G: 나는 사랑에서 가장 중요한 것은 존중이라고 생각해.
   B: 동의해. 서로의 다름을 존중하는 것이 매우 중요해.
2. **B:** 에펠탑을 좀 봐.
   G: 정말 크고 아름답다!
   B: 에펠탑에 대해 너에게 해 주고 싶은 이야기가 있어. 사람들이 처음엔 이것을 좋아하지 않았대.
   G: 정말? 하지만 이건 요즘 파리에서 가장 유명한 장소 중 하나잖아!

Tina: 안녕, 모두들. 내 이름은 Tina이고 나는 여행 작가야. 오늘 나는 너희들에게 내가 여행에서 배운 중요한 교훈에 대해 말해 주고 싶어. 내가 처음 한국에 방문했을 때, 나는 많은 한국인들이 내 나이를 물었기 때문에 무례하다고 생각했어. 그런데 나중에 나는 이것이 그들의 문화 때문이라는 것을 알았어. 한국인들은 그들보다 나이가 많은 사람들에게는 언어를 다르게 쓰는데, 그래서 다른 사람들의 나이를 알 필요가 있는 거였어. 이 경험은 나에게 다른 문화를 배우고 이해하는 것의 중요성을 알게 해 주었어.

(전화가 울린다)
Suji: 여보세요, 저 수지인데요.
Diego: 안녕, 나야 Diego. 얘기할 시간 있니?
Suji: 응, 무슨 일이야?
Diego: 문화적 차이들에 관한 사회 숙제를 하고 있거든. 그런데 올바른 정보를 찾는 데 어려움이 있어.
Suji: "Culture Shock"이라고 불리는 웹 사이트에 대해 말해 주고 싶어. 나는 그 웹 사이트에서 사람들이 다른 문화들에 대해 질문하고 답해 준다고 들었어.
Diego: 그것 참 완벽하게 들린다. 도와줘서 고마워.
Suji: 천만에. 숙제 잘하기를 바라.

[01~02] 다음 대화를 읽고 물음에 답하시오.

> G: I'm going camping with my family tomorrow!
> B: Hmm.... (A)<u>나는 내일 비가 올 거라고 들었어.</u> (heard, that, will)
> G: What? It can't be true.
> B: I'm sorry, but it was on the news.

01 위 대화의 밑줄 친 (A)의 우리말을 주어진 단어를 사용하여 영작하시오.

➡ _____

02 위 대화에서 알 수 있는 소녀의 기분 변화로 적절한 것은?

① excited → disappointed
② angry → nervous
③ sad → happy
④ sad → excited
⑤ nervous → angry

[03~04] 다음 대화를 읽고 물음에 답하시오.

> Somi: (A)_____
> Brian: Really? I'm interested in science.
> Somi: Then you should sign up. There is a big prize for the winner.
> Brian: Great! Thanks for telling me.

03 위 대화의 빈칸 (A)에 들어갈 말을 〈보기〉에 주어진 단어를 모두 배열하여 영작하시오.

┌─ 보기 ├─

that / next / is / I / a / heard / contest / science / there / week

➡ _____

04 위 대화의 내용과 일치하지 <u>않는</u> 것은?

① 다음 주에 과학 대회가 있다.
② Brian은 과학에 관심이 있다.
③ Somi는 Brian에게 과학 대회에 참가할 것을 권유하였다.
④ 과학 대회의 우승자에게는 큰 상이 있다.
⑤ Somi는 과학 대회 참가를 신청하였다.

01 다음 대화가 자연스럽게 이어지도록 순서대로 배열하시오.

> (A) I'm sorry, but it was on the news.
> (B) I'm going camping with my family tomorrow!
> (C) What? It can't be true.
> (D) Hmm.... I heard that it will rain tomorrow.

➡ _____

[02~03] 다음 대화를 읽고 물음에 답하시오.

Jisu: It will be Halloween soon!
Tony: I heard that people (A)[carve / curve] pumpkins on Halloween. What else do people do?
Jisu: Children wear (B)[starry / scary] costumes and visit houses to get (C)[sweat / sweets].
Tony: ⓐThat sounds interesting.

02 위 대화의 괄호 (A)~(C)에 들어갈 말로 적절한 것끼리 짝지어진 것은?

	(A)	(B)	(C)
①	carve	starry	sweat
②	carve	scary	sweat
③	carve	scary	sweets
④	curve	scary	sweat
⑤	curve	starry	sweets

03 위 대화의 밑줄 친 ⓐ와 바꾸어 쓸 수 있는 것을 모두 고르시오.

① I'm interested in sounds.
② How interesting!
③ I have interests in sounds.
④ That sounds like fun.
⑤ You are funny.

[04~05] 다음 대화를 읽고 물음에 답하시오.

Somi: I heard (A)[that / which] there is a science contest next week.
Brian: Really? I'm (B)[interesting / interested] in science.
Somi: Then you should sign (C)[down / up]. There is a big prize for the winner.
Brian: Great! Thanks for telling me.

04 위 대화의 괄호 (A)~(C)에 들어갈 말로 바르게 짝지어진 것은?

	(A)	(B)	(C)
①	that	interesting	down
②	that	interested	up
③	that	interested	down
④	which	interested	up
⑤	which	interesting	down

05 위 대화를 읽고 대답할 수 없는 것은?

① What did Somi hear?
② When will a science contest be held?
③ What is Brian interested in?
④ What will the winner get at the science contest?
⑤ When should Brian sign up for the science contest?

[06~07] 다음 대화를 읽고 물음에 답하시오.

G: I'm going camping with my family tomorrow!
B: Hmm.... I heard that it will rain tomorrow.
G: What? (a)It can't be true.
B: (A)_____

06 위 대화의 빈칸 (A)에 들어갈 말로 적절한 것은?

① I don't agree with you.

② I don't think so.

③ That's good news.

④ I'm sorry, but it was on the news.

⑤ I'm glad to hear that.

07 위 대화의 밑줄 친 (a)와 바꾸어 쓸 수 있는 것을 <u>모두</u> 고르시오.

① That's interesting.

② I'm very satisfied.

③ I can't believe it.

④ Unbelievable!

⑤ Excellent!

[08~09] 다음 대화를 읽고 물음에 답하시오.

Mina: Alex, do you have some time?

Alex: Yes, Mina, what is it?

Mina: I heard ⓐthat you went to Spain this summer!

Alex: Yes, I went on a family trip.

Mina: Can you tell me more about your trip? I'm thinking of ⓑvisiting Spain this winter.

Alex: I see. I think Spain is a really nice country ⓒto visit. There are many interesting places.

Mina: Where do you recommend ⓓthat I go?

Alex: I recommend ⓔto visit the Prado Museum in Madrid. It's one of the most famous museums in the world.

Mina: Thanks for the help!

08 위 대화의 ⓐ~ⓔ 중 어법상 <u>어색한</u> 것을 찾아 바르게 고치시오.

➡ _____

09 위 대화를 읽고 대답할 수 <u>없는</u> 것은?

① Where did Alex visit with his family this summer?

② What does Mina ask for Alex?

③ Where does Alex recommend to Mina?

④ What is one of the most famous museums in Madrid?

⑤ Where is the most interesting place in Spain?

[10~11] 다음 대화를 읽고 물음에 답하시오.

G: (A)_____

B: What is it?

G: I think the most important thing in love is respect.

B: I agree with you. Respecting each other's differences is very important.

10 위 대화의 빈칸 (A)에 들어갈 말을 <보기>에 주어진 단어들을 모두 배열하여 영작하시오.

┌─ 보기 ┤

something / love / I'd / tell / about / like / to / you

➡ _____

11 What do the girl and the boy agree about love?

➡ _____

01 다음 대화의 내용과 일치하도록 미나의 설명을 완성하시오.

> Mina: Alex, do you have some time?
>
> Alex: Yes, Mina, what is it?
>
> Mina: I heard that you went to Spain this summer!
>
> Alex: Yes, I went on a family trip.
>
> Mina: Can you tell me more about your trip? I'm thinking of visiting Spain this winter.
>
> Alex: I see. I think Spain is a really nice country to visit. There are many interesting places.
>
> Mina: Where do you recommend that I go?
>
> Alex: I recommend visiting the Prado Museum in Madrid. It's one of the most famous museums in the world.
>
> Mina: Thanks for the help!

> Mina: Today, I met Alex, who went on (A)_____ to Spain this summer, and got some useful information from him. I made the plan to visit (B)_____ this winter, so I needed some information about it. Alex said that Spain was (C)_____ and there were (D)_____. Among them, he advised me to (E)_____, which is one of the most famous museums in the world. I decided to visit it. I can't wait to visit Spain this winter.

[02~03] 다음 글을 읽고 물음에 답하시오.

> Tina: Hello, everyone. My name is Tina and I'm a travel writer. Today, I'd like to tell you an important lesson that I learned while ⓐtraveling. When I first visited Korea, I thought Koreans were rude ⓑbecause many people asked me my age. However, I later found out that this was ⓒbecause their culture. Koreans use language differently to people who are ⓓolder than them, so they need to know the other person's age. This experience ⓔhas taught me the importance of learning and understanding other cultures.

02 위 글의 밑줄 친 ⓐ~ⓔ 중 어법상 어색한 것을 찾아 바르게 고치시오.

➡ _____

03 Why did Tina think that Koreans were rude? ("It was …" 로 시작할 것.)

➡ _____

04 우리말과 일치하도록 주어진 단어를 모두 배열하여 완성하시오.

> 내가 그에게 나를 도와줄 것인지 물었을 때, 그가 고개를 끄덕였다.
> (if / I / he / nodded / he / him / would / me / when / asked / help)

➡ _____

Grammar

교과서

① 목적격 관계대명사

> • The boy **whom** you met is my brother. 네가 만난 소년은 내 남동생이야.
> • The jacket **which** you bought looks great on you. 네가 산 외투는 너에게 잘 어울려.

■ 관계대명사는 두 개의 문장을 하나로 이어주는 접속사 역할을 하면서 동시에 (대)명사 역할을 한다. 전치사의 목적어 혹은 동사의 목적어였던 (대)명사를 목적격 관계대명사로 만들어 문장을 하나로 이어준다.

- The game **which** Tom is enjoying looks very fun. <동사의 목적어> Tom이 즐기고 있는 게임은 아주 재미있어 보여.
- The girl **who[whom]** you are looking at is beautiful. 네가 보고 있는 그 소녀는 아름답다.

■ 목적격 관계대명사 who(m), which는 that으로 대체할 수 있으며, 생략 가능하다. 관계대명사가 전치사의 목적어로 사용된 경우 전치사는 동사 뒤에 그대로 두거나, 전치사를 관계대명사 앞으로 보낼 수 있다. 단, 관계대명사 that은 전치사 다음에 쓸 수 없음에 유의한다.

- Mr. Jefferson is the doctor **who[whom/that]** I work for. Jefferson씨는 내가 고용되어 일하는 의사이다.
  = Mr. Jefferson is the doctor **for whom** I work.
  Mr. Jefferson is the doctor for that I work. (×)

- This is the house **which[that]** I was born **in**. 이곳은 내가 태어난 집이야.
  = This is the house **in which** I was born.
  This is the house in that I was born. (×)

- She is the director (**who[whom]**) I saw on television. 그녀는 내가 텔레비전에서 본 감독이다.

핵심 Check

1. 다음 우리말과 일치하도록 빈칸에 알맞은 말을 쓰시오.

(1) Nick은 내 여동생이 정말로 사랑하는 남자야.

➡ Nick is the man _____ my sister really loves.

(2) 이것은 내가 어제 산 사전이야.

➡ This is the dictionary _____ I bought yesterday.

(3) 나는 당신이 누구에 관해 이야기하고 있는지 모르겠네요.

➡ I don't know _____ _____ you are talking.

(4) 이것은 내가 흥미 있어 하는 책이야.

➡ This is the book in _____ I am interested.

② 관계대명사 what

- That is **what** I want. 저것은 내가 원하는 것이야.
- Did you understand **what** she told you? 그녀가 네게 말한 것을 이해했니?

■ 관계대명사 what은 선행사를 포함하는 관계대명사로 'the thing(s) which[that]'의 의미이다.
  - She told me **what** she prepared for the project. 그녀는 자기가 프로젝트를 위해 준비하는 것을 내게 말해 주었다.
    = She told me the thing. She prepared the thing for the project.
  - I know **what** you cooked for dinner.
    = I know the thing **that[which]** you cooked for dinner.

■ 관계대명사 what이 이끄는 관계대명사절은 명사절 역할을 하며, 문장 안에서 주어, 목적어, 보어로 쓰인다. 이때 해석은 '~하는 것'이라고 한다.
  - I don't understand **what** I have just read. 내가 방금 읽은 것을 이해할 수 없어요.
    = I don't understand the thing **which** I have just read.
  - **What** is important is that you lied to me. 중요한 것은 네가 나에게 거짓말을 했다는 거야.
    = The thing **which** is important is that you lied to me.
  - **What** you need to do now is to relax. 네가 지금 할 필요가 있는 것은 쉬는 것이야.
    = The thing **which** you need to do now is to relax.

핵심 Check

2. 다음 우리말과 일치하도록 빈칸에 알맞은 말을 쓰시오.
   (1) 네 가방 안에 가지고 있는 것을 내게 보여 줘.
      ⇒ Show me the thing _____ you have in your bag.
      ⇒ Show me _____ you have in your bag.
   (2) 나는 그들이 말한 것을 믿지 않아.
      ⇒ I don't believe the thing _____ they said.
      ⇒ I don't believe _____ they said.
   (3) 나는 네가 말하는 것에 동의하지 않아.
      ⇒ I disagree with the thing _____ you say.
      ⇒ I disagree with _____ you say.

01 적절한 관계대명사를 이용하여 다음 두 문장을 하나의 문장으로 쓰시오.

(1) There were many children at the zoo. Tom and Jane visited the zoo.

➡ _____

(2) Those boys look very cute. The woman is looking after them.

➡ _____

_____

(3) I want to wear the dress. Elizabeth made the dress.

➡ _____

(4) I have the book. Molly really liked it.

➡ _____

02 다음 빈칸에 알맞은 관계대명사를 쓰시오. (필요하면 전치사와 함께 쓸 것.)

(1) Is this _____ you wanted to have?
(2) Where is the girl _____ you talked about?
(3) The music _____ she is listening to is very beautiful.
(4) Jason is the student _____ Mr. Han is waiting.
(5) Chris is looking for the wallet _____ he lost yesterday.

03 같은 의미의 문장이 되도록 빈칸에 알맞은 말을 쓰시오.

(1) The hotel is famous for its breakfast. You are staying in the hotel.
　= The hotel _____ you are staying in is famous for its breakfast.
　= The hotel _____ you are staying is famous for its breakfast.
(2) You must do the thing. The thing is right.
　= You must do the thing _____ is right.
　= You must do _____ is right.
(3) The thing is true. I said it.
　= The thing _____ I said is true.
　= _____ I said is true.

01 다음 빈칸에 들어갈 말로 적절한 것을 <u>모두</u> 고르시오.

> Is this the jacket _____ you lost yesterday?

① which ② whom ③ who
④ that ⑤ what

 02 다음 중 밑줄 친 부분을 생략할 수 <u>없는</u> 것은?

① Do you like the ring <u>which</u> James gave to you?
② Bell is the man <u>who</u> we invited to the party last week.
③ That is the table <u>which</u> Brian sold to me.
④ Is this the student <u>whom</u> you think the most reliable?
⑤ The doctor has a son <u>who</u> likes to invent many things.

03 다음 주어진 문장의 밑줄 친 부분과 쓰임이 같은 것은?

> Where is the chair <u>that</u> you borrowed from the store?

① I know <u>that</u> somebody broke into Amy's house.
② The fact <u>that</u> the list didn't have my name surprised me.
③ We realized <u>that</u> they didn't come to the party.
④ Are the pants <u>that</u> you are wearing bought by your brother?
⑤ Did you think <u>that</u> he would keep the promise?

04 지시에 맞게 다음 우리말을 영어로 쓰시오.

> 나는 네가 지난여름에 한 일을 알고 있다.

(1) which를 사용하여
➡ _____

(2) what을 사용하여
➡ _____

05 다음 빈칸에 들어갈 말이 바르게 짝지어진 것은?

> • David is the man _____ I play tennis.
> • Traveling all around the world is _____ I like to do most.

① whom – what ② in which – which
③ with whom – what ④ what – what
⑤ about whom – what

 06 다음 빈칸에 공통으로 들어갈 말로 가장 적절한 것은?

> • Kate will get the job _____ she applied for.
> • Kate will get the job for _____ she applied.

① which ② that ③ what
④ who ⑤ whom

서답형
07 다음 빈칸에 알맞은 말을 쓰시오.

> Ann bought the thing. I want to see the thing.
> = I want to see _____ Ann bought.

Grammar 23

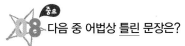

08 다음 중 어법상 **틀린** 문장은?

① The children who are playing outside look happy.
② Robert is the man who we trust most.
③ She doesn't know what I know.
④ The flower which you picked it up is still fresh.
⑤ That is the chocolate box you threw away.

09 다음 중 빈칸에 관계대명사 that이 들어갈 수 **없는** 것은?

① Can you see the vase _____ my grandmother made?
② Jamie wants the dog _____ Brian raised last year.
③ Look at the building in _____ my father worked.
④ Don't use the machine _____ I put on the table.
⑤ One of the cups _____ you brought here is very pretty.

10 다음 빈칸에 들어갈 말로 가장 적절한 것은?

> Focus on _____ you have to do now.

① which   ② whom   ③ that
④ who   ⑤ what

서답형

11 주어진 단어를 활용하여 다음 우리말을 12단어로 이루어진 한 문장의 영어로 쓰시오.

> 그녀는 그녀의 꿈에서 본 남자를 찾고 있어.
> (looking for / see in one's dream)

➡ _____
_____

12 다음 빈칸에 들어갈 말로 적절하지 **않은** 것은?

> The health-care workers _____ were helpful.

① who I spoke to   ② that I spoke to
③ to whom I spoke   ④ I spoke to
⑤ whom I spoke to them

13 다음 중 주어진 문장의 빈칸에 들어갈 말과 같은 말이 들어가는 것은?

> Food is _____ we need most now.

① The book _____ she wrote last year sells well.
② _____ matters is to do your best.
③ The bread _____ Amelia baked tastes good.
④ The big picture _____ hung on the wall was drawn by my father.
⑤ Did you buy the guitar _____ you wanted to buy?

14 다음 중 어법상 옳은 문장의 개수는?

> ⓐ The tree which you planted it last spring grows well.
> ⓑ The singer that you like most are known to people all around the world.
> ⓒ The rate at that hair grows can be surprisingly slow.
> ⓓ Lions used to walk around the field which we lived in.
> ⓔ I don't understand which she is trying to say to us.

① 1개   ② 2개   ③ 3개   ④ 4개   ⑤ 5개

서답형

15 일곱 개의 단어를 써서 다음 문장을 영어로 옮길 때 여섯 번째로 오는 단어는?

> 네가 가지고 온 그 커피는 어디에 있니?

➡ _____

16 다음 빈칸에 들어갈 말로 적절한 것을 모두 고르시오.

> 사람들이 찾던 소녀는 기차역에서 발견되었다.
> The girl _____ was found at the train station.

① who people were looking

② who was looking at people

③ who was looking for people

④ that people were looking for

⑤ for whom people were looking

서답형

17 주어진 문장과 같은 의미가 되도록 빈칸에 알맞은 말을 쓰시오.

> Sherlock is the man. We depend on him when we are in danger.
> = Sherlock is the man _____
> _____ .

18 다음 우리말을 영어로 바르게 옮긴 것을 모두 고르시오.

> 나는 네가 원하는 것을 네게 줄게.

① I'll give you the thing I want.

② I'll give you the thing what you want.

③ I'll give you which want the thing.

④ I'll give you what you want.

⑤ I'll give you the thing you want.

19 다음 빈칸에 알맞은 말을 쓰시오. (3 words)

> 내가 쓴 것은 그녀에 의해 읽히지 않았어.
> _____ wasn't read by her.

➡ _____

20 다음 대화의 빈칸에 공통으로 들어갈 말은? (대·소문자 무시)

> A: Tell me _____ you want for your birthday present.
> B: _____ I want is a basketball.

① that   ② which   ③ who

④ whose   ⑤ what

 21 다음 중 밑줄 친 부분을 관계대명사 that으로 바꿀 수 없는 것은?

① The book which she wrote is very interesting.

② The dog which you saw the other day is Tom's.

③ Where are the socks which Jimmie bought for me?

④ Do you know the girl about whom people keep talking?

⑤ I can't see the children whom you are looking at.

22 다음 빈칸 ⓐ와 ⓑ에 들어갈 말이 바르게 짝지어진 것은?

> Culture shock is an experience ⓐ_____ we can have when we move to a cultural environment ⓑ_____ is different from our own.

① what – which   ② that – what

③ that – which   ④ who – what

⑤ which – who

23 다음 중 어법상 어색한 것을 고르시오.

> Please show me ①what you bought at the market. ②Seeing ③that other people bought ④makes me ⑤excited.

01 다음 두 문장을 관계대명사 that을 써서 하나의 문장으로 쓰시오.

Tell me about the cats. You take care of them on the streets.

➡ _____

_____

02 다음 두 문장을 한 문장으로 쓸 때, 빈칸을 알맞게 채우시오.

She is the woman. I told you about her.

➡ She is the woman _____ about.

➡ She is the woman _____ you.

03 적절한 관계대명사를 이용하여 다음 두 문장을 하나의 문장으로 쓰시오.

(1) The woman was very kind. I met her last week.

➡ _____

(2) Shrek is the movie. I liked it the most when I was young.

➡ _____

_____

(3) I will return the money. I borrowed it from my friends yesterday.

➡ _____

_____

(4) Is this the camera? You have been looking for the camera.

➡ _____

_____

04 한 칸에 하나의 단어만 써서 다음 우리말을 영어로 쓰시오.

이것은 그가 내게 준 것이야.

➡ This is _____ _____ _____

_____ _____ _____.

➡ This is _____ _____ _____

_____.

05 주어진 단어를 바르게 배열하여 다음 우리말을 영어로 쓰시오.

네 호주머니에 가지고 있는 것을 내게 보여줘. (pocket / have / me / what / show / in / you / your)

➡ _____

06 다음 대화에서 어법상 틀린 것을 바르게 고쳐 쓰시오.

A: Do you know the boys with that Mina is running?
B: Oh, they are her classmates.

➡ _____

07 다음 빈칸에 알맞은 말을 쓰시오.

저녁으로 내가 먹고 싶은 것은 피자야.

➡ _____ for dinner is pizza.

08 적절한 관계대명사를 이용하여 다음 문장을 완성하시오.

네가 어제 본 영화는 재미있었니?
➡ Was the movie _____ interesting?

09 한 칸에 하나의 단어만 써서 문장을 완성하시오.

(1) The planet _____ we live on is moving.

➡ The planet _____ _____ we live is moving.

(2) Do you remember the girl _____ David danced with?

➡ Do you remember the girl _____ _____ David danced?

(3) The subject _____ I am interested in is a computer science.

➡ The subject _____ _____ I am interested is a computer science.

(4) _____ made me upset is your attitude.

10 다음 문장을 두 개의 문장으로 쓰시오.

(1) He is the singer whom I have wanted to meet in person.

➡ _____

(2) Paul is my friend on whom I can rely.

➡ _____

(3) Is this the rabbit which you are taking care of?

➡ _____

(4) The museum which I wanted to visit was closed.

➡ _____

(5) This is what John gave to me on my birthday.

➡ _____
_____

11 다음 우리말을 영어로 옮기시오.

나는 Tom이 함께 춤췄던 소녀를 알아.

➡ _____

12 주어진 단어를 활용하여 다음 우리말을 여섯 단어로 이루어진 한 문장의 영어로 쓰시오.

너는 그가 제안한 것을 받아들여야만 해. (accept, offer)

➡ _____

13 다음 두 문장을 하나의 문장으로 쓸 때 빈칸에 알맞은 말을 쓰시오. 한 칸에 하나의 단어만 쓰시오.

What is the name of the boy? You met him at the station.

➡ What is the name of the boy _____ _____ _____ at the station?

➡ What is the name of the boy _____ _____ at the station?

14 다음 대화의 빈칸에 알맞은 말을 다섯 단어로 쓰시오.

A: Jake, what do you want to read?
B: This science fiction novel is _____ _____ .

15 주어진 단어를 활용하여 다음 우리말을 영어로 쓰시오.

내가 수요일에 본 그 소년은 미국인이야. (9 words) (Wednesday)

➡ _____

Reading

Cultures Around the World

Welcome to "Culture Shock"! If you are interested in cultures around
조건의 부사절을 이끄는 접속사(~라면)
the world, this is the website that you are looking for! You can ask and
목적격 관계대명사(생략 가능)
answer any questions you may have about other cultures. Let's take a
(that) you may have about other cultures   살펴보다
look!

Suji: I'm very upset. There is a new student from Greece in my school.
~ 출신의
I asked her to be friends with me but she shook her head. How rude!
to부정사를 목적격 보어로 취하는 동사   How rude (she is)!

⌐→ **Ocean:** Calm down. I'm sure what she really meant was "yes."
관계대명사(= the thing which)
In some countries like Greece, Turkey, and Iran, nodding your head
~와 같은
means "no" and shaking your head means "yes."

Shao: Help! I'm a Chinese boy who has been invited to a Kenyan
동명사 주어: 단수 취급   주격 관계대명사   현재완료 수동태
friend's house. But I don't know anything about Kenya. Are there any
부정문에서 쓰이는 anything
manners I need to know? Please give me some advice!
예의(주로 복수형으로 쓰임)   셀 수 없는 명사

shock: 충격, 쇼크
be interested in: ~에 흥미가 있다
look for: ~을 찾다
other: 다른
shake: 고개를 젓다
rude: 무례한
nod: 고개를 끄덕이다
manners: 예의, 예절
mean: 의미하다
advice: 충고

 확인문제

- 다음 문장이 본문의 내용과 일치하면 T, 일치하지 <u>않으면</u> F를 쓰시오.

1 The website is for people who have an interest in cultures around the world. ☐

2 The new student from Greece came to Suji and asked her to be friends with her. ☐

3 When a man who came from Iran nods his head, it means "no." ☐

4 Ocean knows about cultures of countries like Greece, Turkey, and Iran. ☐

5 Shao knows a lot about the culture of Kenya. ☐

↳ **Clever**: I heard that when Chinese people are invited to
  명사절 접속사(+완전한 절)
someone's house, they leave some food on their plate. It shows that
there was enough food for the guest. However, with Kenyan people,
                                      접속부사(그러나)
please finish all the food the host has prepared. If you leave food, it
                          (that) the host has prepared
means that you didn't like it.
     명사절 접속사(+완전한 절)
  Diego: Does anyone speak German? Today, I was 5 minutes late for
                                                              ~에 늦은
an appointment with my German friend. When I finally met him, he
looked very angry. He said that I must try to keep my "Termin" better.
                      명사절 접속사 that
What does it mean?
        "Termin"을 가리키는 말
  ↳ **Smile**: "Termin" means "appointment" in German. Germans
think that it's important to be on time. In Germany, there is a saying,
          가주어 it   진주어
"What is set should be kept." So, please be punctual with Germans.
=The thing that
  Did you find the information you needed? We hope that what
                                (that) you needed   명사절 접속사 that
you have read was helpful and interesting. Understanding cultural
= the thing which you have read   동명사
differences can make a difference in your life. Please visit our website
again!

invite: 초대하다
someone 어떤 사람
plate: 접시
finish: 끝내다, 모두 먹다
German: 독일의; 독일어
appointment: 약속
on time: 정시에
saying: 속담, 격언
punctual: 시간을 엄수하는
helpful: 유용한
interesting: 흥미로운
life: 삶, 생활

 확인문제

● 다음 문장이 본문의 내용과 일치하면 T, 일치하지 <u>않으면</u> F를 쓰시오.

1   To be polite, you should finish your plate when you are invited to a Chinese house. ☐

2   Kenyan people don't prepare any food for their guests. ☐

3   It is a good idea to eat all the food on your plate in your Kenyan friend's house. ☐

4   Diego was not on time for the appointment. ☐

5   It is important to be punctual for the appointment with German. ☐

6   German people don't care about whether or not people are late for the appointment. ☐

● 우리말을 참고하여 빈칸에 알맞은 말을 쓰시오.

Cultures Around the World

1 _____ _____ "Culture Shock"!

2 If you _____ _____ _____ cultures around the world, this is the website _____ you are looking for!

3 You can ask and answer any questions you may have _____ _____ _____. Let's take _____ _____!

4 Suji: I'm very _____.

5 There is a new student _____ _____ in my school.

6 I asked _____ _____ _____ _____ with me but she _____ her head.

7 How _____!

8 Ocean: Calm _____. I'm sure _____ she really _____ _____ "yes."

9 In some _____ like Greece, Turkey, and Iran, _____ your head _____ "no" and _____ your head means "yes."

10 Shao: Help! I'm a Chinese boy _____ _____ _____ _____ to a Kenyan friend's house.

11 But I don't know _____ _____ Kenya.

12 Are there any _____ _____ _____ _____ _____? Please give _____ _____ _____!

13 Clever: I heard _____ when Chinese people _____ _____ to someone's house, they _____ some food _____ their plate.

14 It shows _____ there was _____ _____ for the guest.

세계의 문화

1 "Culture Shock"에 오신 것을 환영합니다!

2 만약 당신이 세계 각국의 문화에 관심이 있다면, 이곳이 바로 당신이 찾던 웹 사이트입니다.

3 당신은 다른 문화에 대해 가지고 있는 질문을 묻고 답할 수 있습니다. 함께 살펴봅시다!

4 Suji: 나는 굉장히 속상해요.

5 우리 학교에는 그리스에서 새로 온 학생이 있어요.

6 나는 그녀에게 나와 친구가 되자고 했지만, 그녀는 고개를 저었어요.

7 정말 무례해요!

8 Ocean: 진정해요. 나는 그녀가 진짜 의미했던 것은 "응"이었다고 확신해요.

9 그리스, 터키, 이란과 같은 몇몇 나라에서는 고개를 끄덕이는 것이 "싫다"는 의미이고 고개를 흔드는 것이 "좋다"를 의미해요.

10 Shao: 도와주세요! 나는 케냐인 친구 집에 초대된 중국 소년이에요.

11 하지만 저는 케냐에 대해서 아무것도 몰라요.

12 제가 알아야 할 예의가 있나요? 저에게 조언을 해 주세요!

13 Clever: 제가 알기로는, 중국 사람들이 누군가의 집에 초대되었을 때, 접시에 음식을 남겨둔다고 들었어요.

14 그것은 손님에게 충분한 음식이 제공되었음을 보여줘요.

15 _____, with Kenyan people, please _____ all the food the host _____ _____.

16 _____ you _____ food, it means _____ you didn't like it.

17 Diego: Does _____ _____ German?

18 Today, I was 5 _____ _____ _____ an appointment with my German friend.

19 _____ I finally met him, he _____ very _____.

20 He said _____ I must _____ _____ _____ my "Termin" better. What _____ it _____?

21 Smile: "Termin" means "_____" _____ _____.

22 Germans think _____ it's important _____ _____ _____ _____.

23 In Germany, there is a saying, "What _____ _____ should _____ _____."

24 So, please _____ _____ with Germans.

25 Did you find _____ _____ _____ _____?

26 We hope that _____ _____ _____ read _____ helpful and interesting.

27 _____ _____ _____ can make a difference in your life.

28 Please _____ our website again!

15 하지만, 케냐 사람들과 함께 하는 경우, 주인이 준비한 음식을 모두 드세요.

16 만약에 음식을 남기면, 그것은 당신이 그 음식을 좋아하지 않았다는 것을 의미해요.

17 Diego: 혹시 여기 독일어 하는 사람이 있나요?

18 오늘, 저는 독일 친구와의 약속에 5분 늦었어요.

19 마침내 그를 만났을 때, 그는 매우 화가 나 보였어요.

20 그는 내가 "Termin"을 더 잘 지키도록 노력해야 한다고 말했어요. 그것은 무엇을 뜻하나요?

21 Smile: "Termin"은 독일어로 약속을 의미합니다.

22 독일인들은 제시간에 오는 것이 중요하다고 생각해요.

23 독일에서는 "정해진 것은 지켜져야 한다."는 말이 있어요.

24 그러니, 독일인들과 함께 할 때는 시간을 잘 지키세요.

25 당신에게 필요했던 정보를 찾았나요?

26 우리는 당신이 읽은 것이 도움이 되고 재미있기를 바랍니다.

27 문화 차이를 이해하는 것은 당신의 삶을 변화시킬 겁니다.

28 저희 웹 사이트를 또 방문해 주세요!

● 우리말을 참고하여 본문을 영작하시오.

1 "Culture Shock"에 오신 것을 환영합니다!

➡ _____

2 만약 당신이 세계 각국의 문화에 관심이 있다면, 이곳이 바로 당신이 찾던 웹 사이트입니다.

➡ _____

3 당신은 다른 문화에 대해 가지고 있는 질문을 묻고 답할 수 있습니다. 함께 살펴봅시다!

➡ _____

4 Suji: 나는 굉장히 속상해요.

➡ _____

5 우리 학교에는 그리스에서 새로 온 학생이 있어요.

➡ _____

6 나는 그녀에게 나와 친구가 되자고 했지만, 그녀는 고개를 저었어요.

➡ _____

7 정말 무례해요!

➡ _____

8 Ocean: 진정해요. 나는 그녀가 진짜 의미했던 것은 "응"이었다고 확신해요.

➡ _____

9 그리스, 터키, 이란과 같은 몇몇 나라에서는 고개를 끄덕이는 것이 "싫다"는 의미이고 고개를 흔드는 것이 "좋다"를 의미해요.

➡ _____

_____

10 Shao: 도와주세요! 나는 케냐인 친구 집에 초대된 중국 소년이에요.

➡ _____

11 하지만 저는 케냐에 대해서 아무것도 몰라요.

➡ _____

12 제가 알아야 할 예의가 있나요? 저에게 조언을 해 주세요!

➡ _____

13 Clever: 제가 알기로는, 중국 사람들이 누군가의 집에 초대되었을 때, 접시에 음식을 남겨둔다고 들었어요.

➡ _____

_____

14 그것은 손님에게 충분한 음식이 제공되었음을 보여줘요.

➡ _____

15 하지만, 케냐 사람들과 함께 하는 경우, 주인이 준비한 음식을 모두 드세요.

➡ _____

16 만약에 음식을 남기면, 그것은 당신이 그 음식을 좋아하지 않았다는 것을 의미해요.

➡ _____

17 Diego: 혹시 여기 독일어 하는 사람이 있나요?

➡ _____

18 오늘, 저는 독일 친구와의 약속에 5분 늦었어요.

➡ _____

19 마침내 그를 만났을 때, 그는 매우 화가 나 보였어요.

➡ _____

20 그는 내가 "Termin"을 더 잘 지키도록 노력해야 한다고 말했어요. 그것은 무엇을 뜻하나요?

➡ _____

21 Smile: "Termin"은 독일어로 약속을 의미합니다.

➡ _____

22 독일인들은 제시간에 오는 것이 중요하다고 생각해요.

➡ _____

23 독일에서는 "정해진 것은 지켜져야 한다."는 말이 있어요.

➡ _____

24 그러니, 독일인들과 함께 할 때는 시간을 잘 지키세요.

➡ _____

25 당신에게 필요했던 정보를 찾았나요?

➡ _____

26 우리는 당신이 읽은 것이 도움이 되고 재미있기를 바랍니다.

➡ _____

27 문화 차이를 이해하는 것은 당신의 삶을 변화시킬 겁니다.

➡ _____

28 저희 웹 사이트를 또 방문해 주세요!

➡ _____

[01~05] 다음 글을 읽고 물음에 답하시오.

Welcome to "Culture Shock"! If you are interested in cultures around the world, this is the website that you are looking for! You can ask and answer any questions you may have about other cultures. Let's take a look!

Suji: I'm very upset.

There is a new student from Greece in my school. I asked her to be friends with me but she shook her head. How ⓐ_____!

└, Ocean: Calm down. I'm sure what she really meant was "yes." In some countries like Greece, Turkey, and Iran, nodding your head means "no" and shaking your head means "yes."

01 다음 중 빈칸 ⓐ에 들어갈 말로 가장 적절한 것은?

① exciting   ② happy   ③ rude
④ fortunate   ⑤ boring

서답형

02 How did Suji feel when she posted the message?

➡ _____

중요

03 다음 중 위 글을 읽고 답할 수 있는 것은?

① How many visitors does the website have?
② Where did Suji come from?
③ How does Ocean know the culture of Greece?
④ Where did a new student come from?
⑤ What kind of website does Suji like to visit the most?

04 위 글의 내용에 맞게 빈칸에 들어갈 알맞은 말을 고르시오.

One of Jake's friends came from Turkey. One day, Jake asked him to help him do his homework. After _____, he helped Jake.

① crossing his arms
② nodding his head
③ touching my head
④ shaking his head
⑤ scratching his head

서답형

05 다음 빈칸에 들어갈 말을 위 글에서 찾아 쓰시오.

If you _____, you move your head downwards and upwards to show that you are answering 'yes' to a question, or to show agreement, understanding, or approval.

[06~08] 다음 글을 읽고 물음에 답하시오.

Shao Help!

I'm a Chinese boy who has been invited to a Kenyan friend's house. But I don't know anything about Kenya. Are there any manners I need to know? Please give me some advice!

└, Clever: I heard that when Chinese people are invited to someone's house, they leave some food on their plate. It shows that there was enough food for the guest. However, with Kenyan people, please finish all the food ⓐ _____ the host has prepared. If you leave food, it means that you didn't like it.

서답형

06 빈칸 ⓐ에 적절한 말을 모두 쓰시오.

➡ _____

서답형

07 According to the passage, what is polite to do when we are invited to a Chinese friend's home?

➡ _____

중요

08 다음 중 위 글의 내용을 바르게 이해한 사람은?

① Jason: I will clean the plate when I am invited to my Chinese friend's home for dinner.

② Polly: It's good to know there is no cultural difference between China and Kenya.

③ Brian: It is interesting that Chinese people don't want to leave the food.

④ Jacob: As Shao didn't know how to behave in Chinese's house, it was a good idea that Shao wanted to get advice.

⑤ Zach: I should be more careful not to leave any food when I am invited to Kenyan people.

[09~12] 다음 글을 읽고 물음에 답하시오.

Diego: Does anyone speak German?
Today, I was 5 minutes late for an appointment with my German friend. When I finally met him, he looked very angry. He said that I must try to keep my "Termin" better. (A)_____

↳ Smile: "Termin" means "appointment" in German. Germans think that it's important to be on time. In Germany, there is a saying, "What is set should be kept." So, please be punctual with Germans.

Did you find the information you needed? We hope that what you have read was helpful and (B)_____. Understanding cultural differences can make a difference in your life. Please visit our website again!

09 다음 중 빈칸 (A)에 들어갈 말로 가장 적절한 것은?

① How did he do that to me?

② What does it mean?

③ What should I do?

④ Where should I get the answer?

⑤ Why is he so mean?

서답형

10 주어진 단어를 어법에 맞게 빈칸 (B)에 쓰시오.

(interest)

➡ _____

서답형

11 Write the reason why Diego's German friend was upset. Answer in English with eight words. Use the phrase "It was because."

➡ _____

중요

12 다음 중 위 글의 내용과 일치하지 <u>않는</u> 것은?

① Diego didn't understand what the word "Termin" meant.

② Diego was late for an appointment with his friend.

③ Germans think that being on time is important.

④ There is a saying about keeping an appointment in Germany.

⑤ Diego was too late to meet his German friend.

[13~15] 다음 글을 읽고 물음에 답하시오.

Welcome to "Culture Shock"! If you are interested in cultures around the world, this is the website ⓐthat you are looking for! You can ask and answer any questions you may have about other cultures. Let's take a look!

Suji I'm very upset.

There is a new student from Greece in my school. I asked her to be friends with me but she shook her head. How rude!

└, Ocean: Calm down. I'm sure what she really meant was "yes." In some countries like Greece, Turkey, and Iran, nodding your head means "no" and shaking your head means "yes."

13 다음 중 위 글의 밑줄 친 ⓐ와 쓰임이 같은 것은?

① I thought that she would do that for us.

② It is impossible that they finish the project on time.

③ The news that he broke into someone's house was shocking.

④ Did they say that you were not allowed to attend the meeting?

⑤ The person that you met at the meeting was my boss.

14 다음 중 위 글의 내용과 일치하는 것은?

① If you don't have an interest in other cultures, the website will be a good choice.

② It is not easy for your questions to be answered at the website.

③ Suji was upset because of a new student from Greece.

④ Ocean is not familiar with cultures of Turkey and Greece.

⑤ Suji asked a question of Ocean.

15 What did the new student do when Suji told her that she wanted to be friends with her? Answer in English with a full sentence.

➡ _____

[16~19] 다음 글을 읽고 물음에 답하시오.

Shao: Help!

I'm a Chinese boy who has been invited to a Kenyan friend's house. But I don't know anything about Kenya. Are there any manners I need to know? Please give me some advice!

└, Clever: I heard that ⓐ_____ Chinese people are invited to someone's house, they leave some food on their plate.

(A) If you leave food, it means that you didn't like it.

(B) However, with Kenyan people, please finish all the food the host has prepared.

(C) It shows that there was enough food for the guest.

16 다음 중 빈칸 ⓐ에 들어갈 말로 가장 적절한 것은?

① because ② unless ③ when

④ before ⑤ although

17 자연스러운 글이 되도록 (A)~(C)를 바르게 배열한 것은?

① (A) – (C) – (B) ② (B) – (A) – (C)

③ (B) – (C) – (A) ④ (C) – (A) – (B)

⑤ (C) – (B) – (A)

18 Where has Shao been invited? Answer in English with a full sentence.

➡ _____

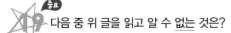 **19** 다음 중 위 글을 읽고 알 수 없는 것은?

① Shao is from China.

② Shao has a Kenyan friend.

③ Shao is not familiar with Kenyan culture.

④ Shao invited a Kenyan friend to his house.

⑤ Shao wants some advice about manners he should keep in mind.

[20~22] 다음 글을 읽고 물음에 답하시오.

Diego: Does anyone speak German?

Today, I was 5 minutes late for an appointment with my German friend. When I finally met him, he looked very angry. He said that I must try to keep my "Termin" better. What does it mean?

└ Smile: "Termin" means "appointment" in German. Germans think that it's important to be on time. In Germany, there is a saying, "What (A)_____ should be kept." So, please be punctual with Germans.

Did you find the information you needed? We hope that what you have read was helpful and interesting. Understanding cultural differences can make a difference in your life. Please visit our website again!

서답형
20 단어 set을 어법에 맞게 빈칸 (A)에 쓰시오.

➡ _____

서답형
21 위 글의 내용에 맞게 빈칸에 알맞은 말을 쓰시오.

> If there is any information _____ _____ _____, you can visit the website. It will provide _____ _____ _____ information.

22 다음 중 위 글을 읽고 답할 수 있는 것은?

① Why was Diego late for an appointment?

② When did the German friend come to the location of the appointment?

③ Why was Diego's friend angry?

④ How did Diego go to the location of the appointment?

⑤ What is the most important thing in Germany?

[23~24] 다음 글을 읽고 물음에 답하시오.

Dear Mira,

Hello, Mira. I'm visiting Korea this winter and I am very ①excited about the trip. But ② what worries me are the cultural differences. So, I was hoping ③to get some ④advices from you.

Love, David

Dear David,

I'd like to tell you about a mistake ⑤that you can make if you don't know Korean culture. In Korea, the oldest person starts eating first and younger people wait for a while. I hope you have a great time in Korea.

Love, Mira

서답형
23 ①~⑤ 중 어법상 바르지 않은 것은?

①　　　②　　　③　　　④　　　⑤

중요
24 미라가 David에게 해준 조언으로 가장 적절한 것은?

① how to say hello in Korea

② a table manner in Korea

③ how to wait for the oldest person

④ how to eat with friends

⑤ how to fix dinner for Korean

[01~04] 다음 글을 읽고 물음에 답하시오.

Welcome to "Culture Shock"! If you are interested in cultures around the world, ⓐ this is the website you are looking! You can ask and answer any questions you may have about other cultures. Let's take a look!

Suji: I'm very upset.

There is a new student from Greece in my school. I asked her to be friends with me but she shook her head. How rude!

└, Ocean: Calm down. I'm sure what she really meant was "(A)_____." In some countries like Greece, Turkey, and Iran, nodding your head means "no" and shaking your head means "(B)_____."

⭐ 1 빈칸 (A)와 (B)에 yes나 no를 문맥에 맞게 쓰시오.

➡ (A) _____ (B) _____

02 주어진 어구를 바르게 배열하여 다음 질문의 답을 완성하시오.

> Q: What kind of website is "Culture Shock?" Answer in English with a full sentence.
> (cultures / it / different / with / is / about / a website / answers / questions / and)

➡ _____

_____

03 Write the reason why Suji was upset with the Greek student. Use the phrase 'It's because.'

➡ _____

_____

⭐ 4 밑줄 친 ⓐ에서 어법상 틀린 것을 찾아 바르게 고쳐 쓰시오.

➡ _____

[05~07] 다음 글을 읽고 물음에 답하시오.

Shao: Help!

I'm a Chinese boy who has been invited to a Kenyan friend's house. But I don't know anything about Kenya. Are there any manners I need to know? Please give me some advice!

└, Clever: I heard that when Chinese people are invited to someone's house, they leave some food on their plate. (A)It shows that there was enough food for the guest. However, with Kenyan people, please finish all the food the host has prepared. If you leave food, it means that you didn't like it.

05 다음 중 위 글의 내용과 일치하지 않는 부분을 두 군데 찾아 바르게 고치시오.

> Shao is a boy from China. He has a Kenyan friend. He invited Shao to his house. Shao knew about Kenya well, so he needed some help. He wanted to know some manners he should keep in the Chinese house.

➡ _____

➡ _____

06 밑줄 친 (A)가 의미하는 것을 우리말로 쓰시오.

➡ _____

07 According to the passage, what does it mean if we don't finish our food in Kenyan's house? Answer in English with a full sentence.

➡ _____

[08~12] 다음 글을 읽고 물음에 답하시오.

Diego: Does anyone speak German?
Today, I was 5 minutes late for an appointment with my German friend. When I finally met him, he looked very angry. He said that I must try to keep my "Termin" better. What does (A)it mean?

└ Smile: "Termin" means "appointment" in German. Germans think that it's important to be on time. In Germany, there is a saying, "(B)정해진 것은 지켜져야 한다." So, please be (C)punctual with Germans.
(D)Did you find the information you needed? We hope that what you have read was helpful and interesting. Understanding cultural differences can make a difference in your life. Please visit our website again!

08 밑줄 친 (A)가 가리키는 것을 위 글에서 찾아 쓰시오.

➡ _____

09 주어진 단어를 활용하여 밑줄 친 우리말 (B)를 영어로 쓰시오.

(set / keep)

➡ _____

10 밑줄 친 (C)를 대신할 수 있는 말을 위 글에서 찾아 쓰시오.

➡ _____

11 위 글의 내용에 맞게 빈칸에 알맞은 말을 쓰시오.

If you visit the website, you can understand _____ _____ which can make a difference in your life.

12 밑줄 친 문장 (D)를 두 개의 문장으로 나누어 쓰시오.

➡ _____

[13~14] 다음 글을 읽고 물음에 답하시오.

Dear Mira,
Hello, Mira. I'm visiting Korea this winter and I am very excited about the trip. But what worries me are the cultural differences. So, I was hoping to get some advice from you.
Love, David

Dear David,
I'd like to tell you about a mistake that you can make if you don't know Korean culture. In Korea, the oldest person starts eating first and younger people wait for a while. I hope you have a great time in Korea.
Love, Mira

13 According to the passage, when will David visit Korea? Answer in English with a full sentence.

➡ _____

14 위 글의 내용에 맞게 빈칸에 알맞은 말을 쓰시오.

If you are a foreigner who doesn't know Korean culture well, you may _____ _____ before _____ _____ _____ starts to eat. But it's a mistake.

구석구석

Project Work Step 1

Hello. Our group would like to tell you about Thanksgiving Day in the United
　　　　　　　　　　　　 ~하고 싶다
States of America. It is celebrated on the fourth Thursday of November.
　　　　　　　　　　 수동태　　　　　　 특정 날짜 앞에 쓰는 전치사
People eat turkey and pumpkin pie. Before eating dinner, families share things
　　　　　　　　　　　　　　　　　　 = Before they eat dinner
that they are thankful for.
목적격 관계대명사

구문해설 ・celebrate: ~을 기념하다 ・turkey: 칠면조 ・share: 공유하다

Check Your Progress 1

W: Hello, everyone. Today, I'd like to tell you a story about myself. As you
　　　　　　　　　　　　　　　　　　　　　　　　 = 주어와 목적어가 같으므로 재귀대명사가 쓰였다.
can see, I'm very thin and weak. Because of my looks, I didn't have any
　　　　　　　　　　　　　　　　 because of+명사(구)
friends when I was young. I was always very nervous when I met new
people. However, I didn't give up on myself. I tried my best to be more
　　　　　　 그러나　　　　 ~을 포기하다　　 = try one's best = do one's best: 최선을 다하다
confident. Now, I travel around the world and give hope to many people. I
hope more people will find the real beauty inside themselves like I did.
　　　　　　　　　　　　　　　　　　　　　　　　　　　　　　 ~처럼(접속사)

구문해설 ・thin: 마른 ・inside: ~ 안에

Check Your Progress 4~6

Dear Mira,

Hello, Mira. I'm visiting Korea this winter and I am very excited about the
　　　　　　 = I will visit
trip. But what worries me are the cultural differences. So, I was hoping to get
　　　　 관계대명사= the thing which)
some advice from you.
　　　 셀 수 없는 명사

Love, David

Dear David,

I'd like to tell you about a mistake that you can make if you don't know
　　　　　　　　　　　　　　　　 목적격 관계대명사　　　　 = unless you know
Korean culture. In Korea, the oldest person starts eating first and younger
　　　　　　　　　　　　　　　　　　　　　　　 = starts to eat
people wait for a while. I hope you have a great time in Korea.
　　　　　 잠시

Love, Mira

구문해설 ・excited: 신이 난 ・cultural difference: 문화 차이 ・advice: 조언 ・mistake: 실수

안녕하세요. 우리 모임은 미국의 추수감사절에 관해 말하고 싶습니다. 이 날은 11월의 넷째 주 목요일에 기념됩니다. 사람들은 칠면조와 호박 파이를 먹습니다. 저녁을 먹기 전에, 가족들은 감사할 무언가를 공유합니다.

W: 안녕, 모두들. 오늘 나는 나에 대한 이야기를 하고 싶어. 너희들도 볼 수 있듯이 나는 매우 마르고 약해. 내 모습 때문에 , 내가 어릴 때 나는 친구들이 없었어. 나는 새로운 사람들을 만날 때 항상 매우 긴장했었어. 그러나 나는 내 스스로를 포기하지 않았어. 나는 좀 더 자신감을 갖기 위해 최선을 다했어. 지금. 나는 세계를 여행하며 많은 사람들에게 희망을 주고 있어. 나는 좀 더 많은 사람들이 내가 했던 것처럼 자신들 안에서 참된 아름다움을 찾길 희망해.

미라에게
미라야, 안녕. 나는 이번 겨울에 한국을 방문할 거고, 굉장히 신이 나 있어. 그런데, 나를 걱정하게 하는 것은 문화 차이야. 그래서, 너에게 조언을 좀 구하고 싶었어.
사랑을 담아서. David가

David에게
네가 한국의 문화에 대해 모르면 할 수 있는 실수에 관해서 알려주고 싶어. 한국에서는 가장 나이가 많은 사람이 먼저 먹기 시작하고, 더 어린 사람들은 잠시 기다려. 네가 한국에서 즐거운 시간을 보내길 바라.
사랑을 담아서, 미라가

영역별 핵심문제

01 다음 짝지어진 단어의 관계가 같도록 빈칸에 알맞은 말을 쓰시오.

perfect : imperfect = believable : _____

02 다음 영영풀이가 가리키는 것을 고르시오.

a person that you have invited to your house or to a particular event that you are paying for

① host　　　② guest
③ traveler　　④ guide
⑤ painter

03 다음 중 밑줄 친 부분의 뜻풀이가 바르지 않은 것은?

① What is the difference between two models? 차이
② Irene is always punctual for class. 주의 깊은
③ Do you know what the capital city of Canada is? 수도
④ I was so upset when my friend broke our appointment yesterday. 약속
⑤ My sister has a great language ability. 언어

04 다음 우리말에 맞게 빈칸에 알맞은 말을 쓰시오.

(1) 음악은 나를 차분하게 만든다.
　➡ Music makes me _____ down.
(2) 나는 네가 음식에 대해 불평하는 것을 멈추었으면 해.
　➡ I want you to stop _____ about the food.
(3) 나는 항상 소금과 설탕을 혼동한다.
　➡ I always _____ salt with sugar.

05 다음 문장의 빈칸에 들어갈 말을 〈보기〉에서 골라 쓰시오.

┌─ 보기 ─
│ sign up / take a look / get rid of / on
│ time / make a difference
└─

(1) You should finish the test _____.
(2) I think you should _____ for the English speech contest.
(3) Now, let's _____ at the pictures.
(4) These two words _____ in the article.
(5) Before studying for the test, I want to _____ stuffs on my desk.

06 다음 주어진 문장의 밑줄 친 capital과 같은 의미로 쓰인 것은?

Do you know what the capital of Japan is?

① The reason of business failure is lack of capital.
② He finally moved to the capital, Oslo, after getting a job.
③ Mike started business with a small capital.
④ The capital of my company has increased by 35 percent.
⑤ Names begin with a capital letter.

[07~08] 다음 대화를 읽고 물음에 답하시오.

Jisu: It will be Halloween soon!

Tony: (A)사람들은 핼러윈에 호박에 조각을 한다고 들었어. (heard, on, that) What else do people do?

Jisu: Children wear scary costumes and visit houses to get sweets.

Tony: That sounds interesting.

07 위 대화의 밑줄 친 (A)의 우리말을 주어진 단어를 사용하여 영작하시오.

➡ _____

08 What do children do on Halloween?

➡ _____

_____

[09~11] 다음 대화를 읽고 물음에 답하시오.

(Phone rings.)

Suji: Hello, Suji speaking.

Diego: Hi, it's me, Diego. Do you have time (A) [taking / to talk]?

Suji: Yes, what's up?

Diego: I'm doing my social studies homework on cultural differences, but I'm having trouble (B)[finding / to find] the right information.

Suji: I'd like to tell you about a website (C) [calling / called] "Culture Shock." I heard that people ask and answer questions about other cultures on that website.

Diego: That sounds perfect. Thank you for your help.

Suji: You're welcome. Good luck with the homework.

09 위 대화의 (A)~(C)에 들어갈 말로 바르게 짝지어진 것은?

	(A)	(B)	(C)
①	talking	finding	calling
②	to talk	finding	called
③	to talk	finding	calling
④	to talk	to find	called
⑤	talking	to find	calling

10 위 대화에서 나타난 Diego의 심경 변화로 알맞은 것은?

① worried → sad

② worried → pleased

③ sad → disappointed

④ happy → worried

⑤ nervous → disappointed

11 위 대화의 내용과 일치하지 <u>않는</u> 것은?

① Diego의 사회 숙제는 문화 차이에 관한 것이다.

② Diego는 올바른 정보를 찾는 데 어려움을 겪고 있었다.

③ 수지는 Diego에게 "Culture Shock"이란 웹 사이트를 소개하였다.

④ 사람들이 "Culture Shock"이란 웹 사이트에서 다른 문화들에 관해 질문하고 답한다.

⑤ Diego는 수지에게 문화 차이에 대한 몇 가지 질문을 하였다.

[12~14] 다음 글을 읽고 물음에 답하시오.

Tina: Hello, everyone. My name is Tina and I'm a travel writer. Today, (a)I'd like to tell you an important lesson that I learned while traveling.(let) When I first visited Korea, I thought Koreans were rude because many people asked me my age. (A)_____, I later found out that this was because of their culture. Koreans use language differently to people who are older than them, so they need to know the other person's age.

12 위 글의 빈칸 (A)에 들어갈 말로 알맞은 것은?

① Therefore ② However
③ Moreover ④ In addition
⑤ On the other hand

13 위 글의 밑줄 친 (a)를 주어진 단어를 사용하여 의미가 같도록 다시 쓰시오.

➡ _____

_____

14 위 글의 내용과 일치하지 않는 것은?

① Tina는 여행 작가이다.
② Tina는 한국인들이 나이를 묻기 때문에 무례하다고 생각했었다.
③ 나중에 Tina는 한국인들이 나이를 묻는 것은 그들의 문화 때문이라는 것을 알았다.
④ 한국인들은 나이가 많은 사람들에게 언어를 다르게 쓴다.
⑤ Tina는 문화에 따른 적절한 언어 사용의 중요성을 알게 되었다.

Grammar

15 다음 중 밑줄 친 부분을 생략할 수 없는 것은?

① Here is the thing <u>that</u> you should remember.
② We are looking at a girl <u>who</u> is wearing a blue dress.
③ This is the chair on <u>which</u> we used to sit together.
④ The drums <u>that</u> you are playing look fancy.
⑤ I am listening to a song <u>which</u> a singer sang.

16 다음 대화의 빈칸에 들어갈 말로 적절한 것을 모두 고르시오.

A: Can you please help me?
B: Okay. Let me see _____ I can do.

① that ② which
③ about which ④ what
⑤ the thing

17 다음 대화의 빈칸에 알맞은 말을 쓰시오.

A: Can you show me the thing that you bought at the store?
B: This dress is _____ _____ _____ at the store.

18 다음 두 문장을 하나의 문장으로 바르게 옮기지 않은 것은?

Do you know the boy? My sister kept talking about him.

① Do you know the boy whom my sister kept talking about?
② Do you know the boy who my sister kept talking about?
③ Do you know the boy my sister kept talking about?
④ Do you know the boy about that my sister kept taking?
⑤ Do you know the boy that my sister kept talking about?

19 다음 두 문장을 하나의 문장으로 쓰시오.

Math is the subject. I studied it hard.

➡ _____

20 다음 중 어법상 옳은 문장은?

① I often visit the market at that I met Christine for the first time.

② The building which my father built are famous for its beauty.

③ Where is the cup who you used yesterday?

④ This is the report Danny handed in.

⑤ That is not the thing what I said.

21 관계대명사 that을 이용하여 다음 우리말을 영어로 쓸 때, 다섯 번째와 열 번째 오는 단어를 바르게 짝지은 것은?

> 이곳은 내가 이 바지를 샀던 가게이다.

① shop – pants　　② that – pants

③ that – at　　　　④ I – at

⑤ bought – pants

22 다음 중 주어진 문장의 밑줄 친 부분과 쓰임이 같은 것은?

> My sister forgot to return the book that she had borrowed.

① Why do you think that she is not coming?

② It is not important that he broke the promise.

③ The news that he was sick worried me.

④ The flower that Mindy gave you is still beautiful.

⑤ That you are with us now makes us relieved.

23 다음 빈칸에 들어갈 말이 바르게 짝지어진 것은?

> • Tell me _____ you think.
> • Who can tell me the year in _____ the Civil War started?
> • Is this the cap _____ you lent to your friend?

① that – that – that

② that – what – that

③ what – which – that

④ what – that – that

⑤ which – what – which

24 다음 대화의 빈칸에 알맞은 말을 쓰시오.

> A: What is the most important thing in your life?
> B: _____ _____ _____ _____ _____ in my life is my family.

25 다음 빈칸에 들어갈 말로 가장 적절한 것은?

> Do you know the year in _____ your parents were born?

① what　　② that　　③ which

④ who　　⑤ whom

26 다음 문장을 어법에 맞게 고쳐 쓰시오.

> My dad is angry because of which I did.

➡ _____

Reading

[27~28] 다음 글을 읽고 물음에 답하시오.

Welcome to "Culture Shock"! If you are interested (A)_____ cultures around the world, this is the website that you are looking for! You can ask and answer any questions you may have about other cultures. Let's take a look!

27 빈칸 (A)에 들어갈 말로 적절한 것은?

① about   ② on   ③ at
④ in   ⑤ for

28 What is the passage mainly talking about?

① what is important in life
② the importance of understanding cultural difference
③ the characteristic of the website
④ the writer's experience of culture shock
⑤ information about other cultures

[29~31] 다음 글을 읽고 물음에 답하시오.

Suji: I'm very upset.
There ①is a new student from Greece in my school. I asked her ②to be friends with me but she shook her head. ③How rude!
⌐, Ocean: Calm down. I'm sure ④that she really meant was "yes." In some countries ⑤like Greece, Turkey, and Iran, nodding your head means "no" and (A)_____ your head means "yes."

29 글의 흐름상 빈칸 (A)에 들어갈 알맞은 말을 쓰시오.

➡ _____

30 ①~⑤ 중 어법상 바르지 않은 것은?

①   ②   ③   ④   ⑤

31 According to the passage, people of what countries express "no" by nodding their head? Answer in English with a full sentence.

➡ _____
_____

[32~34] 다음 글을 읽고 물음에 답하시오.

Diego: Does anyone speak German?
Today, I was 5 minutes ①late for an appointment with my German friend. When I finally met him, he looked very angry. He said that I must try to ②keep my "Termin" better. What does it mean?
⌐, Smile: "Termin" means "③appointment" in German. Germans think that it's ④important to be on time. In Germany, there is a saying, "What is set should be kept." (A)_____, please be ⑤honest with Germans.

32 빈칸 (A)에 들어갈 말로 가장 적절한 것은?

① However   ② So
③ Though   ④ For example
⑤ On the other hand

33 ①~⑤ 중 글의 흐름상 어색한 것은?

①   ②   ③   ④   ⑤

34 위 글의 내용과 일치하지 않는 것은?

① Diego has a friend who came from Germany.
② Diego's friend was angry because Diego was late.
③ Diego was on time for his appointment.
④ Diego doesn't speak German.
⑤ Smile knows what the word "Termin" means.

01 다음 대화를 읽고 대답할 수 <u>없는</u> 것은?

> B: Look at the Eiffel Tower.
> G: It's really tall and pretty!
> B: I'd like to tell you something about the Eiffel Tower. People didn't like it at first.
> G: Really? But it has become one of the most popular places in Paris these days!

① What are the boy and the girl looking at?

② What does the girl think about the Eiffel Tower?

③ What does the boy want to tell her about the Eiffel Tower?

④ Why didn't people like the Eiffel Tower at first?

⑤ What has the Eiffel Tower become in Paris these days?

[02~03] 다음 글을 읽고 물음에 답하시오.

> Tina: Hello, everyone. My name is Tina and I'm a travel writer. (A) Today, I'd like to tell you an important lesson that I learned while traveling. (B) When I first visited Korea, I thought Koreans were rude because many people asked me my age. (C) Koreans use language differently to people who are older than them, so they need to know the other person's age. (D) This experience has taught me the importance of learning and understanding other cultures. (E)

02 위 글의 (A)~(E) 중 주어진 문장이 들어가기에 적절한 곳은?

> However, I later found out that this was because of their culture.

① (A)　② (B)　③ (C)　④ (D)　⑤ (E)

03 위 글을 읽고 대답할 수 <u>없는</u> 것은?

① What is Tina's speech about?

② Why is Tina giving a speech?

③ Why did Tina think that Koreans were rude?

④ What message does Tina want to give to people?

⑤ What do Koreans do to understand other cultures?

[04~06] 다음 대화를 읽고 물음에 답하시오.

> Mina: Alex, do you have some time?
> Alex: Yes, Mina, what is it?
> Mina: (A) I heard that you went to Spain this summer!
> Alex: (B) Yes, I went on a family trip.
> Mina: (C) I'm thinking of visiting Spain this winter.
> Alex: (D) I see. I think Spain is a really nice country to visit. There are many interesting places.
> Mina: (E) Where do you recommend that I go?
> Alex: ⓐ<u>I recommend visiting the Prado Museum in Madrid.</u> It's one of the most famous museums in the world.
> Mina: Thanks for the help!

04 위 대화의 (A)~(E) 중 주어진 문장이 들어가기에 적절한 곳은?

> Can you tell me more about your trip?

① (A)　② (B)　③ (C)　④ (D)　⑤ (E)

05 위 대화의 밑줄 친 @와 바꾸어 쓸 수 없는 것은?

① How about visiting the Prado Museum in Madrid?

② I advise you to visit the Prado Museum in Madrid.

③ Why don't you visit the Prado Museum in Madrid?

④ I think you should visit the Prado Museum in Madrid.

⑤ I'm doubtful if you can visit the Prado Museum in Madrid.

06 위 대화의 내용과 일치하지 않는 것은?

① Alex는 이번 여름에 가족 여행으로 스페인을 다녀왔다.

② Mina는 이번 겨울에 스페인을 방문하려고 생각 중이다.

③ Alex는 스페인이 방문하기에 정말 좋은 나라라고 생각한다.

④ Alex는 Madrid에 있는 Prado 박물관을 방문할 것을 추천하였다.

⑤ Mina는 세계에서 유명한 박물관들 중의 한 곳을 방문하였다.

[07~09] 다음 대화를 읽고 물음에 답하시오.

(Phone rings.)

Suji: Hello, Suji speaking.

Diego: Hi, it's me, Diego. Do you have time to talk?

Suji: Yes, what's up?

Diego: I'm doing my social studies homework on cultural differences, but I'm having trouble finding the right information.

Suji: I'd like to tell you about a website called "Culture Shock." I heard that people ask and answer questions about other cultures on that website.

Diego: That sounds perfect. Thank you for your help.

Suji: You're welcome. Good luck with the homework.

07 What's the matter with Diego?

➡ _____

08 What does Suji advise Diego to do?

➡ _____
_____

09 What do people do on the website called "Culture Shock"?

➡ _____
_____

10 다음 대화에서 대화의 흐름이 자연스럽게 이어지도록 순서대로 배열하시오.

Mina: Alex, do you have some time?

Alex: Yes, Mina, what is it?

Mina: I heard that you went to Spain this summer!

(A) Where do you recommend that I go?

(B) Can you tell me more about your trip? I'm thinking of visiting Spain this winter.

(C) I recommend visiting the Prado Museum in Madrid. It's one of the most famous museums in the world.

(D) Yes, I went on a family trip.

(E) I see. I think Spain is a really nice country to visit. There are many interesting places.

Mina: Thanks for the help!

➡ _____

11 다음 주어진 문장에서 밑줄 친 부분과 바꾸어 쓸 수 있는 것은?

> This is the thing which I want to buy.

① which   ② what   ③ that
④ whom   ⑤ whose

12 다음 우리말을 영어로 바르게 옮긴 것을 모두 고르시오.

> Mrs. Han은 우리가 존경하는 선생님이다.

① Mrs. Han is the teacher whom we look up.
② Mrs. Han is the teacher to whom we look up.
③ Mrs. Han is the teacher we look up to.
④ Mrs. Han is the teacher to that we look up.
⑤ Mrs. Han is the teacher to which we look up.

13 다음 빈칸에 이어질 말로 가장 적절한 것은?

> The man _____.

① whom we met with the children were kind
② we met with the children were kind
③ that we met with the children was kind
④ with whom we met children with was kind
⑤ who we met with was kind

14 다음 빈칸에 알맞은 말을 쓰시오.

> 내가 도서관에서 빌린 책들은 지루해.
> ➡ The books _____ boring.

15 다음 우리말을 영어로 옮길 때 빈칸에 적절한 말을 쓰시오. 한 칸에 하나의 단어만 쓰시오.

> 내가 Judy에게서 들은 것을 너에게 말해 줄게.

➡ I will tell you _____ _____ _____
_____ _____ from Judy.

➡ I will tell you _____ _____
from Judy.

16 주어진 단어를 활용하여 다음 우리말을 지시에 맞게 영어로 쓰시오.

> 이것은 너를 아름답게 만들어 주는 것이야.
> (this / make)

(1) 목적격 관계대명사를 이용하여
➡ _____

(2) what을 이용하여
➡ _____

17 다음 중 어법상 바르지 않은 것은?

① This is the river that I swam in last week.
② Where is the girl you had lunch with?
③ What you need right now is to take a deep breath.
④ A bottle of water is the thing what I want to drink.
⑤ The woman who stole my car was arrested.

[18~21] 다음 글을 읽고 물음에 답하시오.

Shao: Help!
I'm a Chinese boy who has been invited to a Kenyan friend's house. But I don't know anything about Kenya. Are ①there ②any manners ③that ④I need ⑤to know? Please give me some advice!

└ **Clever:** I heard that when Chinese people are invited to someone's house, they leave some food on their plate. It shows that there was enough food for the guest. (A)_____, with Kenyan people, please finish all the food the host has prepared. If you leave food, it means that you didn't like it.

출제율 95%

18 다음 중 빈칸 (A)에 들어갈 말로 가장 적절한 것은?

① For example ② Therefore
③ However ④ Moreover
⑤ As a result

출제율 95%

19 ①~⑤ 중 생략할 수 있는 것은?

①   ②   ③   ④   ⑤

출제율 85%

20 위 글의 내용에 맞게 빈칸에 알맞은 말을 쓰시오.

> Chinese people leave some food on their plate to show that _____
> _____.

출제율 100%

21 위 글의 내용과 일치하지 <u>않는</u> 것은?

① Shao asked some advice.
② Shao's friend invited Shao to his house to have dinner.
③ Shao knew nothing about Kenya.
④ It is recommended to eat all the food on your plate when you are invited to a house of Kenyan people.
⑤ There is a cultural difference between China and Kenya.

[22~25] 다음 글을 읽고 물음에 답하시오.

Dear Mira,
Hello, Mira. I'm visiting Korea this winter and I am very excited about the trip. But ①<u>what worries me</u> are the cultural differences. So, I was hoping to get ②<u>some</u> advice from you.
                              Love, David

Dear David,
I'd like to tell you about a mistake (A)<u>that</u> you can make ③<u>if you don't know</u> Korean culture. In Korea, the oldest person starts eating first and younger people wait ④<u>for a while</u>. I hope ⑤<u>that</u> you have a great time in Korea.
                              Love, Mira

출제율 85%

22 다음 중 밑줄 친 (A)를 대신하여 쓰일 수 있는 것은?

① which ② whose ③ who
④ whom ⑤ what

출제율 90%

23 According to the letter, how does David feel about the trip? Answer in English with a full sentence.

➡ _____

출제율 90%

24 In Korea, who starts to eat first? Answer in English with a full sentence.

➡ _____

출제율 100%

25 다음 중 ①~⑤에 관한 설명으로 바르지 <u>않은</u> 것은?

① 'the thing which worries me'로 바꾸어 쓸 수 있다.
② 셀 수 있는 명사와 셀 수 없는 명사를 모두 수식할 수 있다.
③ 'unless you know'로 바꾸어 쓸 수 있다.
④ 'for a long time'으로 바꾸어 쓸 수 있다.
⑤ 명사절 접속사로 완전한 문장을 이끈다.

[01~03] 다음 대화를 읽고 물음에 답하시오.

Mina: Alex, do you have some time?

Alex: Yes, Mina, what is it?

Mina: I heard that you went to Spain this summer!

Alex: Yes, I went on a family trip.

Mina: Can you tell me more about your trip? I'm thinking of visiting Spain this winter.

Alex: I see. I think Spain is a really nice country to visit. There are many interesting places.

Mina: Where do you recommend that I go?

Alex: I recommend visiting the Prado Museum in Madrid. It's one of the most famous museums in the world.

Mina: Thanks for the help!

01 Where did Alex visit this summer?

➡ _____

02 중요 Why does Mina ask some information about Spain? Use the phrase "It's because."

➡ _____

_____

03 What does Alex recommend visiting in Spain?

➡ _____

_____

04 다음 빈칸에 들어갈 알맞은 말을 쓰시오.

A: Did you hear that the boy _____ we saw on the street was a famous actor?

B: Yes. That's _____ I heard.

05 지시에 맞게 다음 두 문장을 하나의 문장으로 쓸 때 빈칸을 알맞게 채우시오.

Where is the chair? Mindy was sitting on the chair.

➡ (1) Where is the chair _____ on?

➡ (2) Where is the chair _____ sitting?

06 중요 다음 주어진 단어를 이용하여 우리말을 영어로 옮길 때 빈칸에 들어갈 알맞은 말을 쓰시오.

내가 그린 것을 너에게 보여줄게. (draw)
➡ Let me show you _____.

07 다음 대화의 빈칸에 알맞은 말을 다섯 단어로 쓰시오.

A: What kind of fruit do you like the most?

B: Strawberry is the fruit _____ _____.

08 다음 문장과 같은 의미의 문장을 10단어로 쓰시오.

> The thing that I want to buy today is a new computer.

➡ _____

[09~11] 다음 글을 읽고 물음에 답하시오.

Diego: Does anyone speak German?
[A] When I finally met him, he looked very angry.
[B] Today, I was 5 minutes late for an appointment with my German friend.
[C] He said that I must try to keep my "Termin" better. What does it mean?

ㄴ Smile: "Termin" means "appointment" in German. Germans think that it's important to be on time. In Germany, there is a saying, "What is set should be kept." So, please be punctual with Germans.
Did you find the information you needed? (A)<u>문화 차이를 이해하는 것은 당신의 삶을 변화시킬 겁니다.</u> We hope that what you have read was helpful and interesting. Please visit our website again!

09 자연스러운 글이 되도록 [A]~[C]를 바르게 배열하시오.

➡ _____

10 주어진 어구를 바르게 배열하여 우리말 (A)를 영어로 쓰시오. 필요하다면 어형을 바꾸시오.

> (cultural / understand / make / differences / a difference / can / in your life)

➡ _____
_____

11 위 글의 내용에 맞게 빈칸에 알맞은 말을 쓰시오.

> When you make an appointment with a German friend, it is important to _____ _____ .

[12~13] 다음 글을 읽고 물음에 답하시오.

Shao: Help!
I'm a Chinese boy who has been invited to a Kenyan friend's house. But I don't know anything about Kenya. Are there any manners I need to know? Please give me some advice!

ㄴ Clever: I heard that when Chinese people are invited to someone's house, they leave some food on their plate. It shows that there was enough food for the guest. However, with Kenyan people, please finish all the food the host has prepared. If you leave food, it means that you didn't like it.

12 위 글의 내용에 맞게 빈칸에 알맞은 말을 쓰시오.

> Q: In China, how can we express that we are full because there was enough food?
> A: By leaving some food on your plate, you can show that _____ _____ _____ _____ made you full enough.

13 위 글의 내용에 맞게 빈칸에 알맞은 말을 쓰시오.

> In Kenya, there is a _____ _____ that guests should _____ all the food _____ _____ .

01 다음 대화의 내용과 일치하도록 Brian의 일기를 완성하시오.

> Somi: I heard that there is a science contest next week.
>
> Brian: Really? I'm interested in science.
>
> Somi: Then you should sign up. There is a big prize for the winner.
>
> Brian: Great! Thanks for telling me.

> Mon, Oct 28th, 2019
>
> I have lots of interests in (A)_____. I heard good news from Somi today. She told me that a science contest will (B)_____. She encouraged me to (C)_____ for it. She said that there is (D)_____ for the winner. I decided to give it a try. I really appreciated that she told me about that.

02 관계대명사 what과 주어진 동사를 활용하여 여러 가지 문장을 쓰시오.

> eat / see / hear / want / need

(1) _____

(2) _____

(3) _____

03 다음 대화를 읽고 기모노를 소개하는 글을 완성하시오.

> A: I'd like to tell you about Kimono, traditional Japanese clothes. Usually, a flower pattern is drawn on the clothing and it is very colorful.
>
> B: It must be very pretty.
>
> A: You can see many Japanese people wearing it at a festival.

> Hello. Our group would like to tell you about Kimono. It is _____.
> We can see _____ drawn on the clothing. The pattern makes the clothes _____. Japanese people wear it _____. You will think it is very pretty.

단원별 모의고사

1 다음 영영풀이가 가리키는 것을 고르시오.

> the most important town or city of a country, usually where the central government operates from

① capital   ② prize   ③ respect
④ plate   ⑤ tower

2 다음 우리말에 맞게 빈칸에 알맞은 말을 쓰시오.

(1) 나는 나의 나라에 이 편지를 보내고 싶어요.
   ➡ I want to send this letter to my
   _____.

(2) 그것들 간에 차이점은 없습니다.
   ➡ There's no _____ between them.

(3) 독일 축구팀이 경기에서 우승했다.
   ➡ The _____ soccer team won the game.

3 다음 문장에 공통으로 들어갈 말을 고르시오.

> • How about trying this seafood _____?
> • I could see how hungry she was from the way she cleared her _____.
> • The sink was full of _____s.

① plate   ② prize
③ meal   ④ pumpkin
⑤ wave

4 다음 우리말에 맞게 주어진 단어를 사용하여 영작하시오.

(1) 이번 주 금요일 우리 약속이 몇 시니? (this, time)
   ➡ _____

(2) 아시아에서 사람들은 만날 때 보통 고개를 숙인다. (usually, when)
   ➡ _____

5 다음 대화가 자연스럽게 이어지도록 순서대로 배열하시오.

> (A) I agree with you. Respecting each other's differences is very important.
> (B) What is it?
> (C) I'd like to tell you something about love.
> (D) I think the most important thing in love is respect.

➡ _____

[06~07] 다음 대화를 읽고 물음에 답하시오.

B: Look at the Eiffel Tower.
G: It's really tall and pretty!
B: (A)I'd like to tell you something about the Eiffel Tower. People didn't like it at first.
G: Really? But it has become one of the most popular places in Paris these days!

6 위 대화의 밑줄 친 (A)와 바꾸어 쓰기가 어색한 것은?

① Let me tell you something about the Eiffel Tower.
② I want to tell you something about the Eiffel Tower.
③ I'd like to say something about the Eiffel Tower.
④ I'll tell you something about the Eiffel Tower.
⑤ I heard about something about the Eiffel Tower.

07 What has the Eiffel Tower become in Paris these days?

➡ _____

[08~09] 다음 대화를 읽고 물음에 답하시오.

> G: I'd like to tell you something about love.
> B: What is it?
> G: I think the most important thing in love is
> (A)_____.
> B: (B)I agree with you. Respecting each other's differences is very important.

08 위 대화의 빈칸 (A)에 들어갈 말을 대화에서 찾아 알맞은 형태로 쓰시오.

➡ _____

09 위 대화의 밑줄 친 (B)와 바꾸어 쓸 수 없는 것은?

① I think so.
② I'm with you.
③ I can't agree with you more.
④ I think that's right.
⑤ I'm afraid that's not right.

[10~11] 다음 대화를 읽고 물음에 답하시오.

> Somi: I heard that there is a science contest next week.
> Brian: Really? I'm interested in science.
> Somi: Then you should sign up. There is a big prize for the winner.
> Brian: Great! Thanks for telling me.

10 What does Brian have an interest in?

➡ _____

11 What is prepared for the winner of the science contest?

➡ _____

12 다음 짝지어진 대화가 어색한 것은?

① A: I'd like to tell you something about love.
   B: What is it?
② A: I heard that it will rain tomorrow.
   B: What? It can be true.
③ A: Where do you think I should go?
   B: I recommend visiting the Prado Museum in Madrid.
④ A: I heard that you went to Spain this summer!
   B: Yes, I went on a family trip.
⑤ A: Look at the Eiffel Tower.
   B: It's really tall and pretty!

13 다음 중 빈칸에 들어갈 말로 적절한 것을 모두 고르시오.

> _____ happened last week was not Sally's fault.

① The thing   ② That   ③ What
④ The thing that ⑤ When

14 다음 문장과 같은 의미의 문장을 쓰시오.

> The thing that he said an hour ago is not true.

➡ _____

15 다음 중 어법상 옳은 문장의 개수는?

> ⓐ Julia has many toys which she likes to play with.
> ⓑ Do you know the story of the man who he told you?
> ⓒ This is the house in that we used to live some time together.
> ⓓ Pizza is the only food that I can make.
> ⓔ This is what I made for you.

① 1개　② 2개　③ 3개　④ 4개　⑤ 5개

16 다음 빈칸에 알맞은 말을 다섯 단어로 쓰시오.

> 내가 미래에 되고 싶은 것은 의사야.
> ➡ _____ in the future is a doctor.

17 다음 빈칸에 들어갈 말이 바르게 짝지어진 것은?

> • The Genie can give Aladin _____ he wants.
> • He got rid of the mice _____ the village people didn't like.
> • The woman _____ I spoke gave me good advice.

① which – that – whom
② who – that – that
③ whom – which – to whom
④ what – which – whom
⑤ what – which – to whom

[18~19] 다음 글을 읽고 물음에 답하시오.

Shao: Help!
I'm a Chinese boy who has been invited to a Kenyan friend's house. But I don't know anything about Kenya. Are there any manners I need to know? Please give me some advice!
└ Clever: I heard that when Chinese people are invited to someone's house, (A)they leave some food on their plate. It shows that there was enough food for the guest. However, with Kenyan people, please finish all the food the host has prepared. If you leave food, (B)it means that you didn't like it.

18 다음 중 밑줄 친 (A)와 (B)가 지칭하는 것이 바르게 짝지어진 것은?

① Kenyan people – the food
② Chinese people – leaving food
③ Chinese people – finishing food
④ Kenyan people – leaving food
⑤ Kenyan people – finishing food

19 다음 중 위 글을 읽고 답할 수 있는 것은?

① Where is Clever from?
② Why does Clever know a lot about Kenyan culture?
③ What is a polite table manner in China?
④ When was Shao invited by his Kenyan friend?
⑤ What kinds of food do Chinese people prepare for their guests?

[20~22] 다음 글을 읽고 물음에 답하시오.

Diego: Does anyone speak German?
Today, I was 5 minutes late for an appointment with my German friend. When I finally met him, he looked very angry. He said that I must

try to keep my "Termin" better. What does it mean?

ㄴ Smile: "Termin" means "appointment" in German. Germans think that (A)_____. In Germany, there is a saying, "What is set should be kept." So, please be punctual with Germans.

Did you find the information you needed? We hope that what you have read was helpful and interesting. Understanding cultural differences can make a difference in your life. Please visit our website again!

20 다음 중 빈칸 (A)에 들어갈 말로 가장 적절한 것은?

① it's necessary to call first
② it's impossible to keep time well
③ it's unnecessary to be punctual
④ it's important to be on time
⑤ it's happy to meet friends

21 다음 중 Diego가 글을 올린 목적으로 가장 적절한 것은?

① To make an excuse about his being late.
② To find out how he can make friends with the German boy again.
③ To explain why he was late.
④ To blame his German friend.
⑤ To ask what a German word means.

22 다음 문장에서 This에 해당되는 말을 위 글에서 찾아 쓰시오.

> This is a sentence that people often say and that gives advice or information about human life and experience.

➡ _____

[23~25] 다음 글을 읽고 물음에 답하시오.

Welcome to "Culture Shock"! If you are interested in cultures around the world, this is the website (A)[that / what] you are looking for! You can ask and answer any questions you may have about (B)[other / another] cultures. Let's take a look!

Suji: I'm very upset.
There is a new student from Greece in my school. I asked her to be friends with me but she shook her head. How rude!

ㄴ Ocean: Calm down. I'm sure ⓐ그녀가 진짜 의미했던 것 was "yes." In some countries like Greece, Turkey, and Iran, nodding your head means "no" and (C)[shake / shaking] your head means "yes."

23 밑줄 친 우리말 (A)를 네 단어의 영어로 쓰시오.

➡ _____

24 (A)~(C)에서 어법상 옳은 것끼리 바르게 짝지어진 것은?

① what – other – shake
② what – another – shaking
③ that – other – shaking
④ that – other – shake
⑤ that – another – shaking

25 According to the passage, what did Suji ask the new student from Greece? Answer in English with a full sentence.

➡ _____

Take Control of Your Life

🎤 의사소통 기능

- 능력 부인하기
  I don't know how to be on a good diet.

- 충고하기
  Make sure you have at least some beans or eggs.

🎙 언어 형식

- too+형용사/부사+to부정사
  I am **too** old **to** run.

- 가정법과거
  If I **were** free, I **would be** so happy.

Words & Expressions

Key Words

- **add** [æd] 동 추가하다, 덧붙여 말하다
- **advice** [ædváis] 명 조언, 충고
- **amount** [əmáunt] 명 양, 총액
- **asleep** [əslíːp] 형 잠이 든
- **bean** [biːn] 명 콩
- **beg** [beg] 동 구걸하다, 간청하다
- **bitter** [bítər] 형 쓴
- **bottle** [bátl] 명 병
- **brave** [breiv] 형 용감한
- **butterfly** [bʌ́tərflai] 명 나비
- **cap** [kæp] 명 뚜껑, 모자
- **career** [kəríər] 명 직업, 경력
- **case** [keis] 명 용기, 경우
- **catch** [kætʃ] 동 잡다
- **caterpillar** [kǽtərpìlər] 명 애벌레
- **certain** [sə́ːrtn] 형 어떤, 확실한
- **chew** [tʃuː] 동 씹다
- **claw** [klɔː] 명 (동물의) 발톱
- **clever** [klévər] 형 똑똑한, 영리한
- **comfortable** [kʌ́mfərtəbl] 형 편안한
- **concentrate** [kánsəntrèit] 동 집중하다
- **curious** [kjúəriəs] 형 호기심 많은
- **diligent** [dílədʒənt] 형 부지런한, 근면한
- **empty** [émpti] 형 텅 빈 동 비우다

- **expensive** [ikspénsiv] 형 비싼
- **fat** [fæt] 형 뚱뚱한, 살찐
- **greedy** [gríːdi] 형 욕심 많은, 탐욕스러운
- **harmful** [háːrmfəl] 형 해로운
- **healthy** [hélθi] 형 건강한
- **instead** [instéd] 부 대신에
- **pant** [pænt] 동 헐떡거리다
- **posture** [pástʃər] 명 자세
- **press** [pres] 동 누르다
- **pretend** [priténd] 동 ～인 척하다
- **recommend** [rèkəménd] 동 추천하다
- **regularly** [régjulərli] 부 규칙적으로
- **rest** [rest] 명 휴식 동 쉬다
- **rude** [ruːd] 형 무례한
- **salty** [sɔ́ːlti] 형 짠
- **scissors** [sízərz] 명 가위
- **screen** [skriːn] 명 화면
- **shape** [ʃeip] 명 모양, 형태
- **stage** [steidʒ] 명 무대
- **stupid** [stúːpid] 형 어리석은, 멍청한
- **sunshine** [sʌ́nʃain] 명 햇빛
- **throw** [θrou] 동 던지다
- **weak** [wiːk] 형 약한
- **weapon** [wépən] 명 무기

Key Expressions

- **add up** 합산하다
- **as well** 또한
- **be in good shape** 건강하다, 몸매가 좋다
- **be on a diet** 다이어트[식이요법] 중이다
- **be tired of** ～에 싫증이 나다
- **be used to -ing** ～하는 데 익숙하다
- **get rid of** ～을 제거하다, ～을 없애다

- **make sure** 반드시 ～하다, ～을 확실히 하다
- **no longer** 더 이상 ～ 아니다
- **out of breath** 숨이 가쁜
- **put off** ～을 미루다
- **run away** 달아나다
- **run after** ～을 쫓다

Word Power

※ 서로 반대되는 뜻을 가진 어휘

- ☐ **clever** 영리한 ↔ **foolish** 어리석은
- ☐ **empty** 텅 빈 ↔ **full** 가득 찬
- ☐ **regularly** 규칙적으로 ↔ **irregularly** 불규칙적으로
- ☐ **rude, impolite** 무례한 ↔ **polite** 예의 바른
- ☐ **healthy** 건강한 ↔ **sick** 병에 걸린
- ☐ **expensive** 비싼 ↔ **cheap** 값이 싼
- ☐ **fail** 실패하다 ↔ **succeed** 성공하다

- ☐ **fat** 뚱뚱한 ↔ **thin** 마른
- ☐ **throw** 던지다 ↔ **catch** 잡다
- ☐ **weak** 약한 ↔ **strong** 건강한
- ☐ **diligent** 부지런한 ↔ **lazy** 게으른
- ☐ **asleep** 잠이 든 ↔ **awake** 깨어 있는
- ☐ **brave** 용감한 ↔ **cowardly** 비겁한, 겁이 많은
- ☐ **high** 높은 ↔ **low** 낮은

English Dictionary

- ☐ **advice** 조언, 충고
  - → an opinion or a suggestion about what somebody should do in a particular situation
    누군가가 특정한 상황에서 해야 하는 것에 대한 의견이나 제안
- ☐ **beg** 간청하다, 구걸하다
  - → to ask somebody for something especially in an anxious way because you want or need it very much
    당신이 매우 원하거나 필요하기 때문에 특히 열망하는 방식으로 무언가를 누군가에게 요청하다
- ☐ **butterfly** 나비
  - → a flying insect with a long thin body and four large, usually brightly coloured wings
    길고 가는 몸과 보통 밝은 색의 4개의 큰 날개를 가진 나는 곤충
- ☐ **catch** 잡다
  - → to stop and hold a moving object, especially in your hands
    특히 당신의 손으로 움직이는 물체를 멈추어 잡다
- ☐ **chew** 씹다
  - → to bite food into small pieces in your mouth with your teeth to make it easier to swallow 더 삼키기 쉽게 만들기 위해 입속에서 치아로 음식을 작은 조각으로 물어뜯다
- ☐ **claw** 발톱
  - → one of the sharp curved nails on the end of an animal's or a bird's foot
    동물이나 새의 발끝에 날카롭고 굴곡진 발톱의 하나
- ☐ **comfortable** 편안한
  - → making you feel physically relaxed
    신체적으로 편안하게 느끼도록 만드는

- ☐ **empty** 텅 빈
  - → with no people or things inside
    안에 사람이나 물건이 없는
- ☐ **greedy** 탐욕스러운
  - → wanting more money, power, food, etc. than you really need
    정말로 필요한 것보다 더 많은 돈, 힘, 음식 등을 원하는
- ☐ **harmful** 해로운
  - → causing damage or injury to somebody/something, especially to a person's health or to the environment
    누군가 또는 무언가에, 특히 사람의 건강이나 환경에 해나 손상이나 부상을 야기하는
- ☐ **healthy** 건강한
  - → good for your health 당신의 건강에 좋은
- ☐ **rude** 무례한
  - → having or showing a lack of respect for other people and their feelings
    다른 사람과 그들의 감정에 대한 존중의 부족함을 갖거나 보여주는
- ☐ **scissors** 가위
  - → a tool for cutting paper or cloth, that has two sharp blades with handles, joined together in the middle
    가운데에 묶여 있는 손잡이를 가진 두 개의 날카로운 날을 가진 종이나 옷을 자르기 위한 도구
- ☐ **weapon** 무기
  - → an object such as a knife, gun, bomb, etc. that is used for fighting or attacking somebody
    누군가와 싸우거나 공격하기 위해 사용되는 칼, 총, 폭탄 등과 같은 물체

서답형
01 다음 짝지어진 단어의 관계가 같도록 빈칸에 알맞은 말을 쓰시오.

> fat : thin = sick : _____

02 다음 영영풀이가 가리키는 것을 고르시오.

> an opinion or a suggestion about what somebody should do in a particular situation

① rest   ② posture
③ stage   ④ amount
⑤ advice

중요
03 다음 중 밑줄 친 부분의 뜻풀이가 바르지 <u>않은</u> 것은?

① Catch the ball that I throw. 던지다
② I drink tea instead of coffee. 대신에
③ I'm looking for a comfortable chair. 편안한
④ Do you know that you have a bad posture? 자세
⑤ I don't like greedy people. 탐욕스러운

04 다음 주어진 문장의 밑줄 친 shape과 같은 의미로 쓰인 것은?

> Can you tell me what you do to be in good shape?

① Shape the dough into a ball.
② I like to keep in shape, so I go to the gym every day.
③ This tool is used for shaping the cookies.
④ This house is in shape of a triangle.
⑤ The island was originally circular in shape.

중요
05 다음 문장에 공통으로 들어갈 말을 고르시오.

> • Jane is panting out _____ breath after the game.
> • This pill will get rid _____ your headache.
> • I'm tired _____ this music. I'm looking for new genre.

① with   ② to   ③ of
④ on   ⑤ at

서답형
06 다음 우리말을 영작하시오.

(1) 그 무기가 전쟁에서 그들이 이기도록 도와주었다.
   ➡ _____
(2) 모든 병들이 비어 있었다.
   ➡ _____
(3) 나는 그 비싼 펜을 살 수 없다.
   ➡ _____

서답형
07 다음 문장의 빈칸에 들어갈 말을 〈보기〉에서 골라 쓰시오.

> ┤ 보기 ├
> shape / catch / diligent / scissors / screen

(1) She must be so _____ to get up so early.
(2) Cut the paper with the _____.
(3) Please look at the TV _____ here.
(4) The pool is in the _____ of a heart.
(5) The animals use their sharp teeth to _____ food.

1 다음 짝지어진 단어의 관계가 같도록 빈칸에 알맞은 말을 쓰시오.

> expensive : cheap = _____ : full

2 다음 문장의 빈칸에 들어갈 말을 〈보기〉에서 골라 쓰시오.

> ┌─ 보기 ─┐
>
> make sure / out of breath / used to / get rid of / be in good shape

(1) I'm _____ writing a diary every day.

(2) What can I do to _____ ?

(3) We were _____ after running for 5 minutes.

(4) _____ that you should arrive at the station on time.

(5) I need to _____ waste before my parents come back home.

3 다음 우리말에 맞게 빈칸에 알맞은 말을 쓰시오.

(1) 그는 달리기 후에 여전히 헐떡거리고 있었다.
➡ He was still _____ after his run.

(2) 그녀는 나를 못 본 척했다.
➡ She _____ that she didn't see me.

(3) 너의 건강을 위해 규칙적으로 운동해라.
➡ Exercise _____ for your health.

04 다음 우리말을 주어진 단어를 이용하여 영작하시오.

(1) 쿠키들이 너무 딱딱해서 그것들을 씹을 수가 없어요. (so, that)
➡ _____

(2) 호랑이들과 사자들은 날카로운 발톱을 갖고 있다. (sharp)
➡ _____

(3) 나는 수업 중에 집중할 수 없다. (during)
➡ _____

(4) 나쁜 습관을 없애기는 쉽지 않다. (it, rid)
➡ _____

05 다음 주어진 우리말과 일치하도록 주어진 어구를 배열하여 영작하시오.

(1) 나는 이 병을 어떻게 여는지 모른다.
(to / I / how / bottle / don't / open / know / this)
➡ _____

(2) 나는 체중을 줄이기 위해 다이어트 중이야.
(on / I'm / weight / a diet / lose / to)
➡ _____

(3) 미루지 말아야 한다는 것을 명심해.
(put / not / sure / should / make / off / you)
➡ _____

(4) 나는 이 채소들이 맛이 쓰기 때문에 싫어해.
(these / taste / I / bitter / hate / they / vegetables / because)
➡ _____

Conversation

① 능력 부인하기

I don't know how to be on a good diet. (나는 좋은 다이어트를 하는 법을 모르겠어.)

■ 상대방에게 자신의 능력을 부인할 때 'I don't know ~.', 'I can't ~.', 'I'm not good at ~.' 등의 표현을 사용하여 표현할 수 있다.

능력을 부인할 때 쓰는 표현

- I can't move these boxes. (이 상자들을 옮길 수 없어.)
- I'm not good at playing soccer. (나는 축구를 잘하지 못해.)
- I'm poor at drawing. (나는 그림을 못 그려.)
- I have no idea how to use this machine. (나는 이 기계를 어떻게 사용하는지 몰라.)
- I don't know how to find my phone. (나는 내 전화기를 어떻게 찾아야 할지 모르겠어.)
- It's not easy to open this bottle. (이 병을 여는 게 쉽지 않아.)

부탁하는 표현

- Can you help me? (나 좀 도와줄 수 있니?)
- Would you mind opening the window? (창문을 열어 주시겠어요?)
- Could I ask you a favor? (부탁 좀 드려도 될까요?)
- Please give me a hand. (나 좀 도와주세요.)
- Would you do me a favor? (부탁 좀 들어주시겠어요?)
- May I ask a favor of you? (부탁 좀 할까요?)

핵심 Check

1. 다음 주어진 우리말과 일치하도록 괄호 안에 알맞은 말을 쓰시오.

(1) A: I _____ _____ _____ _____ _____ my future career.

(나는 어떻게 내 미래 진로를 선택해야 할지 모르겠어.)

B: _____ _____ _____ talk to your career teacher and do some tests?

(진로 선생님과 이야기하고 몇몇 검사들을 해보는 게 어때?)

(2) A: I'm not _____ at math. I'm afraid of taking the math test today.

(나는 수학을 잘하지 못해. 나는 오늘 수학 시험 보는 게 두려워.)

B: _____ _____ solve the easy problems first. (너는 쉬운 문제들을 먼저 푸는 게 낫겠어.)

② 충고하기

Make sure you have at least some beans or eggs.
(최소한 콩이나 계란을 먹어야 하는 것을 명심해.)

- 상대방에게 충고나 조언을 할 때 'Make sure ~.', 'Why don't you ~?', 'You'd better ~.', 'Don't ~.' 등의 표현을 사용하여 충고할 수 있다.

충고할 때 쓰는 표현

- Make sure you don't exercise too hard. (운동을 너무 많이 하지 말 것을 명심해.)
- You should get enough sleep. (충분히 잠을 자야 해.)
- Why don't you get some fresh air? (신선한 공기 좀 마시는 게 어때?)
- You'd better ask your teacher's opinion. (네 선생님의 의견을 묻는 게 낫겠어.)
- Don't press the power button. (전원 단추를 누르지 마.)
- Be careful not to catch a cold. (감기에 걸리지 않게 조심해.)
- Watch out for cars. (차 조심해.)

충고를 구할 때 쓰는 표현

- What should I do? (제가 어떻게 해야 하나요?)
- Do you think I should see a doctor? (제가 병원에 가야 한다고 생각하시나요?)
- Can I get your advice on this matter? (이 문제에 대해 조언을 얻을 수 있을까요?)
- What would you do if you could win the contest? (대회에서 우승하면 뭐 할 거예요?)

충고에 답하는 표현

- Okay. I will. (알겠어요. 제가 할게요.)
- I'll try next time. (다음에 할게.)
- I'll try not to. (그렇지 않도록 할게.)

핵심 Check

2. 다음 주어진 우리말과 일치하도록 괄호 안에서 알맞은 말을 선택하시오.

   (1) A: I'm trying to get better _____. But it is not _____.

      (나는 더 나은 시력을 얻기 위해 노력하고 있어. 하지만 쉽지 않네.)

      B: _____ _____ you don't look at your phone during the night.

      (너는 밤 동안에는 네 핸드폰을 보지 말 것을 명심해.)

   (2) A: I want to improve my grades, so I'm studying very hard.

      (나는 내 성적을 향상시키고 싶어서 공부를 열심히 하고 있어.)

      B: _____ _____ get enough sleep as well. (너는 또한 잠도 충분히 자야 해.)

Everyday English 1 B Listening Activity

Ms. Kim: Minjae, can I ❶have a word with you? It won't take long.

Minjae: Of course, Ms. Kim.

Ms. Kim: I saw that you are not ❷concentrating and ❸falling asleep ❹during classes.

Minjae: Oh, I'm sorry.

Ms. Kim: What's the matter?

Minjae: I just can't fall asleep easily. I tried to go to bed early but ❺ failed. I don't know how to get a good night's sleep.

Ms. Kim: ❻Maybe you should try to go to bed regularly, not early.

Minjae: Oh, then I will try doing that.

Ms. Kim: 민재야, 나하고 얘기 좀 할까? 길게 걸리지는 않을 거야.
Minjae: 물론이지요. 김 선생님.
Ms. Kim: 나는 네가 수업 시간에 집중하지 않고 잠든 것을 보았어.
Minjae: 아, 죄송해요.
Ms. Kim: 무슨 일 있니?
Minjae: 단지 쉽게 잠이 들지 못해요. 일찍 잠자리에 들려고 노력하지만 실패해요. 잠을 잘 자는 법을 모르겠어요.
Ms. Kim: 아마 규칙적으로 잠자리에 들려고 노력해야 할 거야. 일찍 자려고 하는 것이 아니라.
Minjae: 아, 그러면 그렇게 노력해 볼게요.

❶ have a word with: ~와 잠깐 이야기하다 ❷ concentrate: 집중하다
❸ fall asleep: 잠들다 ❹ during+명사, while+주어+동사
❺ 동사로 tried와 병렬구조이다.
❻ 충고하는 표현으로 'Make sure you should try to go to bed regularly, not early.'로 바꾸어 쓸 수 있다.

Check(√) True or False

(1) Minjae has difficulty falling asleep easily at night.　　T ☐ F ☐

(2) Ms. Kim advises Minjae to go to bed early.　　T ☐ F ☐

Everyday English 2 B Listening Activity

M: Today, I'd like to talk about your eyes. The eyes are really important parts of our body, but ❶more and more students are having eye problems. Some students cannot see without glasses or have ❷dry eyes. If you do not want these problems, ❸try to take some time to rest your eyes. When you study, try to look outside ❹for a while. ❺Make sure you don't look at computer or phone screens for too long.

M: 오늘, 저는 여러분의 눈에 대해 이야기하려고 합니다. 눈은 정말로 중요한 우리 신체의 일부분입니다. 그러나 점점 더 많은 학생들이 안구 문제를 겪고 있습니다. 몇몇 학생들은 안경이 없이는 볼 수 없거나 안구 건조증을 겪습니다. 만약 여러분이 이러한 문제를 겪는 것을 원하지 않는다면 여러분의 눈이 쉴 수 있는 시간을 가지도록 노력해 보세요. 여러분이 공부를 할 때, 잠시 동안이라도 바깥을 보려고 노력하세요. 컴퓨터나 휴대폰 화면을 너무 오래 보지 않도록 명심하세요.

❶ more and more: 더욱 더, 점점 더 ❷ dry: 건조한 ↔ wet: 습한, 촉촉한
❸ 동사원형으로 시작하는 명령문이다. ❹ for a while: 잠시 동안
❺ 충고하는 표현으로 'You should not look at computer or phone screens for too long.'으로 바꾸어 쓸 수 있다.

Check(√) True or False

(3) The speaker explains how to prevent eye problems.　　T ☐ F ☐

(4) The speaker recommends taking a rest for your eyes.　　T ☐ F ☐

Everyday English 1 A. Function Practice 2-(1)

G: Did you see my phone?

B: No, I didn't. Call your phone with ❶mine.

G: My phone will not ❷ring. I don't know how to find my phone.

B: Don't worry. ❸I'll help you. We will find ❹it soon.

❶ mine은 소유대명사로 'my phone'을 의미한다.
❷ ring은 '울리다'를 의미한다.
❸ 도움을 제공하는 표현으로 'I'll give you a hand.'로 바꾸어 쓸 수 있다.
❹ it은 소녀의 전화기를 가리킨다.

Everyday English 1 A. Function Practice 2-(2)

G: Oh, this flower is the one I'm ❶looking for. I'll take it.

M: Here it is. ❷Take good care of ❸it.

G: I don't know how to care.

M: Don't ❹water it too often. And it should get enough light.

❶ look for: ~을 찾다
❷ take care of: ~을 돌보다
❸ it은 여자가 구매한 the flower를 가리킨다.
❹ water는 동사로 쓰여서 '물을 주다'를 뜻한다.

Everyday English 2 A. Function Practice 2-(1)

G: My back and leg ❶hurt.

B: I think it's because you always ❷cross your legs.

G: Oh, do you think so? I didn't know I have poor ❸posture.

B: ❹Make sure you don't cross your legs when you sit in a chair.

❶ hurt는 '아프다'를 뜻한다.
❷ cross one's legs: 다리를 꼬다
❸ posture: 자세
❹ make sure는 '~을 명심하다'는 뜻으로 충고할 때 쓰인다. 'You should not cross your legs when you sit in a chair.'로 바꾸어 쓸 수 있다.

Everyday English 2 A. Function Practice 2-(2)

G: Your hands are ❶shaking. Are you okay?

B: It may be ❷because of the energy drink. I drank three cans for today's test.

G: That's too much! Make sure you don't drink ❸that much next time.

B: ❹Okay, I won't.

❶ shake: 흔들다
❷ because of 뒤에는 명사구가 이어진다.
❸ that much: 그렇게 많이
❹ 충고에 대한 대답으로 'I try not to.'로 바꾸어 대답할 수 있다.

In Real Life

Olivia: You're eating only rice, again!

Junho: You know ❶I'm on a diet for health reasons, ❷don't you?

Olivia: Of course. But I don't think that only eating rice will be very healthy.

Junho: What do you mean?

Olivia: Your body needs a ❸certain amount of meat.

Junho: But people said that I needed to avoid meat.

Olivia: That's not right. They mean eating too much meat will be ❹harmful.

Junho: I don't know how to be on a good diet! It's too difficult!

Olivia: Make sure you have ❺at least some beans or eggs. Oh, and ❻don't forget to eat some vegetables too.

❶ be on a diet: 다이어트 중이다
❷ 부가의문문으로 '그렇지 않니?'를 뜻한다.
❸ certain: 어느 정도의
❹ harmful: 해로운
❺ at least: 적어도
❻ don't forget to = remember to

● 다음 우리말과 일치하도록 빈칸에 알맞은 말을 쓰시오.

Everyday English 1 A. Function Practice (1)

1. G: Did you see my phone?

   B: No, I didn't. _____ your phone with _____.

   G: My phone will not _____. I don't _____ _____ _____ _____ find my phone.

   B: _____ _____. I'll _____ you. We will _____ _____ soon.

2. G: Oh, this flower is the one I'm _____ _____. I'll _____ _____.

   M: _____ it is. _____ good _____ of it.

   G: I don't know _____ _____ _____.

   M: Don't _____ it too often. And it should get _____ _____.

Everyday English 1 B. Listening Activity

Ms. Kim: Minjae, can I _____ _____ _____ with you? It won't _____ _____.

Minjae: Of _____, Ms. Kim.

Ms. Kim: I saw that you are not _____ and _____ _____ during classes.

Minjae: Oh, I'm _____.

Ms. Kim: What's _____ _____?

Minjae: I just can't _____ _____ _____. I _____ to go to bed early but _____. I don't know _____ _____ a good night's sleep.

Ms. Kim: Maybe you _____ _____ to go to bed regularly, not _____.

Minjae: Oh, then I will _____ _____ that.

해석

1. G: 내 휴대폰 보았니?
   B: 아니, 못 봤어. 내 것으로 네 휴대폰에 전화해 봐.
   G: 내 전화는 울리지 않을 거야. 난 내 전화를 찾는 법을 모르겠어.
   B: 걱정 마. 내가 도와줄게. 우리는 그걸 곧 찾을 거야.

2. G: 오, 이 꽃은 내가 찾던 거예요. 제가 살게요.
   M: 여기 있어요. 잘 돌보세요.
   G: 저는 어떻게 돌보아야 하는지 몰라요.
   M: 물을 너무 자주 주지 마세요. 그리고 충분한 햇빛을 받게 하세요.

Ms Kim: 민재야, 나하고 얘기 좀 할까? 길게 걸리지는 않을 거야.
Minjae: 물론이지요. 김 선생님.
Ms Kim: 나는 네가 수업 시간에 집중하지 않고 잠든 것을 보았어.
Minjae: 아, 죄송해요.
Ms Kim: 무슨 일 있니?
Minjae: 단지 쉽게 잠이 들지 못해요. 일찍 잠자리에 들려고 노력하지만 실패해요. 잠을 잘 자는 법을 모르겠어요.
Ms Kim: 아마 규칙적으로 잠자리에 들려고 노력해야 할 거야. 일찍 자려고 하는 것이 아니라.
Minjae: 아, 그러면 그렇게 노력해 볼게요.

Everyday English 2 A. Function Practice

1. **G:** My back and leg _____.

   B: I think it's because you always _____ _____ _____.

   G: Oh, do you think so? I didn't know I have _____ _____.

   B: _____ _____ you don't cross your legs when _____ _____ in a chair.

2. **G:** Your hands are _____. Are you _____?

   B: It may be because of the _____ _____. I _____ three cans for _____ _____.

   G: That's _____ _____! _____ _____ you don't drink that much next time.

   B: Okay, _____ _____.

Everyday English 2 B. Listening Activity

M: Today, I'd like to talk about your _____. The eyes are really _____ parts of our body, but _____ and _____ students are having eye problems. Some students cannot see without _____ or have _____ eyes. _____ you do not want these problems, _____ _____ take some time to _____ your eyes. When you study, try to _____ _____ for a while. _____ _____ you don't look at _____ or _____ _____ for too long.

In Real Life

Olivia: You're eating only _____, again!

Junho: You know I'm _____ _____ _____ for _____ _____, don't you?

Olivia: Of course. But I don't think that _____ _____ _____ will be very _____.

Junho: What do you _____?

Olivia: Your body needs a _____ _____ of _____.

Junho: But people said that I _____ to _____ meat.

Olivia: That's not right. They mean eating too much meat will be _____.

Junho: I don't know how to _____ _____ _____ _____ _____ diet! It's _____!

Olivia: Make sure you have _____ _____ some _____ or _____. Oh, and _____ _____ to eat some _____ too.

해석

1. G: 등과 다리가 아파.
   B: 내 생각에 그건 네가 항상 다리를 꼬아서 앉기 때문이야.
   G: 어머, 너 그렇게 생각하니? 나는 내가 자세가 좋지 않은지 몰랐어.
   B: 의자에 앉을 때 다리를 꼬지 않도록 명심해.

2. G: 네 손들이 떨리고 있어. 괜찮니?
   B: 아마도 에너지 음료 때문일 거야. 내가 오늘 시험을 위해 세 캔을 마셨거든.
   G: 그건 너무 많아! 너는 다음에는 그렇게 많이 마시지 말아야 한다는 것을 명심해.
   B: 알았어. 안 그럴게.

M: 오늘, 저는 여러분의 눈에 대해 이야기하려 합니다. 눈은 정말로 중요한 우리 신체의 일부분입니다. 그러나 점점 더 많은 학생들이 안구 문제들을 겪고 있습니다. 몇몇 학생들은 안경이 없이는 볼 수 없거나 안구 건조증을 겪습니다. 만약 여러분이 이러한 문제를 겪는 것을 원하지 않는다면 여러분의 눈이 쉴 수 있는 시간을 가지도록 노력해 보세요. 여러분이 공부를 할 때, 잠시 동안이라도 바깥을 보려고 노력하세요. 컴퓨터나 휴대폰 화면을 너무 오래 보지 않도록 명심하세요.

Olivia: 너 또 밥만 먹고 있구나!
Junho: 내가 건강상의 이유로 다이어트 중인 것 알지, 그렇지 않니?
Olivia: 물론이지. 그런데 나는 밥만 먹는 것이 매우 건강하다고 생각하지 않아.
Junho: 무슨 의미야?
Olivia: 너의 몸은 특정한 양의 고기를 필요로 해.
Junho: 그런데 사람들은 내가 고기를 피해야 할 필요가 있다고 말해.
Olivia: 그건 옳지 않아. 그들이 의미하는 건 고기를 너무 많이 먹는 것이 해롭다는 거야.
Junho: 나는 좋은 다이어트를 하는 법을 모르겠어. 너무 어려워!
Olivia: 최소한 콩이나 계란을 먹어야 하는 것을 명심해. 아, 그리고 채소를 먹는 것도 잊지 마.

[01~02] 다음 대화를 읽고 물음에 답하시오.

G: Oh, this flower is the one I'm ⓐlooking for. I'll take it.
M: Here it is. Take ⓑgood care of it.
G: I don't know ⓒwhat to care.
M: Don't water it too ⓓoften. And it should get ⓔenough light.

01 위 대화의 밑줄 친 ⓐ~ⓔ 중 대화의 흐름상 어색한 것을 찾아 바르게 고치시오.

➡ _____

02 위 대화의 내용과 일치하지 않는 것은?

① 소녀는 꽃을 사기로 결정했다.
② 소녀는 꽃을 어떻게 관리해야 하는지 모른다.
③ 꽃에 너무 자주 물을 주면 안 된다.
④ 꽃은 충분한 햇빛을 받아야 한다.
⑤ 남자는 소녀가 꽃을 잘 관리하지 못할까봐 걱정했다.

[03~04] 다음 글을 읽고 물음에 답하시오.

Mr. Kim: Today, I'd like to talk about your eyes. (A) The eyes are really important parts of our body, but more and more students are having eye problems. (B) If you do not want these problems, try to take some time to rest your eyes. (C) When you study, try to look outside for a while. (D) Make sure you don't look at computer or phone screens for too long. (E)

03 위 대화의 (A)~(E) 중 주어진 문장이 들어가기에 적절한 곳은?

> Some students cannot see without glasses or have dry eyes.

① (A)   ② (B)   ③ (C)   ④ (D)   ⑤ (E)

04 위 대화를 읽고 대답할 수 없는 것은?

① What is Mr. Kim talking about?
② What are many students suffering from?
③ What should students do not to have eye problems?
④ What do students need to do to protect their eyes when they study?
⑤ How long should students take a rest after looking at computer or phone screens?

[01~03] 다음 대화를 읽고 물음에 답하시오.

Ms. Kim: Minjae, ⓐcan I have a word with you? It won't take long.

Minjae: Of course, Ms. Kim.

Ms. Kim: I saw that you are not concentrating and falling asleep (A)[while / during] classes.

Minjae: Oh, I'm sorry.

Ms. Kim: What's the matter?

Minjae: I just can't fall asleep easily. I tried to go to bed early but (B)[fail / failed]. I don't know (C)[what / how] to get a good night's sleep.

Ms. Kim: Maybe you should try to go to bed regularly, not early.

Minjae: Oh, then I will try doing that.

서답형

01 위 대화의 밑줄 친 ⓐ를 우리말로 옮기시오.

➡ _____

중요

02 위 대화의 (A)~(C)에 들어갈 말로 바르게 짝지어진 것은?

	(A)	(B)	(C)
①	while	fail	what
②	while	failed	how
③	during	failed	what
④	during	failed	how
⑤	during	fail	what

03 위 대화의 내용과 일치하지 않는 것은?

① 민재는 수업 시간에 집중하지 않고 잠이 들었다.

② 민재는 밤에 잠이 쉽게 들지 못한다.

③ 민재는 일찍 잠을 자려고 노력하지만 실패한다.

④ 민재는 잠을 잘 자는 법을 모른다.

⑤ 김 선생님은 민재에게 일찍 잠자리에 들 것을 권하였다.

[04~06] 다음 대화를 읽고 물음에 답하시오.

G: Did you see my phone?

B: No, I didn't. Call your phone with mine.

G: My phone will not ⓐring. (A)_____

B: Don't worry. I'll help you. We will find it soon.

서답형

04 빈칸 (A)에 들어갈 말을 〈보기〉에 주어진 단어들을 모두 배열하여 영작하시오.

┌─ 보기 ├─

don't / find / to / I / my / know / phone / how

➡ _____

중요

05 위 대화에서 나타난 소녀의 심정으로 적절한 것은?

① excited   ② angry   ③ worried
④ pleased   ⑤ satisfied

06 위 대화의 밑줄 친 ⓐ와 다른 의미로 쓰인 것은?

① Did you hear the bell ringing in the morning?

② I don't know why my telephone doesn't ring.

③ If you need any help, ring the bell anytime.

④ Although it rang several times, he didn't answer the phone.

⑤ You can't imagine how sad I was when I lost my ring.

[07~09] 다음 대화를 읽고 물음에 답하시오.

Sue: My back and leg hurt.

Brian: ⓐI think it's because of you always cross your legs.

Sue: Oh, do you think so? I didn't know I have poor posture.

Brian: (A)_____ when you sit in a chair.

07 위 대화의 빈칸 (A)에 들어갈 말로 나머지와 의미가 <u>다른</u> 것은?

① Don't cross your legs

② You should not cross your legs

③ Be careful not to cross your legs

④ Make sure you don't cross your legs

⑤ Try to cross your legs

08 위 대화의 밑줄 친 ⓐ에서 어법상 <u>어색한</u> 것을 바르게 고치시오.

➡ _____

09 According to Brian, why does Sue have a pain on her back and leg?

➡ _____

[10~11] 다음 대화를 읽고 물음에 답하시오.

Suji: Your hands are shaking. Are you okay?

Minsu: It may be because of the energy drink. I drank three cans for today's test.

Suji: That's too much! (A)Make sure you don't drink that much next time.

Minsu: Okay, I won't.

10 위 대화의 밑줄 친 (A)와 바꾸어 쓰기에 <u>어색한</u> 것은?

① I think you should not drink that much next time.

② Be careful not to drink that much next time.

③ You'd better not drink that much next time.

④ Don't drink that much next time.

⑤ Why don't you drink that much next time?

11 위 대화의 내용과 일치하지 <u>않는</u> 것은?

① 민수는 손을 떨고 있다.

② 민수는 오늘 시험이 있다.

③ 민수는 오늘 세 캔의 에너지 드링크를 마셨다.

④ 수지는 에너지 드링크를 너무 많이 마시지 말 것을 충고하였다.

⑤ 민수는 손이 떨려서 공부를 못하고 있다.

12 다음 짝지어진 대화가 <u>어색한</u> 것은?

① A: I don't know how to use this machine.
   B: Oh, let me teach you.

② A: I don't know how to open this bottle.
   B: Maybe you should press the cap first.

③ A: What should I do to be in good shape?
   B: Make sure you should exercise regularly.

④ A: Why did you stay up so late?
   B: You should not be late again.

⑤ A: I'm trying to exercise every morning. But it is really difficult.
   B: Don't exercise too hard at the beginning.

[01~03] 다음 대화를 읽고 물음에 답하시오.

Ms. Kim: Minjae, can I have a word with you? It won't take long.

Minjae: Of course, Ms. Kim.

Ms. Kim: I saw that you are not concentrating and falling asleep during classes.

Minjae: Oh, I'm sorry.

Ms. Kim: What's the matter?

Minjae: I just can't fall asleep easily. I tried to go to bed early but failed. I don't know how to get a good night's sleep.

Ms. Kim: Maybe you should try to go to bed regularly, not early.

Minjae: Oh, then I will try doing that.

01 Why couldn't Minjae concentrate on classes?

➡ _____

02 What did Ms. Kim advise to Minjae?

➡ _____

03 위 대화의 내용과 일치하도록 민재의 일기를 완성하시오.

Mon, Dec 2th, 2019
Today, I felt so sorry for Ms. Kim. I couldn't (A)_____ on her class and (B)_____ during classes. She asked me what the problem was. I explained why I couldn't focus on her classes. The reason was that (C)_____ easily even though I tried to go to bed early. I was confused because I didn't know (D)_____.
Then, she recommended (E)_____ _____, not early. I hope I can fall asleep easily tonight.

[04~05] 다음 대화를 읽고 물음에 답하시오.

Suji: Your hands are shaking. Are you okay?

Minsu: It may be because of the energy drink. I drank three cans for today's test.

Suji: That's too much! Make sure you don't drink that much next time.

Minsu: Okay, I won't.

04 Why are Minsu's hands shaking?

➡ _____
_____

05 What does Suji advise to Minsu?

➡ _____
_____

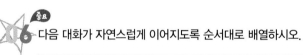
6 다음 대화가 자연스럽게 이어지도록 순서대로 배열하시오.

(A) Don't worry. I'll help you. We will find it soon.
(B) No, I didn't. Call your phone with mine.
(C) Did you see my phone?
(D) My phone will not ring. I don't know how to find my phone.

➡ _____

Grammar

1 too+형용사/부사+to부정사

- He is **too** young **to** travel with us. 그는 너무 어려서 우리와 함께 여행할 수 없어.
- They are **too** heavy **for** you **to** lift. 그것들은 네가 들기엔 너무 무거워.

■ 'too ~ to V'는 '너무 ~해서 V할 수 없는'이라는 의미이다.

- I am **too** exhausted **to** watch the show. 나는 너무 지쳐서 그 쇼를 볼 수 없다.
- The knife is **too** dangerous **to** play with. 그 칼은 너무 위험해서 가지고 놀 수 없어.

■ 'too+형용사/부사+to V'는 'so+형용사/부사+that+주어+can't+동사원형'으로 바꾸어 쓸 수 있다.

- She is **too** weak **to** lift the sofa. 그녀는 너무 약해서 그 소파를 들 수 없어.
  = She is **so** weak **that** she can't lift the sofa.
- It is **too** thin **to** be used for this. 그것은 너무 가늘어서 이것을 위해 사용될 수 없어.
  = It is **so** thin **that** it can't be used for this.

■ 반면에, '충분히 ~해서 …할 수 있다'는 의미를 나타낼 때에는 '형용사/부사+enough+to부정사'를 쓰고, 이는 'so+형용사/부사+that+주어+can+동사원형'과 같다.

- They are kind **enough to** show us how to get there.
  = They are **so** kind **that** they can show us how to get there.
  그들은 우리에게 그곳에 가는 길을 보여 줄 만큼 친절해.
- Molly is slim **enough to** wear the pants. Molly는 그 바지를 입기에 충분히 날씬해.
  = Molly is **so** slim **that** she can wear the pants.

핵심 Check

1. 다음 우리말과 일치하도록 빈칸에 알맞은 말을 쓰시오.

   (1) 그는 너무 피곤해서 나와 대화할 수 없어.

   ➡ He is _____ _____ _____ _____ with me.

   ➡ He is _____ _____ _____ _____ _____ _____ with me.

   (2) 그 노래는 따라 부르기에 충분히 쉬워.

   ➡ The song is _____ _____ for us _____ sing along with.

   ➡ The song is so _____ _____ _____ can sing along with it.

---

② 가정법과거

- If I **were** a musician, I **could write** many songs. 내가 음악가라면, 나는 많은 곡을 쓸 수 있을 텐데.
- If you **saw** the movie, you **would be** moved. 네가 그 영화를 본다면, 감동 받을 텐데.

■ 가정법과거는 '만약 (지금) ~라면'이라는 의미로 쓰이며 'If+주어+과거동사, 주어+과거형 조동사+동사원형'으로 표현한다. 현재의 사실에 반대되는 것을 가정할 때 쓰인다.

- If I **were** a butterfly, I **would fly** in the warm spring air. 내가 나비라면, 나는 따뜻한 봄 하늘을 날 텐데.
  (= As I am not a butterfly, I won't fly in the warm spring air.)
- If I **were** the president of this country, I **could get** rid of exams.
  내가 이 나라의 대통령이라면, 나는 시험을 없앨 수 있을 텐데.
  (= As I am not the president of this country, I can't get rid of exams.)
- If I **were** old enough, I **would do** what I want to do.
  내가 충분히 나이가 들면, 나는 내가 하고 싶은 것을 할 텐데.
  (= As I am not old enough, I won't do what I want to do.)

■ 가정법과거는 현재의 실행 가능성이 매우 희박한 일을 나타낼 때도 쓰인다.

- If I **were** a doctor, I **would make** you healthy. 내가 의사라면, 널 건강하게 해 줄 텐데.
  (= As I am not a doctor, I won't make you healthy)
- If it **were** summer, we **would enjoy** at the beach. 여름이라면, 우리는 해변에서 즐길 수 있을 텐데.
  (= As it is not summer, we won't enjoy at the beach.)

핵심 Check

2. 다음 문장을 직설법과 가정법으로 쓸 때 빈칸에 알맞은 말을 쓰시오.

(1) 만약 공부를 하지 않아도 된다면, 나는 행복할 텐데.
→ If I _____ _____ _____ study, I _____ _____ happy.
→ As I _____ _____ study, I _____ _____ happy.

(2) 만약 내가 충분한 돈을 가지고 있다면, 새 스마트폰을 살 수 있을 텐데.
→ If I _____ enough money, I _____ _____ a new smartphone.
→ As I _____ _____ enough money, I _____ _____ a new smartphone.

01 다음 문장에서 어법상 <u>어색한</u> 부분을 바르게 고쳐 쓰시오.

(1) I am too poor to saving any money.

_____ ➡ _____

(2) He is too nervous that he can't interview the actor.

_____ ➡ _____

(3) If he were more careful, he can arrive there safely. But he is too careless.

_____ ➡ _____

(4) If I go home early, I would take a bath. But I can't go home early.

_____ ➡ _____

02 다음 주어진 단어를 어법에 맞게 빈칸에 쓰시오.

(1) If I _____ much money, I would buy a car. (have)

(2) If I _____ the appointment, I would remember it. (make)

(3) If he _____ on time, we could meet him. (arrive)

(4) If I _____ a bird, I could fly high in the sky. (be)

(5) If you _____ the bus, you could get there soon. (take)

03 다음 문장을 같은 의미의 문장으로 다시 쓰시오.

(1) Kevin is too lazy to exercise regularly.

➡ _____

(2) The room is big enough to hold twenty people.

➡ _____

(3) Molly is too lazy to take the job.

➡ _____

(4) This ladder is long enough to reach there.

➡ _____

(5) The machine is too old for me to operate well.

➡ _____

01 주어진 문장과 같은 의미의 문장은?

> The man is so diligent that he can do the work.

① The man is too diligent to do the work.
② The man is very diligent doing the work.
③ The man is diligent enough to do the work.
④ The man is diligent and he does the work.
⑤ The man is too diligent for doing the work.

02 다음 문장을 가정법으로 쓸 때 빈칸에 들어갈 말로 가장 적절한 것은?

> As I haven't much money, I can't buy the house.
> ➡ If I _____ much money, I _____ the house.

① have – can buy   ② had – can buy
③ had – could buy   ④ had – bought
⑤ have – could have bought

03 다음 빈칸에 들어갈 말로 가장 적절한 것은?

> I _____ pick you up. Let me pick you up.

① drive well so that
② drive so well that
③ drive too well that
④ drive too well to
⑤ drive well enough to

04 주어진 단어를 활용하여 다음 우리말을 영어로 쓰시오.

> 내가 그녀의 전화번호를 기억한다면, 그녀에게 전화할 수 있을 텐데. (call)

➡ _____

05 다음 우리말을 영어로 바르게 옮긴 것을 <u>모두</u> 고르시오.

> 그 집은 살기에 충분히 따뜻해.

① The house is too warm to live in.
② The house is so warm that we can live in it.
③ The house is very warm so we live in the house.
④ The house is warm enough to live in.
⑤ The house is too warm that we can't live in.

06 다음 문장이 의미하는 것으로 가장 적절한 것은?

> I am so sorry that I am too tired to climb the mountain.

① As I am not very tired, I want to climb the mountain.
② If I were tired, I would climb the mountain.
③ I am very tired, so I am not going to climb the mountain.
④ If I were not so tired, I would climb the mountain.
⑤ As I am sorry, I will go climbing the mountain.

07 다음 중 어법상 바르지 <u>않은</u> 것은?

① If I made a mistake, I would apologize to you.
② If they came here early, I would serve them some food.
③ He is too tall to fit in the car.
④ If I were a student, I will study harder.
⑤ The book is interesting enough to be read by people of all ages.

08 다음 문장과 같은 의미의 문장을 쓰시오.

> He was too upset to think clearly.

➡ _____

09 다음 빈칸에 들어갈 말로 가장 적절한 것은?

> I was too embarrassed _____ your face.

① seeing   ② that I can't see
③ to see   ④ that I can see
⑤ to seeing

10 다음 우리말을 영어로 바르게 옮긴 것은?

> 내가 너라면, 나는 그곳에 가지 않을 텐데.

① If I am you, I will not go there.
② If I were you, I will not go there.
③ If I were you, I would go there.
④ If I were you, I would not go there.
⑤ If I was you, I would go there.

11 다음 대화의 빈칸에 들어갈 말로 가장 적절한 것은?

> A: You look upset. What's up?
> B: I have to move this sofa, but I can't. It's because I _____.

① am too tired to do my homework
② am very weak to lift it
③ am so weak that I can't move it
④ am so tired that I can move it
⑤ am strong enough to move it

12 주어진 문장을 가정법으로 바르게 나타낸 것은?

> As I am not sick, I won't go see a doctor.

① If I am sick, I will go see a doctor.
② If I were sick, I will go see a doctor.
③ If I were not sick, I would go see a doctor.
④ If I were sick, I would go see a doctor.
⑤ If I were sick, I wouldn't go see a doctor.

13 다음 중 빈칸에 들어갈 알맞은 것은?

> He is _____ say 'no'.

① kind enough to   ② too kind that
③ so kind that   ④ too kind to
⑤ enough kind to

14 다음 가정법을 직설법으로 전환하시오.

> If I traveled more often, I could tell you many interesting things.

➡ _____
_____

15 9개의 단어를 사용하여 다음 우리말을 영어로 옮길 때 다섯 번째와 일곱 번째로 오는 단어를 바르게 묶은 것은?

> 이 장미들은 많은 사람들을 끌어 모으기에 충분히 아름답다.

① are – to
② beautiful – attract
③ enough – many
④ enough – attract
⑤ beautiful – to

16 다음 대화의 빈칸에 들어갈 말로 가장 적절한 것은?

> A: As you live so far away, we can't meet you as often as we want.
> B: Right. If _____, we _____.

① we live close – meet more often
② we lived close – can meet more often
③ we lived close – could meet more often
④ we didn't live close – could meet more often
⑤ we lived close – can't meet more often

서답형
17 다음 우리말과 같도록 빈칸에 알맞은 말을 쓰시오.

> 잠자기에 너무 밝아요.
> ➡ It is _____ _____ _____ _____
> _____ _____.

서답형
18 다음 문장과 같은 의미의 문장을 쓰시오.

> You look too tired to work with us right now.

➡ _____
_____

19 다음 중 어법상 바르지 않은 것은?

> The problem is ①too difficult ②to solve. If ③it ④were more easy, I ⑤can solve it.

①　　　②　　　③　　　④　　　⑤

서답형
20 다음 상황에 해 줄 수 있는 조언을 가정법과거를 사용하여 쓰시오.

> Amelia gets in trouble. She needs some help from people who she trusts. You think it is good idea for her to ask her parents for some help. In this situation, what would you say to Amelia?

➡ If I _____
_____.

 21 다음 중 어법상 바른 문장은?

① My coffee is too hot to drinking.
② You are lazy enough to do it every day.
③ If the TV were not so loud, I could sleep.
④ If they came here, I felt happy.
⑤ You are polite enough not to telling her the story.

서답형
22 다음 문장을 가정법으로 전환하시오.

> As you don't help me, I won't help you.

➡ _____

서답형
23 주어진 단어를 활용하여 다음 우리말을 영어로 쓰시오.

> 밖에 나가기엔 너무 추워.
> (it / cold / to)

➡ _____

01 다음 가정법을 직설법으로 전환하시오.

If I had a car, I could go there to see you.

➡ ____________________

02 중요 주어진 형용사와 to부정사를 활용하여 빈칸을 알맞게 채우시오.

shy / dark / famous

(1) She is ______________ be noticed by many people.

(2) James is ______________ talk in front of many people.

(3) It's ______________ read a book. Can you please turn on the light?

03 다음 상황을 읽고 Kate가 할 말을 완성하시오.

Kate wants to go to a party. But she doesn't have nice shoes. So she can't go to the party. She says, "If I ______________, I would ______________."

04 고난이도 다음 우리말을 지시에 맞게 영어로 쓰시오.

그는 비싼 자동차를 살 만큼 충분히 부자다.

(1) to부정사를 사용하여

➡ ____________________

(2) that을 사용하여

➡ ____________________

05 다음 대화의 빈칸에 알맞은 말을 가정법과거를 활용하여 쓰시오.

A: ____________________

B: Do you mean that you clean your room because you don't live alone?

A: Yes. You are right.

06 중요 다음 빈칸에 알맞은 말을 쓰시오.

그는 나에게 진실을 말해 줄 만큼 충분히 정직해.

= He is ________ ________ ________ tell me the truth.

= He is ________ ________ ________ ________ ________ tell me the truth.

07 다음 주어진 단어를 활용하여 다음 우리말을 영어로 쓰시오.

그 소녀의 발은 너무 작아서 그 신발을 신을 수 없어. (that)

➡ ____________________

____

08 중요 다음 인어 공주에 관한 직설법 문장을 가정법 문장으로 바꾸어 쓰시오.

As the little mermaid doesn't have two legs, she can't go and meet the prince.

➡ ____________________

____

09 다음 문장을 직설법은 가정법으로, 가정법은 직설법으로 전환 하시오.

(1) As I don't know your e-mail address, I can't send you an e-mail.

➡ _____

(2) If I were not busy, I would help you.

➡ _____

(3) As the socks are too expensive, I won't buy them.

➡ _____

(4) If we were close friends, I would tell you the secret.

➡ _____

(5) As they visit the museum, I will follow them.

➡ _____

10 대화의 빈칸에 알맞은 말을 네 단어로 쓰시오.

A: I'm looking for a shirt.
B: How about this?
A: It's _____. Is there a smaller size of it?
B: Sure. Here you are.

11 다음 문장과 같은 의미의 문장을 쓰시오.

We are too young to drive.

➡ _____

12 다음 대화의 밑줄 친 부분을 바르게 가정법으로 바꿔 쓰시오.

A: Was David invited to Jane's birthday party?
B: No, he wasn't. Jane doesn't like him. If Jane likes him, she will invite him.

➡ _____

13 다음 대화의 빈칸에 알맞은 말을 쓰시오.

A: This is a present for you.
B: This bike is for seven-year-old children. I am ten years old. I am _____ such a small bike. I want a bigger one.

14 주어진 말을 써서 다음 빈칸에 알맞은 말을 쓰시오

내가 기차역에 정시에 도착한다면, 그 기차를 탈 수 있을 텐데. (catch)
➡ If I _____ on time, I _____ the train.

15 다음은 나무에 매달린 포도를 보며 여우가 한 말이다. 주어진 단어와 to부정사를 활용하여 영어로 쓰시오.

그것은 너무 높이 있어서 닿을 수 없어. 그것은 너무 시어서 먹을 수 없을 거야.
(reach / eat)

➡ _____

Reading

The Cat Just Couldn't Help It

Scene #1.

An old and tired mouse enters.

Mouse: (*He is out of breath.*) I'm tired of running from Cat. I am
  _{동명사(전치사 of의 목적어)} = I am so
  too old to run. If I were free, I would be so happy. (*He thinks*
  old that I can't run. = As I am not free, I won't be so happy.
  for a while.) Oh, I have an idea!

Scene #2.

*Mouse goes and gets something from the back of the stage. Cat enters
and catches Mouse.*

Mouse: (*He pretends to beg.*) I'm too smelly for you to eat!
  = I'm so smelly that you can't eat me!
  Instead, have this, please. (*He gives a box of sugar to Cat.*)
  = eat = He gives Cat a box of sugar.

Cat: (*He tastes it. His eyes get bigger.*) What is it? Give me more!

Mouse: It's sugar. If you let me go, I'll bring you some every day.
  사역동사+목적어+동사원형

Scene #3.

*It is at Cat's house. Cat, now fat, is eating sugar. He has only a few
teeth. Dog is watching him.*
  아주 소수의

Dog: (*He is worried.*) Cat, my friend, be careful. The sugar will get
  You will be in danger because of sugar.'를 의미.
  bitter.

Cat: What do you mean by that?

Dog: Look at yourself! You are too fat to run, and your teeth are too
  재귀대명사 = You are so fat that you can't run. = your teeth are so weak that you can't chew!
  weak to chew!

---

just: 단지, 정말, 좀
tired: 피곤한, 지루한
enter: 들이오다
out of breath: 숨이 찬
be tired of: ~에 싫증이 나다
for a while: 잠시
pretend: ~인 척하다
beg: 빌다, 간청하다
smelly: 냄새 나는
instead: 대신에
tooth: 이, 치아
chew: 씹다

 확인문제

● 다음 문장이 본문의 내용과 일치하면 T, 일치하지 <u>않으면</u> F를 쓰시오.

1 Mouse didn't like being chased by Cat. ☐

2 Mouse wanted to be free. ☐

3 Cat's eyes got bigger because sugar was very tasty. ☐

4 Cat didn't allow Mouse to go. ☐

5 Dog was worried about Cat that ate too little sugar. ☐

Cat: *(He eats more.)* Why should I run or chew? Sugar is the only
<u>much의 비교급</u>
thing I need. I can't live without it.
= (that) I need (목적격 관계대명사 생략)

Dog goes out sadly.

Scene #4.

Cat has almost emptied the box of sugar. Mouse enters.

Mouse: *(He smiles.)* I think my plan has worked.

Cat: *(He is angry.)* It's almost empty! Mouse, tell me <u>where you get it.</u>
간접의문문(의문사+주어+동사)

Mouse: I have a friend <u>who</u> makes sugar. But he's scared of your
= that(주격 관계대명사)
claws. If you get rid of <u>them</u>, you can meet him soon.
your claws

Cat: Okay!

Scene #5.

Mouse hands Cat a pair of scissors and Cat cuts his claws.
건네준다   가위 한 개

Cat: I'm ready! Now take me to your friend!

Mouse: *(He laughs at Cat.)* You stupid cat! <u>If you were fast, and

had your sharp teeth and claws, I'd listen to you.</u> But you no
= As you are not fast. and don't have your sharp teeth and claws. I won't listen to you.
longer have <u>them</u> now! You <u>have lost</u> your biggest weapons!
your sharp teeth and claws   현재완료(결과)
Why should I listen to <u>what</u> you say now? *(He runs away.)*
the thing which
Cat: What! *(He tries to run after Mouse, but fails.)* Oh! I'm <u>too fat to

run after him!</u>
= I am so fat that I can't run after him!

sadly: 슬프게
work: 효과가 있다
empty: 텅 빈; 비우다
scared: 무서워하는
claw: (동물의) 발톱
get rid of: ~을 없애다
stupid: 어리석은, 멍청한
sharp: 날카로운, 뾰족한
no longer: 더 이상 ~ 아니다
weapon: 무기
run away: 달아나다
fail: 실패하다
run after: ~을 쫓다

📎 **확인문제**

● 다음 문장이 본문의 내용과 일치하면 T, 일치하지 <u>않으면</u> F를 쓰시오.

1 According to Cat, what he needed was only sugar. ☐

2 Cat wanted more sugar from Mouse. ☐

3 Cat agreed to what Mouse suggested. ☐

4 Cat's claws were cut by Mouse. ☐

5 Cat is not fast any more. ☐

6 Cat succeeded in catching Mouse. ☐

● 우리말을 참고하여 빈칸에 알맞은 말을 쓰시오.

The Cat Just Couldn't Help It

Scene #1.

1 *An old and _____ mouse _____ .*

2 Mouse: *(He is _____ _____ _____ .)* I'm tired of _____ _____ Cat.

3 I am _____ _____ _____ run. If I _____ free, I _____ _____ so happy. *(He thinks _____ a while.)* Oh, I _____ _____ !

Scene #2.

4 *Mouse goes and _____ something _____ the back of the stage.*

5 Cat _____ and _____ Mouse.

6 Mouse: *(He _____ _____ beg.)* I'm _____ _____ _____ _____ to eat! _____ , have this, please. *(He _____ a box of sugar _____ Cat.)*

7 Cat: *(He _____ _____ . His eyes get _____ .)* What is it? Give me _____ !

8 Mouse: It's sugar. If you _____ me _____ , I'll _____ you some every day.

Scene #3.

9 *It is at Cat's _____ . Cat, now _____ , is eating sugar. He has only _____ _____ teeth. Dog is _____ him.*

10 Dog: *(He is _____ .)* Cat, my friend, _____ _____ . The sugar will get _____ .

11 Cat: What do you _____ _____ _____ ?

12 Dog: Look at _____ ! You are _____ _____ _____ , and your teeth are _____ _____ _____ !

고양이는 정말 어떻게 할 수 없었다

장면 1

1 한 마리의 늙고 지친 쥐가 들어온다.

2 Mouse: *(그는 숨이 차다.)* 나는 고양이로부터 달아나는 것에 질렸어.

3 나는 나이가 너무 들어서 달릴 수 없어. 내가 만약 자유로워진다면, 행복할 텐데. *(그는 잠깐 동안 생각한다.)* 오, 내게 좋은 생각이 났어.

장면 2

4 쥐가 무대 뒤에서 무언가를 가져온다.

5 고양이가 들어와 쥐를 잡는다.

6 Mouse: *(그는 비는 척한다.)* 저는 너무 냄새가 나서 당신이 잡아먹을 수 없어요. 대신, 이걸 드세요. *(그는 설탕 상자를 고양이에게 건넨다.)*

7 Cat: *(그는 그것을 맛본다. 그의 눈이 커진다.)* 이게 뭐야? 더 줘!

8 Mouse: 그것은 설탕이에요. 만약에 당신이 저를 가게 해주면, 제가 매일 가지고 올게요.

장면 3

9 고양이의 집이다. 지금은 뚱뚱해진 고양이가 설탕을 먹고 있다. 그는 오직 몇 개의 이빨만 가지고 있다. 개가 그를 바라보고 있다.

10 Dog: *(그는 걱정된다.)* 내 친구 고양이야, 조심해, 그 설탕은 썩을 거야.

11 Cat: 무슨 말이야?

12 Dog: 너 스스로를 봐! 너는 너무 뚱뚱해서 달릴 수 없고, 너의 이빨은 너무 약해서 씹을 수 없잖아!

13 Cat: *(He eats more.)* _____ should I _____ or _____? Sugar is the only thing _____ _____. I can't live _____ it.

14 *Dog _____ _____ sadly.*

Scene #4.

15 *Cat has almost _____ the box of sugar. Mouse _____.*

16 Mouse: *(He smiles.)* I think my plan _____ _____.

17 Cat: *(He is _____.)* It's almost _____! Mouse, tell me _____ _____ _____ it.

18 Mouse: I have a friend _____ _____ sugar. But he's _____ _____ your claws. If you get rid of _____, you can meet him soon.

19 Cat: _____!

Scene #5.

20 *Mouse _____ Cat a pair of scissors and _____ _____ _____ claws.*

21 Cat: I'm ready! Now _____ me _____ your friend!

22 Mouse: *(He _____ _____ Cat.)* You _____ cat!

23 If you _____ _____, and _____ your sharp teeth and claws, _____ _____ _____ you. But you no longer have _____ now!

24 You _____ _____ your biggest weapons!

25 Why should I listen to _____ _____ _____ now? *(He runs _____.)*

26 Cat: What! *(He tries _____ _____ _____ Mouse, but fails.)* Oh! I'm too _____ _____ _____ after him!

13 Cat: *(그는 더 먹는다.)* 왜 내가 뛰거나 씹어야 해? 나에게 필요한 건 설탕 한 가지야. 나는 그것 없이는 살 수 없어.

14 *개가 슬프게 나간다.*

장면 4

15 *고양이는 설탕 상자를 거의 비웠다. 쥐가 들어온다.*

16 Mouse: *(그가 미소 짓는다.)* 내 계획이 효과가 있는 것 같아.

17 Cat: *(그는 화가 났다.)* 거의 비었잖아! 쥐야, 네가 어디서 이걸 가져오는지 말해!

18 Mouse: 나에게 설탕을 만드는 친구가 하나 있어요. 하지만 그는 당신의 발톱을 무서워한답니다. 만약 당신이 그것들을 없애버리면, 당신은 곧 그를 만날 수 있을 거예요.

19 Cat: 좋아!

장면 5

20 *쥐가 고양이에게 가위를 건네고, 고양이는 자신의 발톱을 자른다.*

21 Cat: 나는 준비가 됐어! 이제 나를 너의 친구에게 데려다줘!

22 Mouse: *(그는 고양이를 비웃는다.)* 멍청한 고양이!

23 만약 당신이 빠르고 당신의 뾰족한 이빨과 발톱을 가지고 있다면, 나는 당신의 말을 들었겠죠! 하지만 당신은 지금은 그것들을 더 이상 가지고 있지 않아요!

24 당신은 당신의 가장 큰 무기들을 잃었어요!

25 내가 왜 당신이 지금 말하는 것을 들어야 하죠? *(그는 도망간다.)*

26 Cat: 뭐? *(고양이가 쥐를 쫓아가려고 하지만 실패한다.)* 오! 나는 너무 뚱뚱해서 그를 쫓아갈 수가 없구나!

우리말을 참고하여 본문을 영작하시오.

The Cat Just Couldn't Help It

Scene #1.

1 한 마리의 늙고 지친 쥐가 들어온다.

➡ _____

2 Mouse: *(그는 숨이 차다.)* 나는 고양이로부터 달아나는 것에 질렸어.

➡ _____

3 나는 나이가 너무 들어서 달릴 수 없어. 내가 만약 자유로워진다면, 행복할 텐데. *(그는 잠깐 동안 생각한다.)* 오, 내게 좋은 생각이 났어.

➡ _____

Scene #2.

4 쥐가 무대 뒤에서 무언가를 가져온다.

➡ _____

5 고양이가 들어와 쥐를 잡는다.

➡ _____

6 Mouse: *(그는 비는 척한다.)* 저는 너무 냄새가 나서 당신이 잡아먹을 수 없어요. 대신, 이걸 드세요. *(그는 설탕 상자를 고양이에게 건넨다.)*

➡ _____

_____

7 Cat: *(그는 그것을 맛본다. 그의 눈이 커진다.)* 이게 뭐야? 더 줘!

➡ _____

8 Mouse: 그것은 설탕이에요. 만약에 당신이 저를 가게 해주면, 제가 매일 가지고 올게요.

➡ _____

Scene #3

9 고양이의 집이다. 지금은 뚱뚱해진 고양이가 설탕을 먹고 있다. 그는 오직 몇 개의 이빨만 가지고 있다. 개가 그를 바라보고 있다.

➡ _____

10 Dog: *(그는 걱정된다.)* 내 친구 고양이야, 조심해, 그 설탕은 써질 거야.

➡ _____

11 Cat: 무슨 말이야?

➡ _____

12 Dog: 너 스스로를 봐! 너는 너무 뚱뚱해서 달릴 수 없고, 너의 이빨은 너무 약해서 씹을 수 없잖아!

➡ _____

13 Cat: *(그는 더 먹는다.)* 왜 내가 뛰거나 씹어야 해? 나에게 필요한 건 설탕 한 가지야. 나는 그것 없이는 살 수 없어.

➡ _____

14 *개가 슬프게 나간다.*

➡ _____

Scene #4.

15 *고양이는 설탕 상자를 거의 비웠다. 쥐가 들어온다.*

➡ _____

16 Mouse: *(그가 미소 짓는다.)* 내 계획이 효과가 있는 것 같아.

➡ _____

17 Cat: *(그는 화가 났다.)* 거의 비었잖아! 쥐야, 네가 어디서 이걸 가져오는지 말해!

➡ _____

18 Mouse: 나에게 설탕을 만드는 친구가 하나 있어요. 하지만 그는 당신의 발톱을 무서워한답니다. 만약 당신이 그것들을 없애버리면, 당신은 곧 그를 만날 수 있을 거예요.

➡ _____

_____

19 Cat: 좋아!

➡ _____

Scene #5.

20 *쥐가 고양이에게 가위를 건네고, 고양이는 자신의 발톱을 자른다.*

➡ _____

21 Cat: 나는 준비가 됐어! 이제 나를 너의 친구에게 데려다 줘!

➡ _____

22 Mouse: *(그는 고양이를 비웃는다.)* 멍청한 고양이!

➡ _____

23 만약 당신이 빠르고 당신의 뾰족한 이빨과 발톱을 가지고 있다면, 나는 당신의 말을 들었겠죠! 하지만 당신은 지금은 그것들을 더 이상 가지고 있지 않아요!

➡ _____

24 당신은 당신의 가장 큰 무기들을 잃었어요!

➡ _____

25 내가 왜 당신이 지금 말하는 것을 들어야 하죠? *(그는 도망 간다.)*

➡ _____

26 Cat: 뭐? *(고양이가 쥐를 쫓아가려고 하지만 실패한다.)* 오! 나는 너무 뚱뚱해서 그를 쫓아갈 수가 없구나!

➡ _____

[01~03] 다음 글을 읽고 물음에 답하시오.

Scene #1.

An old and tired mouse enters.

Mouse: *(He is out of breath.)* I'm tired of running from Cat. I am too old to run. If I were free, I would be so happy. *(He thinks for a while.)* Oh, I have an idea!

Scene #2.

Mouse goes and gets something from the back of the stage. Cat enters and catches Mouse.

Mouse: *(He pretends to beg.)* I'm too smelly for you to eat! Instead, have this, please. *(He gives a box of sugar to Cat.)*

Cat: *(He tastes it. His eyes get bigger.)* What is it? Give me more!

Mouse: It's sugar. If you let me go, I'll bring you some every day.

01 다음 중 위 글의 종류로 가장 적절한 것은?

① an essay ② a play
③ an article ④ a poem
⑤ a novel

02 다음 중 위 글의 내용과 일치하는 것은?

① Mouse thinks that being chased by Cat is fun.
② The mouse is free now.
③ Mouse eats something in front of the stage.
④ Cat likes what Mouse gave him.
⑤ Mouse promises that he will bring Cat some more cheese every day if he lets him go.

03 In the first scene, what does Mouse look like? Answer in English with a full sentence.

➡ _____

[04~06] 다음 글을 읽고 물음에 답하시오.

Scene #3.

It is at Cat's house. Cat, now fat, is eating sugar. He has only a few teeth. Dog is watching him.

Dog: *(He is worried.)* Cat, my friend, be (A)_____. The sugar will get bitter.

Cat: What do you mean by that?

Dog: Look at yourself! You are too fat to run, and your teeth are too weak to chew!

Cat: *(He eats more.)* Why should I run or chew? Sugar is the only thing I need. I can't live without it.

Dog goes out sadly.

04 다음 중 빈칸 (A)에 들어갈 말로 가장 적절한 것은?

① curious ② creative ③ careful
④ polite ⑤ honest

05 다음 중 위 글을 읽고 답할 수 있는 것은?

① Where does Cat get the sugar?
② How did Dog and Cat know each other?
③ How does Cat look?
④ How much money did Cat spend on buying sugar?
⑤ How much sugar does Cat eat a day?

서답형

06 다음은 고양이가 한 말이다. 빈칸에 알맞은 말을 쓰시오.

> If there _____ _____ _____, I could not live.

[07~10] 다음 글을 읽고 물음에 답하시오.

Scene #4.

Cat has almost emptied the box of sugar. Mouse enters.

Mouse: *(He smiles.)* I think my plan has worked.

Cat: *(He is angry.)* It's almost empty! Mouse, tell me (A)_____.

Mouse: I have a friend who makes sugar. But he's scared of your claws. If you get rid of them, you can meet him soon.

Cat: Okay!

Scene #5.

Mouse hands Cat a pair of scissors and Cat cuts his claws.

Cat: I'm ready! Now take me to your friend!

Mouse: *(He laughs at Cat.)* You stupid cat! If you were fast, and had your sharp teeth and claws, I'd listen to you. But you no longer have them now! You have lost your biggest weapons! Why should I listen to what you say now? *(He runs away.)*

Cat: What! *(He tries to run after Mouse, but fails.)* Oh! I'm too fat to run after him!

07 다음 중 빈칸 (A)에 들어갈 말로 가장 적절한 것은?

① when you get home
② where you get sugar
③ how you make me fat
④ why you make me keep eating sugar
⑤ who you will bring to me

중요

08 위 글의 내용과 일치하지 <u>않는</u> 것은?

① Cat wants to get sugar.
② Cat accepts what Mouse suggests.
③ Cat brings a pair of scissors.
④ Mouse set up a plan and it works.
⑤ Mouse thinks that Cat is stupid.

서답형

09 Write the reason why Cat wants to meet Cat's friend who makes sugar. Answer in English with a full sentence.

➡ _____

서답형

10 위 글의 내용에 맞게 빈칸에 알맞은 말을 쓰시오.

> Mouse wants Cat to _____ _____ _____ _____ _____.

11 자연스러운 글이 되도록 (A)~(C)를 바르게 배열하시오.

> These days, I drink coffee milk and energy drinks.
> (A) Yes, those things did help me, but not as much as coffee milk and energy drinks. I can't focus on what I am doing without them.
> (B) At first, they seemed to help me concentrate better. But as time passed, I realized that it was getting really hard to concentrate without them.
> (C) The people around me were worried. They recommended that I eat apples or drink green tea instead. They said drinking just water would help me too.

➡ _____

[12~16] 다음 글을 읽고 물음에 답하시오.

Scene #1.

An old and tired mouse enters.

Mouse: *(He is ①out of breath.)* I'm tired of running from Cat. I am too old to run. (A)_____. *(He thinks for a while.)* Oh, I have an idea!

Scene #2.

Mouse goes and gets something from the back of the stage. Cat enters and catches Mouse.

Mouse: *(He pretends to beg.)* I'm too smelly (B)_____ you to eat! Instead, have this, please. *(He gives a box of sugar to Cat.)*

Cat: *(He tastes it. His eyes get bigger.)* What is it? Give me ②more!

Mouse: It's sugar. If you let me go, I'll bring you some every day.

Scene #3.

It is at Cat's house. Cat, now fat, is eating sugar. He has only a few teeth. Dog is watching him.

Dog: *(He is ③worried.)* Cat, my friend, be careful. The sugar will get bitter.

Cat: What do you mean by that?

Dog: Look at yourself! You are too fat to run, and your teeth are too ④strong to chew!

Cat: *(He eats more.)* Why should I run or chew? Sugar is the only thing I need. I can't live ⑤without it.

Dog goes out sadly.

12 다음 직설법을 가정법으로 만들어 빈칸 (A)에 쓰시오.

> As I am not free, I will not be happy.

➡ _____

13 다음 중 빈칸 (B)에 들어갈 말로 가장 적절한 것은?

① of ② about ③ for
④ to ⑤ with

14 Write the reason why Mouse can't run well. Use the phrase 'It's because.'

➡ _____

15 ①~⑤ 중 글의 흐름상 어색한 것은?

① ② ③ ④ ⑤

16 다음 중 위 글의 내용과 일치하지 <u>않는</u> 것은?

① Mouse came up with an idea to solve his problem.
② Mouse gave Cat a box of sugar.
③ Cat was very interested in sugar.
④ There were only a few teeth left to Cat.
⑤ Cat is not friends with Dog.

[17~20] 다음 글을 읽고 물음에 답하시오.

Scene #4.

Cat has almost emptied the box of sugar. Mouse enters.

Mouse: *(He smiles.)* I think my plan has worked. ①

Cat: *(He is angry.)* It's almost empty! ② Mouse, tell me where you get it.

Mouse: I have a friend who makes sugar. ③ If you get rid of them, you can meet him soon. ④

Cat: Okay! ⑤

Scene #5.

Mouse hands Cat a pair of scissors and Cat cuts his claws.

Cat: I'm ready! Now take me to your friend!

Mouse: *(He laughs (A)_____ Cat.)* You stupid cat! If you were fast, and had your sharp teeth and claws, I'd listen to you. But you no longer have them now! You have lost your biggest weapons! Why should I listen to what you say now? *(He runs away.)*

Cat: What! *(He tries to run after Mouse, but fails.)* Oh! I'm too fat to run after him!

17 다음 중 빈칸 (A)에 들어가는 말과 같은 말이 들어가는 것은?

① I am not interested _____ studying math.
② Who takes care _____ your plants?
③ We look up _____ Mr. King.
④ They don't care _____ what I need.
⑤ She was surprised _____ the news.

18 ①~⑤ 중 주어진 문장이 들어가기에 가장 적절한 곳은?

But he's scared of your claws.

①　　②　　③　　④　　⑤

19 다음 중 글의 마지막에서 고양이가 느낄 심경으로 가장 적절한 것은?

① happiness　② boredom　③ regret
④ loneliness　⑤ fear

20 다음 중 위 글을 읽고 답할 수 없는 것은?

① Who is eating sugar?
② Who has a friend that makes sugar?
③ What does Mouse want Cat to do?
④ Who cut Cat's claws?
⑤ Where does Mouse's friend live?

[21~23] 다음 글을 읽고 물음에 답하시오.

I am not diligent and I put things off. I cannot get up early in the morning. I always say, "In 10 more minutes..." If I were more diligent, I would have breakfast and would focus on my classes. Of course, I would not be late for school. I would not put off my homework and would finish it. I know my habits are not good ones. I think I will have to make a plan to be more diligent and to be a good student. From now on, I will make a list of things (A) to do. I am also going to get up 30 minutes earlier every morning.

서답형

21 What is the writer's problem? Answer in English with a full sentence.

➡ _____

22 다음 중 밑줄 친 (A)와 쓰임이 같은 것은?

① It is a shame to lie to someone who trusts you.
② Dorothy went to the department store to buy a scarf.
③ Do you have any idea to suggest?
④ Amelia felt sad to hear what they said about her.
⑤ She decided to climb the mountain every month.

23 Which one is NOT true about the passage?

① The writer delays things.
② The writer gets up late in the morning.
③ As the writer is not diligent, he or she can't have breakfast.
④ The writer wants to be a better student.
⑤ The writer plans to get up an hour earlier.

[01~07] 다음 글을 읽고 물음에 답하시오.

Scene #1.

An old and tired mouse enters.

Mouse: *(He is out of breath.)* I'm tired of running from Cat. (A)I am too old to run. If I were free, I would be so happy. *(He thinks for a while.)* Oh, I have an idea!

Scene #2.

Mouse goes and gets something from the back of the stage. Cat enters and catches Mouse.

Mouse: *(He pretends to beg.)* I'm too smelly for you to eat! Instead, have this, please. *(He gives a box of sugar to Cat.)*

Cat: *(He tastes it. His eyes get bigger.)* What is it? Give me more!

Mouse: It's sugar. If you let me go, I'll bring you some every day.

Scene #3.

It is at Cat's house. Cat, now fat, is eating sugar. He has only a few teeth. Dog is watching him.

Dog: *(He is worried.)* Cat, my friend, be careful. The sugar will get bitter.

Cat: What do you mean by that?

Dog: Look at yourself! You are too fat to run, and your teeth are too weak to chew!

Cat: *(He eats more.)* Why should I run or chew? Sugar is the only thing I need. I can't live without (B)it.

Dog goes out sadly.

01 According to the script, what did Mouse give Cat to be freed? Answer in English with a full sentence.

➡ _____

02 주어진 단어를 사용하여 밑줄 친 문장 (A)와 같은 의미의 문장을 쓰시오.

(that)

➡ _____

03 What does Mouse promise to do if Cat lets him go? Answer in English with a full sentence.

➡ _____

04 How does Dog feel when he meets his friend Cat? Answer in English.

➡ _____

05 글의 내용에 맞게 빈칸에 알맞은 말을 쓰시오.

Dog said to Cat that he should be _____ not to eat too much _____. But Cat didn't listen to _____ Dog said.

06 Write the reason why it is hard for Cat to run. Use the phrase below.

(it's because)

➡ _____

07 밑줄 친 (B)가 가리키는 것을 위 글에서 찾아 쓰시오.

➡ _____

[08~11] 다음 글을 읽고 물음에 답하시오.

Scene #4.

Cat has almost emptied the box of sugar. Mouse enters.

Mouse: *(He smiles.)* (A)<u>내 계획이 효과가 있는 것 같아.</u>

Cat: *(He is angry.)* It's almost empty! Mouse, tell me where you get it.

Mouse: I have a friend who makes sugar. But he's scared of your claws. If you get rid of them, you can meet him soon.

Cat: Okay!

Scene #5.

Mouse hands Cat a pair of scissors and Cat cuts his claws.

Cat: I'm ready! Now take me to your friend!

Mouse: *(He laughs at Cat.)* You stupid cat! If you were fast, and had your sharp teeth and claws, I'd listen to you. But you no longer have them now! You have lost (B)<u>your biggest weapons!</u> Why should I listen to what you say now? *(He runs away.)*

Cat: What! *(He tries to run after Mouse, but fails.)* Oh! I'm too fat to run after him!

08 다음 빈칸에 들어가는 말을 위 글에서 찾아 쓰시오.

> If you _____ to do something that you were trying to do, you are unable to do it or do not succeed in doing it.

09 위 글의 내용에 맞게 빈칸에 알맞은 말을 쓰시오.

> According to what Mouse said, his friend is afraid of _____ _____. So he brought Cat _____ _____ _____ _____ to cut them.

10 주어진 단어를 활용하여 밑줄 친 우리말 (A)를 영어로 쓰시오. 필요하다면 어형을 바꾸시오.

> (think / have / work)

➡ _____

11 밑줄 친 (B)가 가리키는 것을 위 글에서 찾아 우리말로 쓰시오.

➡ _____

[12~13] 다음 글을 읽고 물음에 답하시오.

A long time ago, there lived a caterpillar named Bob. He was waiting to become a beautiful butterfly. One day, while he was taking a walk, he found a brown bottle. It was warm and bright inside the bottle. Bob stayed there for a few days. His friends came and said, "Bob, get out. We have to prepare." But Bob didn't want to leave his bottle. "This place is too good to leave. Why do I have to go out?" he thought. When spring came, Bob's friends flew here and there in the warm air. Only Bob was left in the brown bottle, cold and still. "Poor Bob, if he were a butterfly like us, he would enjoy his wonderful sunshine," his friends said.

12 Where was Bob when spring came? Answer in English with a full sentence.

➡ _____

13 Why didn't Bob want to leave the bottle? Answer in English and use the words below.

> (because / so / that)

➡ _____

Think and Write B

I am not diligent and I put things off. I cannot get up early in the morning.
= put off things

I always say, "In 10 more minutes..." If I were more diligent, I would have
As I am not more diligent, I don't have breakfast

breakfast and would focus on my classes. Of course, I would not be late for
and don't focus on my classes.

school. I would not put off my homework and would finish it. I know my
If I were more diligent의 생략

habits are not good ones. I think I will have to make a plan to be more diligent
=habits   think (that)   형용사적 용법

and to be a good student. From now on, I will make a list of things to do. I am
형용사적 용법

also going to get up 30 minutes earlier every morning.
30분 더 일찍

구문해설 · put off: ~을 미루다 · get up: 일어나다 · diligent: 부지런한 · from now on: 지금부터

Check Your Progress 1

G: What's wrong? You look worried.
=What's the matter?   look+형용사: ~하게 보이다

B: Oh, I think I have lost 50 thousand won.

G: What? Did you search carefully?

B: Of course, I had it in my bag, inside my pencil case!
= 50 thousand won
I've saved it for a long time!

G: Why did you put it there? Why did you bring that much money to school?
= in your bag   그렇게

B: That money was for my new soccer ball. I don't know how to get my
= how I should get
money back.

G: First you have to talk to your teacher. Then make sure you don't bring a lot
= bring A to B: A를 B에 가져오다
of money to school again.

구문해설 · carefully: 주의 깊게, 신중하게 · pencil case: 필통 · save: 모으다, 저금하다

Check Your Progress 4

These days, Tom has found a new hobby. It is watching funny videos on the
요즘   = The new hobby 동명사(보어)

Internet with his phone. They are so interesting. Time seems to fly when he
Funny videos   흥미를 유발하는   ~인 것 같다

watches them. The problem is he sometimes stays up late at night to watch
앞에 접속사 that 생략   부사적 용법 중 목적(~하기 위해서)

videos. His friends say, "Tom, make sure you don't take your phone to your
make sure (that)

room when you go to bed." Tom thinks this is a good idea.

구문해설 · hobby: 취미 · funny: 재미있는 · interesting: 흥미로운 · stay up: 깨어 있다

해석

나는 부지런하지 않고 일들을 미룬다. 나는 아침에 일찍 일어날 수 없다. 나는 항상 '10분만 더 …'라고 말한다. 내가 만약 부지런하다면, 나는 아침을 먹을 것이고 수업에 집중할 수 있을 것이다. 물론, 나는 학교에 늦지도 않을 것이다. 나는 내 숙제를 미루지 않고 다 마칠 수 있을 것이다. 나는 이 습관이 전혀 좋지 않다는 것을 잘 안다. 나는 내가 더 부지런해지고 좋은 학생이 될 수 있는 계획을 세워야 한다고 생각한다. 지금부터, 나는 해야 할 일의 목록을 만들 것이다. 또한, 나는 매일 아침 30분 더 일찍 일어날 것이다.

G: 무슨 일이야? 걱정스러워 보여.
B: 오, 나 5만 원을 잃어버린 것 같아.
G: 뭐? 주의 깊게 찾아보았니?
B: 물론이지, 나는 가방에 있는 필통에 돈이 있었어. 나는 오랫동안 돈을 모았었어.
G: 왜 돈을 거기에 놓았니? 왜 그렇게 많은 돈을 학교에 가져왔니?
B: 그 돈은 내 새 축구공을 위한 거였어. 나는 어떻게 내 돈을 돌려받을지 모르겠어.
G: 우선, 네 선생님께 말씀드려야 해. 그리고 학교에 다시는 많은 돈을 가져오지 말 것을 명심해.

요즘 Tom은 새로운 취미를 찾았다. 그것은 그의 핸드폰을 사용해 인터넷으로 재미난 동영상을 보는 것이다. 그것들은 굉장히 흥미롭다. 그가 그것들을 보고 있는 동안 그는 시간 가는 줄 모른다. 문제는, 그가 때때로 동영상들을 보기 위해 밤늦게까지 잠을 안 잔다는 것이다. 그의 친구들은 "Tom, 잠 자러 갈 때 방에 핸드폰을 가지고 가지 않도록 해."라고 말한다. Tom은 그게 좋은 생각이라고 생각한다.

Words & Expressions

01 다음 짝지어진 단어의 관계가 같도록 빈칸에 알맞은 말을 쓰시오.

> fail : succeed = _____ : lazy

02 다음 영영풀이가 가리키는 것을 고르시오.

> a flying insect with a long thin body and four large, usually brightly coloured wings

① butterfly   ② worm
③ snake   ④ caterpillar
⑤ snail

03 다음 중 밑줄 친 부분의 뜻풀이가 바르지 <u>않은</u> 것은?

① It is not good for your health to eat too much <u>salty</u> food. (맛이) 단
② Can you <u>recommend</u> a book for me? 추천하다
③ You should take a <u>rest</u> after watching the screen for a while. 휴식
④ Mike is <u>pretending</u> he doesn't know me at all. ~인 척하다
⑤ I enjoyed a warm spring <u>sunshine</u> with my pet. 햇빛

04 다음 우리말에 맞게 빈칸에 알맞은 말을 쓰시오. (각각 2단어씩 쓸 것.)

(1) 고양이가 나비를 쫓고 있었다.
➡ The cat was _____ a butterfly.
(2) 쥐가 고양이로부터 달아나는 것에 싫증이 났다.
➡ The mouse is tired of _____ from the cat.
(3) 그는 불어를 말하고, 또한 그것을 쓴다.
➡ He speaks French, and writes it _____.

05 다음 문장의 빈칸에 들어갈 말을 〈보기〉에서 골라 쓰시오.

> ┤ 보기 ├
> harmful / meat / weak / stupid / rest

(1) I was _____ to lose the chance.
(2) You should help _____ people.
(3) Eating too much fast food is _____.
(4) Chicken is a kind of white _____.
(5) He won't _____ until he finishes it.

06 다음 주어진 문장의 밑줄 친 fat과 같은 의미로 쓰인 것은?

> You will get <u>fat</u> if you eat too many sweets.

① Fast food can make you <u>fat</u> and unhealthy.
② I didn't know that pork <u>fat</u> is used to make cosmetics.
③ This sausage has too much <u>fat</u> on it.
④ You should cut down on <u>fats</u>.
⑤ How about eating food which is low in <u>fat</u>?

07 다음 문장에 공통으로 들어갈 말을 고르시오.

> • Let's take a _____ for a while.
> • Would you put the _____ of the butter in the refrigerator?

① rest   ② rude
③ shape   ④ pant
⑤ asleep

08 다음 우리말을 주어진 단어를 이용하여 영작하시오.

(1) 나는 매일 공부하는 일에 싫증난다. (tired)

➡ _____

(2) 그는 더 이상 여기에 살고 있지 않아요. (is, longer)

➡ _____

_____

Conversation

[09~11] 다음 대화를 읽고 물음에 답하시오.

Olivia: You're eating only rice, again!

Junho: You know I'm ⓐon a diet for health reasons, don't you?

Olivia: Of course. But I don't think that only ⓑ eating rice will be very healthy.

Junho: What do you mean?

Olivia: Your body needs a ⓒcertain amount of meat.

Junho: But people said that I needed to avoid meat.

Olivia: (A)_____ They mean eating too much meat will be harmful.

Junho: I don't know ⓓhow to be on a good diet! It's too difficult!

Olivia: Make sure you have at least some beans or eggs. Oh, and don't forget ⓔeating some vegetables too.

09 위 대화의 빈칸 (A)에 들어갈 말로 적절한 것은?

① Sounds great.
② That's not right.
③ I agree with you.
④ That's true.
⑤ I think so, too.

10 위 대화의 밑줄 친 ⓐ~ⓔ 중 어색한 것을 찾아 바르게 고치시오.

➡ _____

11 위 대화의 내용과 일치하지 <u>않는</u> 것은?

① Junho는 건강상의 이유로 다이어트 중이다.
② Olivia는 밥만 먹는 것이 건강에 아주 좋다고 생각하지 않는다.
③ 득정한 양의 고기도 신체에 필요하나.
④ 고기를 너무 많이 먹는 것은 해롭다.
⑤ Olivia는 Junho에게 콩이나 계란을 피하고 채소를 먹을 것을 조언하였다.

[12~13] 다음 대화를 읽고 물음에 답하시오.

Sue: My back and leg hurt.

Brian: I think it's because you always cross your legs.

Sue: Oh, do you think so? I didn't know I have poor posture.

Brian: _____ when you sit in a chair.

12 위 대화의 빈칸에 들어갈 말을 보기에 주어진 단어들을 배열하여 영작하시오.

┌─ 보기 ─┐

cross / legs / make / you / your / sure / don't

➡ _____

13 위 대화의 내용과 일치하지 <u>않는</u> 것은?

① Sue는 등과 다리가 아프다.
② Sue는 항상 다리를 꼬아서 앉는다.
③ Sue는 자신이 좋지 않은 자세를 갖고 있다는 것을 몰랐다.
④ Brian은 Sue에게 의자에 앉을 때 다리를 꼬지 말라고 충고하였다.
⑤ Brian은 Sue가 다리를 꼬지 않는다는 것을 확인하였다.

14 다음 대화에서 주어진 (A)~(E)가 자연스럽게 이어지도록 순서대로 배열하시오.

> Ms. Kim: Minjae, can I have a word with you? It won't take long.
> Minjae: Of course, Ms. Kim.
> Ms. Kim: I saw that you are not concentrating and falling asleep during classes.

> (A) I just can't fall asleep easily. I tried to go to bed early but failed. I don't know how to get a good night's sleep.
> (B) What's the matter?
> (C) Oh, then I will try doing that.
> (D) Maybe you should try to go to bed regularly, not early.
> (E) Oh, I'm sorry.

➡ _____

Grammar

15 다음 빈칸에 알맞은 말을 고르시오.

> If I were busy, I _____ the meeting.

① won't hold   ② can't hold
③ couldn't hold   ④ may hold
⑤ can hold

16 다음 (A)~(C)에 들어갈 말이 바르게 짝지어진 것은?

> • If you (A)[go / went] there, you could meet John.
> • The building is (B)[too tall / so tall] that everyone wants to visit there.
> • If I had a sister, I (C)[could / can] play with her.

① go – too tall – could
② go – so tall – can
③ go – too tall – can
④ went – so tall – could
⑤ went – too tall – could

17 주어진 단어를 활용하여 다음 우리말을 영어로 쓰시오.

> 너무 늦어서 컴퓨터 게임을 할 수 없어. (it, late, to)

➡ _____

18 다음 대화의 빈칸에 들어갈 말로 가장 적절한 것은?

> A: The movie is _____ watch.
> B: Really? It doesn't scare me at all.

① so scary that   ② scary enough that
③ too scary to   ④ too scary that
⑤ so scary for

19 다음 두 문장을 지시에 맞게 하나의 문장으로 쓰시오.

> Your room is so messy. We can't use it.

(1) to부정사를 활용하여
➡ _____

(2) that을 활용하여
➡ _____

20 다음 문장과 같은 의미의 문장을 가정법을 활용하여 다시 쓰시오.

> I'm too anxious to watch the game.

➡ _____

21 다음 직설법을 가정법으로 바르게 옮긴 것은?

> As you are under 15, you can't go outside alone.

① If you are under 15, you can go outside alone.

② If you were under 15, you could go outside alone.

③ If you were not under 15, you couldn't go outside alone.

④ If you were not under 15, you could go outside alone.

⑤ If you were 15 years old, you couldn't go outside alone.

22 다음 빈칸에 들어갈 말이 바르게 짝지어진 것은?

> It's too hot for us to take a long walk.
> = It's _____ we can't take a long walk.

① very hot that   ② hot enough that

③ so hot that   ④ not hot enough to

⑤ too hot that

23 다음 문장과 의미가 비슷한 것을 고르시오.

> I want to buy a coat, but I don't have enough money.

① If I have enough money, I would buy a coat.

② If I had enough money, I would buy a coat.

③ If there is enough money, I could buy a coat.

④ If I bought a coat, I would not have enough money.

⑤ If I wanted to buy a coat, I wouldn't have enough money.

24 주어진 단어를 활용하여 다음 우리말을 영어로 쓰시오.

> 내가 일찍 잠자리에 든다면, 나는 아침에 일찍 일어날 수 있을 텐데. (go to bed / get)

➡ _____

_____

25 다음 빈칸에 알맞은 말을 쓰시오.

> If I could swim, I would not take swimming lessons.
> = As I _____, I _____.

26 다음 우리말에 맞게 빈칸에 알맞은 말을 쓰시오.

> 그녀는 좋은 결정을 내릴 만큼 현명해.
> ➡ She is _____ a good decision.

Reading

[27~28] 다음 글을 읽고 물음에 답하시오.

> ①Scene #1.
> *An old and tired mouse ②enters.*
> **Mouse**: *(He is ③out of breath.)* I'm tired of ④ running from Cat. I am too old to run. If I were free, I would be so happy. *(He thinks ⑤for a while.)* Oh, I have an idea!

27 위 글에 이어질 내용으로 가장 적절한 것은?

① a plan to chase after Mouse

② a trick of Mouse not to be chased by Cat

③ an excellent idea of Cat

④ a story of Mouse who wants to be friends with Cat

⑤ the reason why Cat is tired

28 ①~⑤ 중 단어의 의미가 바르지 <u>않은</u> 것은?

① 장면   ② 들어온다
③ 숨 쉴 수 없는   ④ ~로부터 달아나다
⑤ 잠깐 동안

[29~32] 다음 글을 읽고 물음에 답하시오.

Scene #2.

Mouse goes and gets something from the back of the stage. Cat enters and (A)[lets go of / catches] Mouse.

Mouse: *(He pretends to beg.)* I'm too smelly for you to eat! Instead, have this, please. *(He gives a box of sugar to Cat.)*

Cat: *(He tastes it. His eyes get bigger.)* What is it? Give me (B)[more / less]!

Mouse: It's sugar. If you let me go, I'll bring you some every day.

Scene #3.

It is at Cat's house. Cat, now (C)[fat / thin], is eating sugar. He has only a few teeth. Dog is watching him.

Dog: *(ⓐ_____)* Cat, my friend, be careful. The sugar will get bitter.

Cat: ⓑ무슨 말이야?

Dog: Look at yourself! You are too fat to run, and your teeth are too weak to chew!

Cat: *(He eats more.)* Why should I run or chew? Sugar is the only thing I need. I can't live without it.

Dog goes out sadly.

29 다음 중 빈칸 ⓐ에 들어갈 말로 가장 적절한 것은?

① He is happy.   ② He is excited.
③ He is bored.   ④ He is worried.
⑤ He doesn't care.

30 (A)~(C)에서 글의 흐름상 옳은 것끼리 바르게 묶은 것은?

① catches – less – thin
② catches – more – fat
③ lets go of – more – thin
④ lets go of – more – fat
⑤ lets go of – less – thin

31 주어진 단어를 바르게 배열하여 밑줄 친 우리말 ⓑ를 영어로 쓰시오.

that / what / mean / by / you / do

➡ _____

32 다음 중 위 글을 읽고 답할 수 <u>없는</u> 것은?

① From where did Mouse get the sugar?
② What did Mouse say to Cat when he pretended to beg?
③ Without what can't Cat live?
④ How much sugar did Cat eat every day?
⑤ What did Cat do after hearing what Dog said about how he looked?

[33~34] 다음 글을 읽고 물음에 답하시오.

These days, Tom has found a new hobby. It is watching funny videos on the Internet with his phone. (A)They are so interesting. Time seems to fly when he watches them. The problem is he sometimes stays up late at night to watch videos. His friends say, "Tom, make sure you don't take your phone to your room when you go to bed." Tom thinks this is a good idea.

33 밑줄 친 (A)가 지칭하는 것을 위 글에서 찾아 쓰시오.

➡ _____

34 Write the reason why Tom stays up late at night. Answer in English with a full sentence.

➡ _____

[01~03] 다음 대화를 읽고 물음에 답하시오.

Ms. Kim: Minjae, (A)can I have a word with you? It won't take long.

Minjae: Of course, Ms. Kim.

Ms. Kim: I saw ⓐthat you are not concentrating and falling asleep ⓑduring classes.

Minjae: Oh, I'm sorry.

Ms. Kim: What's the matter?

Minjae: I just can't fall asleep easily. I tried to go to bed early but ⓒfail. I don't know how ⓓto get a good night's sleep.

Ms. Kim: Maybe you should try to go to bed ⓔ regularly, not early.

Minjae: Oh, then I will try doing that.

출제율 90%

01 위 대화의 밑줄 친 (A)와 바꾸어 쓸 수 있는 것은?

① can I talk to you now?

② can I let you know a word?

③ would you say something about me?

④ would you teach a word to me?

⑤ can I spell a word?

출제율 95%

02 위 대화의 밑줄 친 ⓐ~ⓔ 중 어법상 어색한 것을 찾아 바르게 고치시오.

➡ _____

출제율 100%

03 위 대화를 읽고 대답할 수 없는 것은?

① Why did Ms. Kim want to talk with Minjae?

② Why did Minjae fall asleep during classes?

③ What did Ms. Kim advise to get a good night's sleep?

④ What did Minjae try to do?

⑤ What subject does Ms. Kim teach?

[04~06] 다음 글을 읽고 물음에 답하시오.

Mr. Kim: Today, I'd like to talk about your eyes. The eyes are really important parts of our body, but more and more students are having eye problems. Some students cannot see without glasses or have dry eyes. If you do not want these problems, try to take some time to rest your eyes. When you study, try to look outside for a while. Make sure you don't look at computer or phone screens for too long.

출제율 90%

04 What does Mr. Kim want to talk about?

➡ _____

출제율 95%

05 What problems do more and more students have?

➡ _____

출제율 90%

06 What should students do to protect their eyes?

➡ _____

[07~08] 다음 대화를 읽고 물음에 답하시오.

Olivia: You're eating only rice, again!

Junho: You know I'm on a diet for health reasons, (A)그렇지 않니?

Olivia: Of course. But I don't think that only eating rice will be very healthy.

Junho: What do you mean?

Olivia: Your body needs a certain amount of meat.

Junho: But people said that I needed to avoid meat.

Olivia: That's not right. They mean eating too much meat will be (B)[healthy / harmful].

Junho: I don't know how to be on a good diet! It's too (C)[easy / difficult]!

Olivia: Make sure you have at least some beans or eggs. Oh, and don't (D)[forget / remember] to eat some vegetables too.

출제율 85%

07 위 대화의 밑줄 친 (A)의 우리말을 두 단어로 영작하시오.

➡ _____

출제율 100%

08 위 대화의 (B)~(D)에 들어갈 말이 바르게 짝지어진 것은?

	(B)	(C)	(D)
①	healthy	easy	forget
②	healthy	difficult	remember
③	harmful	difficult	forget
④	harmful	difficult	remember
⑤	harmful	easy	forget

[09~10] 다음 글을 읽고 물음에 답하시오.

Mr. Kim: Today, (A)I'd like to talk about your eyes. The eyes are really important parts of our body, but more and more students are having eye problems. Some students cannot see without glasses or have dry eyes. If you do not want these problems, try to take some time to rest your eyes. When you study, try to look outside for a while. Make sure you don't look at computer or phone screens for too long.

출제율 90%

09 위 글의 밑줄 친 (A)와 바꾸어 쓸 수 없는 것은?

① Let me tell you about your eyes.

② I'd like to tell you about your eyes.

③ I'd like to say something about your eyes.

④ Let me talk about your eyes.

⑤ Tell me more about your eyes.

출제율 100%

10 위 글의 내용과 일치하지 않는 것은?

① Mr. Kim은 눈 건강에 대해 이야기하고 있다.

② 점점 더 많은 학생들이 안구 문제를 겪고 있다.

③ 몇몇 학생들은 안경 없이는 볼 수 없거나 안구 건조증을 겪는다.

④ 안구 건조를 치료하기 위해 눈이 쉴 수 있는 시간을 갖도록 노력해야 한다.

⑤ 컴퓨터나 휴대폰 화면을 너무 오래 보지 않도록 명심해야 한다.

출제율 95%

11 다음 우리말을 영어로 옮길 때 다섯 번째로 오는 단어는?

> 많은 연필을 가지고 있다면, 나는 많은 것들을 그릴 텐데.

① had ② many ③ pencils

④ I ⑤ would

출제율 95%

12 다음 빈칸에 들어갈 말로 가장 적절한 것은?

> This food smells good, but it is too hot for me to eat right now.
> = This food smells good, but it is _____ right now.

① very hot that I can eat

② so hot that I can eat

③ hot enough to eat

④ so hot that I can't eat it

⑤ very hot to eat it

출제율 95%

13 다음 빈칸에 알맞은 말을 바르게 짝지은 것은?

> If I _____ a one-week vacation, I
> _____ a trip to Japan. But I'm so busy
> these days.

① have – will take   ② have – take

③ had – would take   ④ had – take

⑤ had – will take

출제율 100%

14 다음 중 어법상 바르지 <u>않은</u> 것은?

① The boys are too noisy to be in the library.

② If I called him, he would answer it.

③ June was too sick to go to school.

④ If you met her, you would be surprised.

⑤ He was so fat that he can't walk for a long time.

출제율 95%

15 다음 문장과 같은 의미의 문장을 쓰시오.

> The table was too heavy for her to move.

➡ _____

출제율 85%

16 가정법을 활용하여 다음 두 문장을 하나의 문장으로 쓰시오.

> I don't dance well. So I can't win the school dance contest.

➡ _____

출제율 90%

17 다음 가정법을 직설법 문장으로 전환하시오.

> If he were with us, he would tell many interesting stories.

➡ _____

_____

[18~22] 다음 글을 읽고 물음에 답하시오.

> **Scene #4.**
> *Cat has almost emptied the box of sugar. Mouse enters.*
> Mouse: *(He smiles.)* I think my plan ①has worked.
> Cat: *(He is angry.)* It's almost empty! Mouse, tell me where you get it.
> Mouse: I have a friend ②who makes sugar. But he's ③scared of your claws. If you get rid of them, you can meet him soon.
> Cat: Okay!
> **Scene #5.**
> *Mouse hands Cat a pair of scissors and Cat cuts his claws.*
> Cat: I'm ready! Now take me to ④your friend!
> Mouse: *(ⓐ_____)* You stupid cat! (a)If you were fast, and had your sharp teeth and claws, I'd listen to you. But you no longer have them now! You have lost your biggest weapons! Why should I listen to ⑤what you say now? *(He runs away.)*
> Cat: What! *(He tries to run after Mouse, but fails.)* Oh! I'm too ⓑ_____ to run after him!

출제율 100%

18 다음 중 빈칸 ⓐ에 들어갈 말로 가장 적절한 것은?

① He welcomes Cat.

② He cheers Cat up.

③ He shows the way.

④ He laughs at Cat.

⑤ He laughs with Cat.

19 빈칸 ⓑ에 들어갈 말로 가장 적절한 것은?

① clever ② smart ③ fat
④ weak ⑤ noisy

20 ①~⑤에 대한 설명으로 바르지 <u>않은</u> 것은?

① is effective로 바꾸어 쓸 수 있다.
② that으로 바꾸어 쓸 수 있다.
③ afraid of로 바꾸어 쓸 수 있다.
④ 설탕을 가져오는 친구를 의미한다.
⑤ the thing which로 풀어 쓸 수 있다.

21 단어 as를 활용하여 밑줄 친 (a)와 같은 의미의 문장을 쓰시오.

➡ _____
_____

22 다음 중 위 글의 내용과 일치하는 것은?

① Mouse helped Cat empty the box of sugar.
② Cat wanted to know where Mouse got sugar.
③ One of Cat's friends could make sugar.
④ Mouse cut Cat's claws with a pair of scissors.
⑤ Mouse thought Cat was clever.

[23~25] 다음 글을 읽고 물음에 답하시오.

A long time ago, there lived a caterpillar named Bob. He was waiting to become a beautiful butterfly.
[A] But Bob didn't want to leave his bottle. "This place is too good to leave. Why do I have to go out?" he thought.
[B] Bob stayed there for a few days. His friends came and said, "Bob, get out. We have to prepare."
[C] When spring came, Bob's friends flew here and there in the warm air. Only Bob was left in the brown bottle, cold and still.
[D] One day, while he was taking a walk, he found a brown bottle. It was warm and bright inside the bottle.
"Poor Bob, if he ⓐ_____(be) a butterfly like us, he ⓑ_____(enjoy) his wonderful sunshine," his friends said.

23 주어진 단어를 어법에 맞게 빈칸 ⓐ와 ⓑ에 각각 쓰시오.

➡ ⓐ _____ ⓑ _____

24 자연스러운 글이 되도록 [A]~[D]를 바르게 배열하시오.

➡ _____

25 다음 중 위 글을 읽고 답할 수 <u>없는</u> 것은?

① What is the name of the caterpillar?
② What did Bob want to become?
③ Why did Bob's friends want him to get out of the bottle?
④ How was it inside the bottle?
⑤ What did Bob eat while staying in the bottle?

서술형 실전문제

[01~03] 다음 대화를 읽고 물음에 답하시오.

Olivia: You're eating only rice, again!

Junho: You know I'm on a diet for health reasons, don't you?

Olivia: Of course. But I don't think that only eating rice will be very healthy.

Junho: What do you mean?

Olivia: Your body needs a certain amount of meat.

Junho: But people said that I needed to avoid meat.

Olivia: That's not right. They mean eating too much meat will be harmful.

Junho: I don't know how to be on a good diet! It's too difficult!

Olivia: Make sure you have at least some beans or eggs. Oh, and don't forget to eat some vegetables too.

01 What is the problem with Junho's diet?

➡ _____

02 Why does Junho avoid meat?

➡ _____
_____

03 What is Olivia's advice?

➡ _____
_____

04 다음 문장과 같은 의미의 문장을 to부정사를 활용하여 쓰시오.

> The problems were so difficult that they couldn't be solved in one day.

➡ _____
_____

05 다음 우리말을 지시에 맞게 영어로 쓰시오

> 오늘이 금요일이라면, 수업이 더 일찍 끝날 텐데. But today is Wednesday.
> (school / over / earlier)

(1) 직설법으로

➡ _____

(2) 가정법으로

➡ _____

06 다음 문장을 가정법으로 나타내시오.

> I am too embarrassed to go out.

➡ _____

[07~08] 다음 글을 읽고 물음에 답하시오.

> There is a plant in my garden. (A)그것은 너무 약해서 크게 자랄 수 없어요. I feel sorry because I haven't given it enough water. ⓐ충분히 물을 주면, it would grow taller.

07 동사 water를 활용하여 밑줄 친 ⓐ를 적절한 가정법 문장을 써서 영어로 옮기시오.

➡ _____

8 주어진 단어를 활용하여 밑줄 친 우리말 (A)를 영어로 쓰시오.

> (that / grow tall)

➡ _____

[09~10] 다음 글을 읽고 물음에 답하시오.

Scene #3.

It is at Cat's house. Cat, now fat, is eating sugar. He has only a few teeth. Dog is watching him.

Dog: *(He is worried.)* Cat, my friend, be careful. The sugar will get bitter.

Cat: What do you mean by that?

Dog: Look at yourself! You are too fat to run, and your teeth are too weak to chew!

Cat: *(He eats more.)* Why should I run or chew? Sugar is the only thing I need. I can't live without it.

Dog goes out sadly.

9 위 글을 읽고, 고양이가 뚱뚱해진 이유를 유추하여 영어로 쓰시오. (It's because로 시작할 것.)

➡ _____

10 위 글의 내용에 맞게 빈칸에 알맞은 말을 쓰시오.

> Cat didn't mind not being able to
> _____ _____ _____.

[11~12] 다음 글을 읽고 물음에 답하시오.

I am not diligent and I put things off. I cannot get up early in the morning. I always say, "In 10 more minutes…" If I were ⓐmore diligent, I would have breakfast and

would ⓑfocus on my classes. Of course, I would not be ⓒlate for school. I would not put off my homework and would finish it. I know my habits are not ⓓgood ones. I think I will have to make a plan to be more diligent and to be a good student. (A)지금부터, I will make a list of things to do. I am also going to get up 30 minutes ⓔlater every morning.

11 ⓐ~ⓔ에서 글의 흐름상 어색한 것을 골라 바르게 고쳐 쓰시오.

➡ _____

12 밑줄 친 우리말 (A)를 영어로 쓰시오.

➡ _____

13 다음 희곡을 읽고 글의 내용에 맞게 빈칸에 알맞은 말을 쓰시오.

> **Scene #2.**
>
> *Mouse goes and gets something from the back of the stage. Cat enters and catches Mouse.*
>
> Mouse: *(He pretends to beg.)* I'm too smelly for you to eat! Instead, have this, please. *(He gives a box of sugar to Cat.)*
>
> Cat: *(He tastes it. His eyes get bigger.)* What is it? Give me more!
>
> Mouse: It's sugar. If you let me go, I'll bring you some every day.

> When Mouse was caught by Cat, he said that he was so _____
> _____. And he handed _____ to Cat.

01 다음 대화의 내용과 일치하도록 빈칸을 완성하시오.

> Olivia: You're eating only rice, again!
> Junho: You know I'm on a diet for health reasons, don't you?
> Olivia: Of course. But I don't think that only eating rice will be very healthy.
> Junho: What do you mean?
> Olivia: Your body needs a certain amount of meat.
> Junho: But people said that I needed to avoid meat.
> Olivia: That's not right. They mean eating too much meat will be harmful.
> Junho: I don't know how to be on a good diet! It's too difficult!
> Olivia: Make sure you have at least some beans or eggs. Oh, and don't forget to eat some vegetables too.

> Olivia sees that Junho is eating only (A)_____ again. He is (B)_____ for health reasons. Olivia doesn't think that only eating rice will be healthy because his body needs (C)_____. But Junho heard that he needed to avoid (D)_____. Olivia says that's not right. She says (E)_____ will be harmful. Junho doesn't know how to be on a good diet. It's too difficult for him. Olivia's advice is to eat some (F)_____ too. She adds that he should not forget to eat some (G)_____ as well.

02 다음 빈칸에 알맞은 말을 써서 문장을 완성하시오.

> (1) If she _____, she would clean it every day. It's a pity that she doesn't have her own room.
> (2) If they _____, I would be glad. I'm sad that they don't come to see me.
> (3) If I _____, I would drink lots of water. But I'm not thirsty.

03 다음 대화를 바탕으로 Jamie가 쓴 반성의 글을 완성하시오.

> A: What is your biggest problem?
> B: I don't clean my room.
> A: What can't you do because of your problem?
> B: I can't easily find where I put my things.
> A: What are you going to do to solve your problem?
> B: I will clean my room once a week.

> I am not diligent and _____. Sometimes, my room is so messy that _____. I know my habit is not a good one. So I decide to solve my problem. From now on, I _____.

단원별 모의고사

01 다음 영영풀이가 가리키는 것을 고르시오.

> to bite food into small pieces in your mouth with your teeth to make it easier to swallow

① catch　　② chew　　③ throw
④ beat　　⑤ add

[02~03] 다음 글을 읽고 물음에 답하시오.

Mr. Kim: Today, I'd like to talk about your eyes. The eyes are really important parts of our body, but more and more students are having eye problems. Some students cannot see without glasses or have (A)[wet / dry] eyes. If you do not want these problems, try to take some time to rest your eyes. When you study, try to look (B)[inside / outside] for a while. Make sure you don't look at computer or phone screens for too (C)[long / short].

02 위 글의 (A)~(C)에 들어갈 말이 바르게 짝지어진 것은?

	(A)	(B)	(C)
①	wet	inside	long
②	wet	outside	short
③	dry	outside	long
④	dry	outside	short
⑤	dry	inside	long

03 위 글에서 Mr. Kim의 조언으로 언급되지 <u>않은</u> 것은?

① 눈에 휴식을 주기
② 충분한 수면 취하기
③ 휴대전화 오래 보지 않기
④ 공부할 때 종종 바깥 보기
⑤ 컴퓨터 화면 오래 보지 않기

04 다음 주어진 우리말과 일치하도록 주어진 단어를 모두 배열하여 영작하시오.

(1) 당신은 내게 어떤 식단을 추천하나요?
(do / for / me / what / diet / recommend / you)
➡ _____

(2) 가위로 종이를 자르세요.
(the / cut / paper / the / with / scissors)
➡ _____

05 다음 대화가 자연스럽게 이어지도록 순서대로 배열하시오.

> (A) Here it is. Take good care of it.
> (B) I don't know how to care.
> (C) Don't water it too often. And it should get enough light.
> (D) Oh, this flower is the one I'm looking for. I'll take it.

➡ _____

[06~07] 다음 대화를 읽고 물음에 답하시오.

Olivia: You're eating only rice, again!
Junho: You know I'm on a diet for health reasons, don't you?
Olivia: Of course. But I don't think that only eating rice will be very healthy.
Junho: What do you mean?
Olivia: Your body needs a certain amount of meat.
Junho: But people said that I needed to avoid meat.
Olivia: That's not right. They mean eating too much meat will be harmful.
Junho: I don't know how to be on a good diet! It's too difficult!
Olivia: _____ Oh, and don't forget to eat some vegetables too.

06 위 대화의 빈칸에 들어갈 말을 〈보기〉에 주어진 단어들을 모두 배열하여 영작하시오.

┌─── 보기 ───┐
beans / least / eggs / sure / you / have /
some / at / make / or
└─────────────┘

➡ _____

07 위 대화를 읽고 대답할 수 <u>없는</u> 것은?

① Why is Junho on a diet?
② What is the problem with Junho's diet?
③ What does Olivia think about eating only rice?
④ What is Olivia's advice on Junho's diet?
⑤ What is the good effect of eating only rice?

[08~10] 다음 대화를 읽고 물음에 답하시오.

Ms. Kim: Minjae, can I have a word with you? It won't take long.
Minjae: Of course, Ms. Kim.
Ms. Kim: (A)　I saw that you are not concentrating and falling asleep during classes.
Minjae: (B) Oh, I'm sorry.
Ms. Kim: (C) What's the matter?
Minjae: (D) I tried to go to bed early but failed. I don't know how to get a good night's sleep.
Ms. Kim: (E) Maybe you should try to go to bed regularly, not early.
Minjae: Oh, then I will try doing that.

08 위 대화의 (A)~(E) 중 주어진 문장이 들어가기에 적절한 곳은?

┌─────────────────────────────┐
I just can't fall asleep easily.
└─────────────────────────────┘

① (A)　② (B)　③ (C)　④ (D)　⑤ (E)

09 Who are the two speakers in the dialogue?

① singer – fan
② teacher – student
③ mother – son
④ customer – manager
⑤ traveler – guide

10 위 대화의 내용과 일치하는 것은?

① Ms. Kim has new vocabulary to teach Minjae.
② Minjae has difficulty falling asleep during classes.
③ Minjae knows how to get a good night's sleep.
④ Ms. Kim advises Minjae to go to bed regularly.
⑤ Minjae knows the importance of a good night's sleep in the class.

11 다음 우리말에 맞게 주어진 단어를 사용하여 영작하시오.

(1) 나는 밤에 쉽게 잠들지 못한다. (fall, easily)
➡ _____

(2) 농부가 들판에 콩을 심었다. (field, planted)
➡ _____

(3) 나비들은 봄에 여기저기 날아다닌다. (there, here)
➡ _____

12 다음 대화가 자연스럽게 이어지도록 순서대로 배열하시오.

┌─────────────────────────────────────┐
(A) That's too much! Make sure you don't drink that much next time.
(B) Your hands are shaking. Are you okay?
(C) Okay, I won't.
(D) It may be because of the energy drink. I drank three cans for today's test.
└─────────────────────────────────────┘

➡ _____

13 다음 문장이 의미하는 것으로 가장 적절한 것은?

> The car ran fast. We couldn't stop it.

① The car ran fast enough to be stopped.

② The car ran too fast for us to stop.

③ The car ran very fast to stop a car.

④ The car ran so fast that we can't stop it.

⑤ We couldn't stop the car because it ran away.

14 다음 중 어법상 바르지 않은 것은?

① If it rains tomorrow, I won't go out.

② The water is too cold to drink.

③ If I won the prize, I will be very happy. But I can't get any prize.

④ The movie was so moving that everyone cried.

⑤ If they made me go, they might be in trouble.

15 주어진 단어를 활용하여 다음 문장을 가정법으로 표현하시오.

> The necklace is too expensive for me to buy. (I)

➡ _____

16 다음 직설법을 가정법으로 전환하시오.

> I have many things to do, so I can't watch the movie with you.

➡ _____
_____

17 주어진 문장과 같은 의미의 문장을 쓰시오.

> I am too forgetful to remember what I have to do.

➡ _____
_____

[18~19] 다음 글을 읽고 물음에 답하시오.

Scene #3.

It is at Cat's house. Cat, now fat, is eating sugar. He has only a few teeth. Dog is watching him.

Dog: *(He is worried.)* Cat, my friend, be careful. (A) The sugar will get bitter.

Cat: What do you mean by that?

Dog: Look at yourself! You are too fat to run, and your teeth are too weak to chew!

Cat: *(He eats more.)* Why should I run or chew? Sugar is the only thing I need. I can't live without it.

18 다음 중 위 글의 내용과 일치하는 것은?

① 장면 3의 배경은 개의 집이다.

② 고양이는 아직 이빨이 많이 있다.

③ 개는 고양이를 신경 쓰지 않는다.

④ 고양이의 이빨은 너무 약해서 무언가를 씹을 수 없다.

⑤ 고양이는 개의 말을 귀담아 들었다.

19 밑줄 친 (A)의 의미로 가장 적절한 것은?

① The sugar will go bad.

② You will share the sugar.

③ The sugar will be harmful to you.

④ The sugar will make you happy.

⑤ You will feel nothing.

[20~23] 다음 글을 읽고 물음에 답하시오.

Scene #4.
Cat has almost emptied the box of sugar. Mouse enters.

Mouse: *(He smiles.)* I think my plan has worked.

Cat: *(He is angry.)* It's almost empty! Mouse, tell me where you get it.

Mouse: I have a friend who makes sugar. But he's scared ___ⓐ___ your claws. If you get rid ___ⓑ___ them, you can meet him soon.

Cat: Okay!

Scene #5.
Mouse hands Cat a pair of scissors and Cat cuts his claws.

Cat: I'm ready! Now take me to your friend!

Mouse: *(He laughs at Cat.)* You stupid cat! If you were fast, and had your sharp teeth and claws, I'd listen to you. But you no longer have them now! You have lost your biggest weapons! Why should I listen to (A)_____ you say now? *(He runs away.)*

Cat: What! *(He tries to (B)_____ after Mouse, but fails.)* Oh! I'm too fat to (C)_____ after him!

20 빈칸 ⓐ와 ⓑ에 공통으로 알맞은 전치사는?

① in   ② to   ③ of
④ from   ⑤ with

21 빈칸 (A)에 알맞은 말을 한 단어로 쓰시오.

➡ _____

22 빈칸 (B)와 (C)에 들어갈 말을 위 글에서 찾아 쓰시오.

➡ _____

23 다음 중 위 글의 내용과 일치하지 <u>않는</u> 것은?

① Cat wanted to eat more sugar.
② Cat cut his claws himself.
③ Mouse took Cat to his friend.
④ Cat was laughed at by Mouse.
⑤ Mouse said he brought the sugar from his friend.

[24~25] 다음 글을 읽고 물음에 답하시오.

A long time ago, there lived a caterpillar named Bob. He was waiting ①to become a beautiful butterfly. One day, ②while he was taking a walk, he found a brown bottle. It was warm and bright ③inside the bottle. Bob stayed there for ④a little days. His friends came and said, "Bob, get out. We have to prepare." But Bob didn't want ⑤to leave his bottle. "This place is too good to leave. Why do I have to go out?" he thought. When spring came, Bob's friends flew here and there in the warm air. Only Bob was left in the brown bottle, cold and still. "Poor Bob, if he were a butterfly like us, he would enjoy his wonderful sunshine," his friends said.

24 ①~⑤ 중 어법상 <u>틀린</u> 것은?

①   ②   ③   ④   ⑤

25 위 글의 내용과 일치하도록 빈칸에 알맞은 말을 쓰시오.

Bob's friend told Bob to get out of the bottle to prepare for _____.

INSIGHT
on the textbook

교과서 파헤치기

※ 다음 영어를 우리말로 쓰시오.

01	language	22	greet
02	bow	23	guest
03	capital	24	unbelievable
04	wave	25	host
05	manner	26	perfect
06	nod	27	plate
07	country	28	clothing
08	appointment	29	prepare
09	recommend	30	punctual
10	confuse	31	upset
11	thankful	32	costume
12	respect	33	prize
13	promise	34	stick
14	calm	35	for free
15	confident	36	get rid of
16	rude	37	take part in
17	scary	38	make a difference
18	thin	39	sign up
19	difference	40	have trouble -ing
20	carve	41	on time
21	traditional	42	call upon
		43	shake hands

※ 다음 우리말을 영어로 쓰시오.

01 마른, 얇은 _____

02 추천하다 _____

03 (고개를) 숙이다 _____

04 믿기 어려운 _____

05 무례한, 예의 없는 _____

06 침착한; 진정시키다 _____

07 준비하다 _____

08 존중하다; 존중 _____

09 충고, 조언 _____

10 약속 _____

11 속상한, 화난 _____

12 붙이다 _____

13 새기다, 조각하다 _____

14 인사하다 _____

15 의상 _____

16 전통의 _____

17 나라, 국가 _____

18 차이, 다름 _____

19 언어 _____

20 예의, 예절 _____

21 옷, 의복 _____

22 고개를 끄덕이다 _____

23 손님, 하객 _____

24 주인, 주최자 _____

25 시간을 지키는 _____

26 불평하다 _____

27 무서운 _____

28 약속하다 _____

29 접시 _____

30 자신감 있는 _____

31 감사하는, 고마워하는 _____

32 완벽한, 완전한 _____

33 혼동하다 _____

34 파도; 손을 흔들다 _____

35 무료로 _____

36 ~하는 데 어려움을 겪다 _____

37 ~을 요청하다, ~을 부탁하다 _____

38 ~을 제거하다, ~을 없애다 _____

39 등록하다, 신청하다 _____

40 ~에 참가하다 _____

41 변화를 일으키다 _____

42 악수하다 _____

43 ~에 관심을 갖다 _____

※ 다음 영영풀이에 알맞은 단어를 <보기>에서 골라 쓴 후, 우리말 뜻을 쓰시오.

1 _____ : arriving or doing something at the expected or planned time: _____

2 _____ : having or showing a lack of respect for other people and their feelings: _____

3 _____ : to make objects, patterns, etc. by cutting away material from wood or stone: _____

4 _____ : an opinion or a suggestion about what somebody should do in a particular situation: _____

5 _____ : a raised line of water that moves across the surface of the sea, ocean, etc.: _____

6 _____ : to move your head or the top half of your body forwards and downwards as a sign of respect or to say hello or goodbye: _____

7 _____ : the most important town or city of a country, usually where the central government operates from: _____

8 _____ : to say that you are annoyed, unhappy or not satisfied about somebody/ something: _____

9 _____ : a person who invites guests to a meal, a party, etc. or who has people staying at their house: _____

10 _____ : a feeling of admiration for somebody/something because of their good qualities or achievements: _____

11 _____ : a person that you have invited to your house or to a particular event that you are paying for: _____

12 _____ : an award that is given to a person who wins a competition, race, etc. or who does very good work: _____

13 _____ : to tell somebody that something is good or useful, or that somebody would be suitable for a particular job, etc.: _____

14 _____ : being part of the beliefs, customs or way of life of a particular group of people, that have not changed for a long time: _____

15 _____ : a formal arrangement to meet or visit somebody at a particular time, especially for a reason connected with their work: _____

16 _____ : a strong feeling of surprise as a result of something happening, especially something unpleasant; the event that causes this feeling: _____

보기

bow	prize	recommend	host
respect	shock	advice	guest
appointment	punctual	rude	traditional
capital	wave	complain	carve

※ 다음 우리말과 일치하도록 빈칸에 알맞은 말을 쓰시오.

Everyday English 1 A. Function Practice

1. **G:** I'm _____ _____ _____ my family tomorrow!

   B: Hmm…. I _____ that it _____ _____ tomorrow.

   G: What? It _____ _____ _____ .

   B: I'm sorry, but it was _____ _____ _____ .

2. **G:** I _____ _____ there is a _____ _____ next week.

   B: Really? I'm _____ _____ science.

   G: Then you should _____ _____ . There is a big _____ for the _____ .

   B: Great! _____ _____ _____ me.

3. **G:** It _____ _____ Halloween soon!

   B: I _____ that people _____ _____ on Halloween. _____ _____ do people do?

   G: Children wear _____ _____ and visit houses _____ _____ sweets.

   B: That _____ interesting.

Everyday English 1 B

Mina: Alex, _____ you _____ some _____ ?

Alex: Yes, Mina, _____ is it?

Mina: _____ _____ _____ you _____ _____ _____ this summer!

Alex: Yes, I _____ _____ a family trip.

Mina: Can you tell me _____ _____ _____ _____ ? I'm _____ _____ _____ Spain this winter.

Alex: I see. I think Spain is a really nice country _____ _____ . There are _____ _____ .

Mina: Where do you _____ that I _____ ?

Alex: I _____ _____ the Prado Museum in Madrid. It's _____ _____ _____ _____ _____ _____ in the world.

Mina: _____ _____ the help!

1. **G:** 나는 내일 가족들과 캠핑을 갈 거야.
   B: 흠…. 나는 내일 비가 온다고 들었어.
   G: 뭐? 그럴 리 없어.
   B: 미안하지만, 뉴스에 나왔어.
2. **G:** 나는 다음 주에 과학 대회가 있다고 들었어.
   B: 정말? 나는 과학에 관심이 있어.
   G: 그럼 너는 신청해야 해. 우승자에게는 큰 상이 있어.
   B: 잘됐다! 내게 말해 줘서 고마워.
3. **G:** 곧 핼러윈이야!
   B: 사람들은 핼러윈에 호박에 조각을 한다고 들었어. 사람들은 또 어떤 것들을 하니?
   G: 어린 아이들은 무서운 의상을 차려 입고 사탕을 얻기 위해 여러 집들을 방문해.
   B: 그것 참 흥미롭게 들린다.

Mina: Alex, 너 시간 있니?
Alex: 응, 미나야. 무슨 일인데?
Mina: 네가 이번 여름에 스페인에 갔다는 얘기를 들었어!
Alex: 응, 가족 여행을 갔었어.
Mina: 너의 여행에 대해 더 말해 줄 수 있니? 나도 이번 겨울에 스페인을 방문해 보려고 생각 중이야.
Alex: 알겠어. 나는 스페인이 방문하기에 정말 좋은 나라라고 생각해. 흥미로운 장소들이 많아.
Mina: 내가 갈 만한 장소로 어디를 추천하니?
Alex: 나는 Madrid에 있는 Prado 박물관을 추천해. 세계에서 가장 유명한 박물관 중 하나야.
Mina: 도와줘서 고마워.

Everyday English 2 A. Function Practice

1. **G:** I'd _____ _____ tell you _____ _____ _____.
   B: What is it?
   G: I think _____ _____ _____ thing in love is _____.
   B: I _____ _____ you. _____ each _____ _____ is very important.

2. **B:** _____ _____ the Eiffel Tower.
   G: It's really _____ and _____!
   B: I'd like to tell you _____ _____ the Eiffel Tower. People didn't like it _____ _____.
   G: Really? But it has become one of _____ _____ _____ _____ in Paris _____ _____!

Everyday English 2 B

Tina: Hello, everyone. My name is Tina and I'm a _____ _____. Today, I'd like to tell you an _____ _____ that I learned _____ _____. When I first visited Korea, I thought Koreans were _____ because many people asked me my _____. However, I later _____ _____ that this was _____ _____ their _____. Koreans use language _____ to people who are _____ than them, so they _____ _____ know the other person's age. This _____ has taught me the importance of _____ and _____ _____ _____.

In Real Life

(Phone rings.)

Suji: Hello, Suji _____.
Diego: Hi, it's me, Diego. Do you have _____ _____ _____?
Suji: Yes, what's _____?
Diego: I'm doing my _____ _____ homework on _____ _____, but I'm _____ _____ _____ the _____ _____.
Suji: I'd _____ _____ _____ you about a website _____ "Culture Shock." I heard that people ask and answer questions about _____ _____ on that website.
Diego: That _____ _____. _____ you _____ your help.
Suji: You're _____. _____ luck with the homework.

1. **G:** 사랑에 대해 너에게 해 주고 싶은 이야기가 있어.
   B: 무엇인데?
   G: 나는 사랑에서 가장 중요한 것은 존중이라고 생각해.
   B: 동의해. 서로의 다름을 존중하는 것이 매우 중요해.
2. **B:** 에펠탑을 좀 봐.
   G: 정말 크고 아름답다!
   B: 에펠탑에 대해 너에게 해 주고 싶은 이야기가 있어. 사람들이 처음엔 이것을 좋아하지 않았대.
   G: 정말? 하지만 이건 요즘 파리에서 가장 유명한 장소 중 하나잖아!

Tina: 안녕, 모두들. 내 이름은 Tina이고 나는 여행 작가야. 오늘 나는 너희들에게 내가 여행에서 배운 중요한 교훈에 대해 말해 주고 싶어. 내가 처음 한국에 방문했을 때, 나는 많은 한국인이 내 나이를 물었기 때문에 무례하다고 생각했어. 그런데 나중에 나는 이것이 그들의 문화 때문이라는 것을 알았어. 한국인들은 그들보다 나이가 많은 사람들에게는 언어를 다르게 쓰는데, 그래서 다른 사람들의 나이를 알 필요가 있는 거였어. 이 경험은 나에게 다른 문화를 배우고 이해하는 것의 중요성을 알게 해 주었어.

(전화가 울린다)
Suji: 여보세요, 저 수지인데요.
Diego: 안녕, 나야 Diego. 얘기할 시간 있니?
Suji: 응, 무슨 일이야?
Diego: 문화적 차이들에 관한 사회 숙제를 하고 있거든. 그런데 올바른 정보를 찾는 데 어려움이 있어.
Suji: "Culture Shock"이라고 불리는 웹 사이트에 대해 말해 주고 싶어. 나는 그 웹 사이트에서 사람들이 다른 문화들에 대해 질문하고 답해 준다고 들었어.
Diego: 그것 참 완벽하게 들린다. 도와줘서 고마워.
Suji: 천만에. 숙제 잘하기를 바라.

※ 다음 우리말에 맞도록 대화를 영어로 쓰시오.

Everyday English 1 A. Function Practice

1. G: _____

   B: _____

   G: _____

   B: _____

2. G: _____

   B: _____

   G: _____

   B: _____

3. G: _____

   B: _____

   G: _____

   B: _____

1. G: 나는 내일 가족들과 캠핑을 갈 거야.
   B: 흠…. 나는 내일 비가 온다고 들었어.
   G: 뭐? 그럴 리 없어.
   B: 미안하지만, 뉴스에 나왔어.
2. G: 나는 다음 주에 과학 대회가 있다고 들었어.
   B: 정말? 나는 과학에 관심이 있어.
   G: 그럼 너는 신청해야 해. 우승자에게는 큰 상이 있어.
   B: 잘됐다! 내게 말해 줘서 고마워.
3. G: 곧 핼러윈이야!
   B: 사람들은 핼러윈에 호박에 조각을 한다고 들었어. 사람들은 또 어떤 것들을 하니?
   G: 어린 아이들은 무서운 의상을 차려 입고 사탕을 얻기 위해 여러 집들을 방문해.
   B: 그것 참 흥미롭게 들린다.

Everyday English 1 B

Mina: _____

Alex: _____

Mina: _____

Alex: _____

Mina: _____

Alex: _____

Mina: _____

Alex: _____

Mina: _____

Mina: Alex, 너 시간 있니?
Alex: 응, 미나야. 무슨 일인데?
Mina: 네가 이번 여름에 스페인에 갔다는 얘기를 들었어!
Alex: 응, 가족 여행을 갔었어.
Mina: 너의 여행에 대해 더 말해 줄 수 있니? 나도 이번 겨울에 스페인을 방문해 보려고 생각 중이야.
Alex: 알겠어. 나는 스페인이 방문하기에 정말 좋은 나라라고 생각해. 흥미로운 장소들이 많아.
Mina: 내가 갈 만한 장소로 어디를 추천하니?
Alex: 나는 Madrid에 있는 Prado 박물관을 추천해. 세계에서 가장 유명한 박물관 중 하나야.
Mina: 도와줘서 고마워.

Everyday English 2 A. Function Practice

1. G: _____

   B: _____

   G: _____

   B: _____

2. B: _____

   G: _____

   B: _____

   G: _____
   _____

Everyday English 2 B

Tina: _____
   _____
   _____
   _____
   _____
   _____

In Real Life

(Phone rings.)

Suji: _____

Diego: _____

Suji: _____

Diego: _____
   _____

Suji: _____
   _____

Diego: _____

Suji: _____

1. G: 사랑에 대해 너에게 해 주고 싶은 이야기가 있어.
   B: 무엇인데?
   G: 나는 사랑에서 가장 중요한 것은 존중이라고 생각해.
   B: 동의해. 서로의 다름을 존중하는 것이 매우 중요해.
2. B: 에펠탑을 좀 봐.
   G: 정말 크고 아름답다!
   B: 에펠탑에 대해 너에게 해 주고 싶은 이야기가 있어. 사람들이 처음 엔 이것을 좋아하지 않았대.
   G: 정말? 하지만 이건 요즘 파리에서 가장 유명한 장소 중 하나잖아!

Tina: 안녕, 모두들. 내 이름은 Tina 이고 나는 여행 작가야. 오늘 나는 너희들에게 내가 여행에서 배운 중요한 교훈에 대해 말해 주고 싶어. 내가 처음 한국에 방문했을 때, 나는 많은 한국인들이 내 나이를 물었기 때문에 무례하다고 생각했어. 그런데 나중에 나는 이것이 그들의 문화 때문이라는 것을 알았어. 한국인들은 그들보다 나이가 많은 사람들에게는 언어를 다르게 쓰는데, 그래서 다른 사람들의 나이를 알 필요가 있는 거였어. 이 경험은 나에게 다른 문화를 배우고 이해하는 것의 중요성을 알게 해 주었어.

(전화가 울린다)
Suji: 여보세요, 저 수지인데요.
Diego: 안녕, 나야 Diego. 얘기할 시간 있니?
Suji: 응, 무슨 일이야?
Diego: 문화적 차이들에 관한 사회 숙제를 하고 있거든. 그런데 올바른 정보를 찾는 데 어려움이 있어.
Suji: "Culture Shock"이라고 불리는 웹 사이트에 대해 말해 주고 싶어. 나는 그 웹 사이트에서 사람들이 다른 문화들에 대해 질문하고 답해 준다고 들었어.
Diego: 그것 참 완벽하게 들린다. 도와 줘서 고마워.
Suji: 천만에. 숙제 잘하기를 바라.

※ 다음 우리말과 일치하도록 빈칸에 알맞은 것을 골라 쓰시오.

Cultures Around the World

1 _____ _____ "Culture Shock"!

    A. to   B. welcome

2 If you are _____ in cultures _____ the world, this is the website that you are _____ _____!

    A. looking   B. interested   C. around   D. for

3 You can ask and _____ any questions you _____ have about _____ cultures. Let's _____ a look!

    A. take   B. answer   C. other   D. may

4 Suji: I'm _____ _____.

    A. upset   B. very

5 _____ is a _____ student _____ Greece in my school.

    A. from   B. there   C. new

6 I asked her to _____ friends _____ me but she _____ her head.

    A. be   B. shook   C. with

7 _____ _____!

    A. rude   B. how

8 Ocean: Calm _____. I'm sure _____ she really _____ was "yes."

    A. meant   B. down   C. what

9 In some _____ like Greece, Turkey, and Iran, _____ your head _____ "no" and _____ your head means "yes."

    A. nodding   B. countries   C. shaking   D. means

10 Shao: Help! I'm a Chinese boy who has _____ _____ to a Kenyan _____ house.

    A. invited   B. friend's   C. been

11 But I don't know _____ _____ Kenya.

    A. anything   B. about

12 Are _____ any manners I _____ _____ know? Please give me some _____!

    A. need   B. there   C. advice   D. to

13 Clever: I heard _____ when Chinese people are _____ to someone's house, they _____ some food _____ their plate.

    A. invited   B. on   C. that   D. leave

14 It shows _____ there was _____ _____ for the guest.

    A. enough   B. that   C. food

세계의 문화

1 "Culture Shock"에 오신 것을 환영합니다!

2 만약 당신이 세계 각국의 문화에 관심이 있다면, 이곳이 바로 당신이 찾던 웹 사이트입니다.

3 당신은 다른 문화에 대해 가지고 있는 질문을 묻고 답할 수 있습니다. 함께 살펴봅시다!

4 Suji: 나는 굉장히 속상해요.

5 우리 학교에는 그리스에서 새로 온 학생이 있어요.

6 나는 그녀에게 나와 친구가 되자고 했지만, 그녀는 고개를 저었어요.

7 정말 무례해요!

8 Ocean: 진정해요. 나는 그녀가 진짜 의미했던 것은 "응"이었다고 확신해요.

9 그리스, 터키, 이란과 같은 몇몇 나라에서는 고개를 끄덕이는 것이 "싫다"는 의미이고 고개를 흔드는 것이 "좋다"를 의미해요.

10 Shao: 도와주세요! 나는 케냐인 친구 집에 초대된 중국 소년이에요.

11 하지만 저는 케냐에 대해서 아무것도 몰라요.

12 제가 알아야 할 예의가 있나요? 저에게 조언을 해 주세요!

13 Clever: 제가 알기로는, 중국 사람들이 누군가의 집에 초대되었을 때, 접시에 음식을 남겨둔다고 들었어요.

14 그것은 손님에게 충분한 음식이 제공되었음을 보여줘요.

15 _____, with Kenyan people, please _____ all the food the host _____ _____.

A. finish   B. prepared   C. however   D. has

16 _____ you _____ food, it means _____ you didn't like it.

A. that   B. leave   C. if

17 Diego: Does _____ _____ German?

A. speak   B. anyone

18 Today, I was 5 _____ _____ for an _____ _____ my German friend.

A. with   B. late   C. appointment   D. minutes

19 When I _____ _____ him, he _____ very _____.

A. looked   B. finally   C. angry   D. met

20 He said _____ I must try to _____ my "Termin" _____. What does it _____?

A. keep   B. mean   C. better   D. that

21 Smile: "Termin" _____ "_____" in _____.

A. German   B. means   C. appointment

22 Germans think _____ it's important _____ be _____.

A. that   B. on   C. to   D. time

23 In Germany, there is a _____, "What is _____ should be _____."

A. saying   B. kept   C. set

24 So, please _____ _____ _____ Germans.

A. with   B. be   C. punctual

25 Did you _____ the _____ you _____?

A. information   B. find   C. needed

26 We hope that _____ you _____ read was _____ and interesting.

A. helpful   B. have   C. what

27 _____ cultural differences can make a _____ in your _____.

A. difference   B. understanding   C. life

28 Please _____ our _____ again!

A. website   B. visit

---

15 하지만, 케냐 사람들과 함께 하는 경우, 주인이 준비한 음식을 모두 드세요.

16 만약에 음식을 남기면, 그것은 당신이 그 음식을 좋아하지 않았다는 것을 의미해요.

17 Diego: 혹시 여기 독일어 하는 사람이 있나요?

18 오늘, 저는 독일 친구와의 약속에 5분 늦었어요.

19 마침내 그를 만났을 때, 그는 매우 화가 나 보였어요.

20 그는 내가 "Termin"을 더 잘 지키도록 노력해야 한다고 말했어요. 그것은 무엇을 뜻하나요?

21 Smile: "Termin"은 독일어로 약속을 의미합니다.

22 독일인들은 제시간에 오는 것이 중요하다고 생각해요.

23 독일에서는 "정해진 것은 지켜져야 한다."는 말이 있어요.

24 그러니, 독일인들과 함께 할 때는 시간을 잘 지키세요.

25 당신에게 필요했던 정보를 찾았나요?

26 우리는 당신이 읽은 것이 도움이 되고 재미있기를 바랍니다.

27 문화 차이를 이해하는 것은 당신의 삶을 변화시킬 겁니다.

28 저희 웹 사이트를 또 방문해 주세요!

※ 다음 우리말과 일치하도록 빈칸에 알맞은 말을 쓰시오.

Cultures Around the World

1 _____ _____ "Culture Shock"!

2 If you _____ _____ _____ cultures _____ the world, this is the website _____ you are _____ _____!

3 You can ask and answer any questions you may have _____ _____ _____. Let's _____ _____ _____!

4 Suji: I'm very _____.

5 _____ is a new student _____ _____ in my school.

6 I asked _____ _____ _____ _____ with me but she _____ her _____.

7 How _____!

8 Ocean: _____ _____. I'm _____ _____ she really _____ _____ "yes."

9 In some _____ _____ Greece, Turkey, and Iran, _____ your head _____ "no" and _____ your head means "yes."

10 Shao: Help! I'm a _____ boy _____ _____ _____ _____ _____ a Kenyan friend's house.

11 But I don't know _____ _____ Kenya.

12 Are _____ any _____ _____ _____ _____ _____ _____? Please give _____ _____ _____!

13 Clever: I _____ _____ when Chinese people _____ _____ to someone's house, they _____ some food _____ their _____.

14 It shows _____ there was _____ _____ for the guest.

15 _____, with Kenyan people, please _____ all the food the host _____ _____.

16 _____ you _____ food, it _____ _____ you _____ like it.

17 Diego: Does _____ _____ _____?

18 Today, I was 5 _____ _____ _____ an _____ _____ my German friend.

19 _____ I _____ _____ him, he _____ very _____.

20 He said _____ I _____ _____ _____ _____ my "Termin" better. What _____ it _____?

21 Smile: "Termin" means "_____" _____ _____.

22 Germans think _____ it's important _____ _____ _____ _____.

23 In Germany, there is a saying, "What _____ _____ should _____ _____."

24 So, please _____ _____ _____ _____ _____.

25 Did you find _____ _____ _____ _____ _____?

26 We hope that _____ _____ _____ read _____ helpful and interesting.

27 _____ _____ _____ can _____ _____ _____ in your life.

28 Please _____ _____ _____ again!

15 하지만, 케냐 사람들과 함께 하는 경우, 주인이 준비한 음식을 모두 드세요.

16 만약에 음식을 남기면, 그것은 당신이 그 음식을 좋아하지 않았다는 것을 의미해요.

17 Diego: 혹시 여기 독일어 하는 사람이 있나요?

18 오늘, 저는 독일 친구와의 약속에 5분 늦었어요.

19 마침내 그를 만났을 때, 그는 매우 화가 나 보였어요.

20 그는 내가 "Termin"을 더 잘 지키도록 노력해야 한다고 말했어요. 그것은 무엇을 뜻하나요?

21 Smile: "Termin"은 독일어로 약속을 의미합니다.

22 독일인들은 제시간에 오는 것이 중요하다고 생각해요.

23 독일에서는 "정해진 것은 지켜져야 한다."는 말이 있어요.

24 그러니, 독일인들과 함께 할 때는 시간을 잘 지키세요.

25 당신에게 필요했던 정보를 찾았나요?

26 우리는 당신이 읽은 것이 도움이 되고 재미있기를 바랍니다.

27 문화 차이를 이해하는 것은 당신의 삶을 변화시킬 겁니다.

28 저희 웹 사이트를 또 방문해 주세요!

※ 다음 문장을 우리말로 쓰시오.

1 ▸ Welcome to "Culture Shock"!

➡ _____

2 ▸ If you are interested in cultures around the world, this is the website that you are looking for!

➡ _____

3 ▸ You can ask and answer any questions you may have about other cultures. Let's take a look!

➡ _____

4 ▸ Suji: I'm very upset.

➡ _____

5 ▸ There is a new student from Greece in my school.

➡ _____

6 ▸ I asked her to be friends with me but she shook her head.

➡ _____

7 ▸ How rude!

➡ _____

8 ▸ Ocean: Calm down. I'm sure what she really meant was "yes."

➡ _____

9 ▸ In some countries like Greece, Turkey, and Iran, nodding your head means "no" and shaking your head means "yes."

➡ _____
_____

10 ▸ Shao: Help! I'm a Chinese boy who has been invited to a Kenyan friend's house.

➡ _____

11 ▸ But I don't know anything about Kenya.

➡ _____

12 ▸ Are there any manners I need to know? Please give me some advice!

➡ _____

13 ▸ Clever: I heard that when Chinese people are invited to someone's house, they leave some food on their plate.

➡ _____

14 ▸ It shows that there was enough food for the guest.

➡ _____

15 However, with Kenyan people, please finish all the food the host has prepared.

➡ _____

16 If you leave food, it means that you didn't like it.

➡ _____

17 Diego: Does anyone speak German?

➡ _____

18 Today, I was 5 minutes late for an appointment with my German friend.

➡ _____

19 When I finally met him, he looked very angry.

➡ _____

20 He said that I must try to keep my "Termin" better. What does it mean?

➡ _____

21 Smile: "Termin" means "appointment" in German.

➡ _____

22 Germans think that it's important to be on time.

➡ _____

23 In Germany, there is a saying, "What is set should be kept."

➡ _____

24 So, please be punctual with Germans.

➡ _____

25 Did you find the information you needed?

➡ _____

26 We hope that what you have read was helpful and interesting.

➡ _____

27 Understanding cultural differences can make a difference in your life.

➡ _____

28 Please visit our website again!

➡ _____

※ 다음 괄호 안의 단어들을 우리말에 맞도록 바르게 배열하시오.

1 (to / welcome / Shock"! / "Culture)
➡ _____

2 (you / if / interested / are / cultures / in / the / around / world, / is / this / webiste / the / you / that / looking / are / for!)
➡ _____
_____

3 (can / you / ask / and / any / answer / questions / may / you / have / other / about / cultures. // take / let's / look! / a)
➡ _____
_____

4 (Suji: / very / I'm / upset.)
➡ _____

5 (is / there / new / a / from / student / Greece / my / in / school.)
➡ _____

6 (asked / I / to / her / friends / be / me / with / but / shook / she / head. / her)
➡ _____

7 (rude! / how)
➡ _____

8 (Ocean: / down. / calm // sure / I'm / she / what / meant / really / "yes." / was)
➡ _____

9 (some / in / like / countries / Greece, / and / Turkey, / Iran, / your / nodding / head / means / and / "no" / shaking / your / "yes." / means)
➡ _____
_____

10 (Shao: / help! // a / I'm / Chinese / who / boy / has / invited / been / to / friend's / Kenyan / a / house.)
➡ _____
_____

11 (I / but / know / don't / about / anything / Kenya.)
➡ _____

12 (there / are / manners / any / need / I / know? / to // give / please / some / me / advice!)
➡ _____
_____

13 (Clever: / heard / I / when / that / people / Chinese / invited / are / to / house, / someone's / leave / they / food / some / plate. / their / on)
➡ _____
_____

14 (shows / it / there / that / enough / was / for / food / guest. / the)
➡ _____

세계의 문화

1 "Culture Shock"에 오신 것을 환영합니다!

2 만약 당신이 세계 각국의 문화에 관심이 있다면, 이곳이 바로 당신이 찾던 웹 사이트입니다.

3 당신은 다른 문화에 대해 가지고 있는 질문을 묻고 답할 수 있습니다. 함께 살펴봅시다!

4 Suji: 나는 굉장히 속상해요.

5 우리 학교에는 그리스에서 새로 온 학생이 있어요.

6 나는 그녀에게 나와 친구가 되자고 했지만, 그녀는 고개를 저었어요.

7 정말 무례해요!

8 Ocean: 진정해요. 나는 그녀가 진짜 의미했던 것은 "응"이었다고 확신해요.

9 그리스, 터키, 이란과 같은 몇몇 나라에서는 고개를 끄덕이는 것이 "싫다"는 의미이고 고개를 흔드는 것이 "좋다"를 의미해요.

10 Shao: 도와주세요! 나는 케냐인 친구 집에 초대된 중국 소년이에요.

11 하지만 저는 케냐에 대해서 아무것도 몰라요.

12 제가 알아야 할 예의가 있나요? 저에게 조언을 해 주세요!

13 Clever: 제가 알기로는, 중국 사람들이 누군가의 집에 초대되었을 때, 접시에 음식을 남겨둔다고 들었어요.

14 그것은 손님에게 충분한 음식이 제공되었음을 보여줘요.

15 (with / however, / people, / Kenyan / finish / please / the / all / food / host / the / prepared. / has)

➡ _____

_____

16 (you / if / food, / leave / means / it / you / that / like / didn't / it.)

➡ _____

17 (Diego: / anyone / does / German? / speak)

➡ _____

18 (I / today, / was / 5 / late / minutes / an / for / appointment / my / with / friend. / German)

➡ _____

19 (I / when / finally / him, / met / looked / he / angry. / very)

➡ _____

20 (said / he / that / must / I / to / try / my / keep / better. / "Termin" // does / what / mean? / it)

➡ _____

21 (Smile: / means / "Termin" / in / German. / "appointment")

➡ _____

22 (think / Germans / it's / that / to / important / be / time. / on)

➡ _____

23 (Germany, / in / is / there / saying, / a / is / "what / set / be / should / kept.")

➡ _____

24 (please / so, / punctual / be / Germans. / with)

➡ _____

25 (you / did / the / find / information / needed? / you)

➡ _____

26 (hope / we / what / that / have / you / was / read / interesting. / and / helpful)

➡ _____

27 (cultural / understanding / differences / make / can / difference / a / your / in / life.)

➡ _____

28 (visit / please / webisite / again! / our)

➡ _____

15 하지만, 케냐 사람들과 함께 하는 경우, 주인이 준비한 음식을 모두 드세요.

16 만약에 음식을 남기면, 그것은 당신이 그 음식을 좋아하지 않았다는 것을 의미해요.

17 Diego: 혹시 여기 독일어 하는 사람이 있나요?

18 오늘, 저는 독일 친구와의 약속에 5분 늦었어요.

19 마침내 그를 만났을 때, 그는 매우 화가 나 보였어요.

20 그는 내가 "Termin"을 더 잘 지키도록 노력해야 한다고 말했어요. 그것은 무엇을 뜻하나요?

21 Smile: "Termin"은 독일어로 약속을 의미합니다.

22 독일인들은 제시간에 오는 것이 중요하다고 생각해요.

23 독일에서는 "정해진 것은 지켜져야 한다."는 말이 있어요.

24 그러니, 독일인들과 함께 할 때는 시간을 잘 지키세요.

25 당신에게 필요했던 정보를 찾았나요?

26 우리는 당신이 읽은 것이 도움이 되고 재미있기를 바랍니다.

27 문화 차이를 이해하는 것은 당신의 삶을 변화시킬 겁니다.

28 저희 웹 사이트를 또 방문해 주세요!

※ 다음 우리말을 영어로 쓰시오.

1 "Culture Shock"에 오신 것을 환영합니다!

➡ _____

2 만약 당신이 세계 각국의 문화에 관심이 있다면, 이곳이 바로 당신이 찾던 웹 사이트입니다.

➡ _____

3 당신은 다른 문화에 대해 가지고 있는 질문을 묻고 답할 수 있습니다. 함께 살펴봅시다!

➡ _____

4 Suji: 나는 굉장히 속상해요.

➡ _____

5 우리 학교에는 그리스에서 새로 온 학생이 있어요.

➡ _____

6 나는 그녀에게 나와 친구가 되자고 했지만, 그녀는 고개를 저었어요.

➡ _____

7 정말 무례해요!

➡ _____

8 Ocean: 진정해요. 나는 그녀가 진짜 의미했던 것은 "응"이었다고 확신해요.

➡ _____

9 그리스, 터키, 이란과 같은 몇몇 나라에서는 고개를 끄덕이는 것이 "싫다"는 의미이고 고개를 흔드는 것이 "좋다"를 의미해요.

➡ _____

_____

10 Shao: 도와주세요! 나는 케냐인 친구 집에 초대된 중국 소년이에요.

➡ _____

11 하지만 저는 케냐에 대해서 아무것도 몰라요.

➡ _____

12 제가 알아야 할 예의가 있나요? 저에게 조언을 해 주세요!

➡ _____

13 Clever: 제가 알기론, 중국 사람들이 누군가의 집에 초대되었을 때, 접시에 음식을 남겨둔다고 들었어요.

➡ _____

_____

14 그것은 손님에게 충분한 음식이 제공되었음을 보여줘요.

➡ _____

15 하지만, 케냐 사람들과 함께 하는 경우, 주인이 준비한 음식을 모두 드세요.

➡ _____

16 만약에 음식을 남기면, 그것은 당신이 그 음식을 좋아하지 않았다는 것을 의미해요.

➡ _____

17 Diego: 혹시 여기 독일어 하는 사람이 있나요?

➡ _____

18 오늘, 저는 독일 친구와의 약속에 5분 늦었어요.

➡ _____

19 마침내 그를 만났을 때, 그는 매우 화가 나 보였어요.

➡ _____

20 그는 내가 "Termin"을 더 잘 지키도록 노력해야 한다고 말했어요. 그것은 무엇을 뜻하나요?

➡ _____

21 Smile: "Termin"은 독일어로 약속을 의미합니다.

➡ _____

22 독일인들은 제시간에 오는 것이 중요하다고 생각해요.

➡ _____

23 독일에서는 "정해진 것은 지켜져야 한다."는 말이 있어요.

➡ _____

24 그러니, 독일인들과 함께 할 때는 시간을 잘 지키세요.

➡ _____

25 당신에게 필요했던 정보를 찾았나요?

➡ _____

26 우리는 당신이 읽은 것이 도움이 되고 재미있기를 바랍니다.

➡ _____

27 문화 차이를 이해하는 것은 당신의 삶을 변화시킬 겁니다.

➡ _____

28 저희 웹 사이트를 또 방문해 주세요!

➡ _____

※ 다음 우리말과 일치하도록 빈칸에 알맞은 말을 쓰시오.

Project Work Step 1

1. Hello. Our group _____ _____ _____ _____ you about Thanksgiving Day in the United States of America.

2. It _____ _____ _____ the _____ Thursday of November.

3. People _____ turkey and _____ _____.

4. _____ _____ dinner, families share things that they are _____ _____.

Check Your Progress 1

1. W: Hello, _____.

2. Today, _____ _____ _____ _____ you a story about _____.

3. _____ you can see, I'm very _____ and _____.

4. _____ _____ my looks, I didn't have any friends _____ _____ _____.

5. I _____ _____ very nervous _____ _____ _____ new people.

6. However, I didn't _____ _____ _____ _____.

7. I _____ _____ _____ to be _____ _____.

8. Now, I travel _____ _____ _____ and _____ _____ to many people.

9. I hope more people will find the _____ _____ _____ themselves _____ I _____.

Check Your Progress 4~6

1. _____ Mira,

2. Hello, Mira. I'm _____ Korea this winter and I _____ very _____ _____ the trip.

3. But what _____ me are the _____ _____.

4. So, I was hoping _____ _____ _____ _____ from you.

5. _____, David

---

1. 안녕하세요. 우리 모임은 미국의 추수 감사절에 관해 말하고 싶습니다.
2. 이 날은 11월의 넷째 주 목요일에 기념됩니다.
3. 사람들은 칠면조와 호박 파이를 먹습니다.
4. 저녁을 먹기 전에, 가족들은 감사할 무언가를 공유합니다.

1. W: 안녕, 모두들.
2. 오늘 나는 나에 대한 이야기를 하고 싶어.
3. 너희들도 볼 수 있듯이 나는 매우 마르고 약해.
4. 내 모습 때문에, 내가 어릴 때 나는 친구들이 없었어.
5. 나는 새로운 사람들을 만날 때 항상 매우 긴장했었어.
6. 그러나 나는 내 스스로를 포기하지 않았어.
7. 나는 좀 더 자신감을 갖기 위해 최선을 다했어.
8. 지금, 나는 세계를 여행하며 많은 사람들에게 희망을 주고 있어.
9. 나는 좀 더 많은 사람들이 내가 했던 것처럼 자신들 안에서 참된 아름다움을 찾길 희망해.

1. 미라에게
2. 미라야, 안녕. 나는 이번 겨울에 한국을 방문할 거고, 굉장히 신이 나 있어.
3. 그런데, 나를 걱정하게 하는 것은 문화 차이야.
4. 그래서, 너에게 조언을 좀 구하고 싶었어.
5. 사랑을 담아서, David가

※ 다음 우리말을 영어로 쓰시오.

Project Work Step 1

1. 안녕하세요. 우리 모임은 미국의 추수감사절에 관해 말하고 싶습니다.
   ➡ _____

2. 이 날은 11월의 넷째 주 목요일에 기념됩니다.
   ➡ _____

3. 사람들은 칠면조와 호박 파이를 먹습니다.
   ➡ _____

4. 저녁을 먹기 전에, 가족들은 감사할 무언가를 공유합니다.
   ➡ _____

Check Your Progress 1

1. W: 안녕, 모두들.
   ➡ _____

2. 오늘 나는 나에 대한 이야기를 하고 싶어.
   ➡ _____

3. 너희들도 볼 수 있듯이 나는 매우 마르고 약해.
   ➡ _____

4. 내 모습 때문에, 내가 어릴 때 나는 친구들이 없었어.
   ➡ _____

5. 나는 새로운 사람들을 만날 때 항상 매우 긴장했었어.
   ➡ _____

6. 그러나 나는 내 스스로를 포기하지 않았어.
   ➡ _____

7. 나는 좀 더 자신감을 갖기 위해 최선을 다했어.
   ➡ _____

8. 지금, 나는 세계를 여행하며 많은 사람들에게 희망을 주고 있어.
   ➡ _____

8. 나는 좀 더 많은 사람들이 내가 했던 것처럼 자신들 안에서 참된 아름다움을 찾길 희망해.
   ➡ _____

Check Your Progress 4~6

1. 미라에게
   ➡ _____

2. 미라야, 안녕. 나는 이번 겨울에 한국을 방문할 거고, 굉장히 신이 나 있어.
   ➡ _____

3. 그런데, 나를 걱정하게 하는 것은 문화 차이야.
   ➡ _____

4. 그래서, 너에게 조언을 좀 구하고 싶었어.
   ➡ _____

5. 사랑을 담아서, David가
   ➡ _____

※ 다음 영어를 우리말로 쓰시오.

01	amount	22	harmful
02	bitter	23	recommend
03	career	24	instead
04	throw	25	stupid
05	weak	26	curious
06	shape	27	expensive
07	caterpillar	28	rude
08	claw	29	rest
09	beg	30	pretend
10	comfortable	31	salty
11	regularly	32	weapon
12	diligent	33	clever
13	asleep	34	bean
14	empty	35	get rid of
15	concentrate	36	be in good shape
16	healthy	37	be used to -ing
17	posture	38	put off
18	brave	39	be on a diet
19	chew	40	run away
20	fat	41	add up
21	greedy	42	be tired of
		43	out of breath

※ 다음 우리말을 영어로 쓰시오.

01 콩

02 잠이 든

03 누르다

04 추가하다, 덧붙여 말하다

05 애벌레

06 자세

07 (동물의) 발톱

08 똑똑한, 영리한

09 규칙적으로

10 무기

11 무대

12 부지런한, 근면한

13 텅 빈; 비우다

14 용감한

15 비싼

16 모양, 형태

17 어리석은, 멍청한

18 욕심 많은, 탐욕스러운

19 집중하다

20 해로운

21 양, 총액

22 대신에

23 씹다

24 쓴

25 편안한

26 ~인 척하다

27 추천하다

28 건강한

29 호기심 많은

30 직업, 경력

31 무례한

32 던지다

33 약한

34 화면

35 ~에 싫증이 나다

36 달아나다

37 합산하다

38 숨이 가쁜

39 ~을 제거하다, ~을 없애다

40 ~하는 데 익숙하다

41 더 이상 ~ 아니다

42 ~을 미루다

43 ~을 쫓다

※ 다음 영영풀이에 알맞은 단어를 <보기>에서 골라 쓴 후, 우리말 뜻을 쓰시오.

1 _____ : not physically strong: _____

2 _____ : having a strong, unpleasant taste; not sweet: _____

3 _____ : good for your health: _____

4 _____ : with no people or things inside: _____

5 _____ : to stop and hold a moving object, especially in your hands: _____

6 _____ : making you feel physically relaxed: _____

7 _____ : wanting more money, power, food, etc. than you really need: _____

8 _____ : having or showing a lack of respect for other people and their feelings:
_____

9 _____ : one of the sharp curved nails on the end of an animal's or a bird's foot:
_____

10 _____ : to bite food into small pieces in your mouth with your teeth to make it
easier to swallow: _____

11 _____ : a tool for cutting paper or cloth, that has two sharp blades with handles,
joined together in the middle: _____

12 _____ : an object such as a knife, gun, bomb, etc. that is used for fighting or
attacking somebody: _____

13 _____ : to ask somebody for something especially in an anxious way because
you want or need it very much: _____

14 _____ : causing damage or injury to somebody/something, especially to a
person's health or to the environment: _____

15 _____ : a flying insect with a long thin body and four large, usually brightly
coloured, wings: _____

16 _____ : an opinion or a suggestion about what somebody should do in a
particular situation: _____

보기

rude	catch	beg	advice
claw	healthy	comfortable	butterfly
scissors	chew	greedy	weak
empty	weapon	bitter	harmful

※ 다음 우리말과 일치하도록 빈칸에 알맞은 말을 쓰시오.

Everyday English 1 A. Function Practice (1)

1. **G:** _____ you _____ my phone?

   B: No, I didn't. _____ your phone _____ _____.

   G: My phone will not _____. I don't _____ _____ _____ _____ my phone.

   B: _____ _____. I'll _____ you. We will _____ _____ soon.

2. **G:** Oh, this flower is the one I'm _____ _____. I'll _____ _____.

   M: _____ it is. _____ _____ _____ _____ it.

   G: I don't know _____ _____ _____.

   M: _____ _____ it too often. And it _____ _____ _____ _____.

Everyday English 1 B. Listening Activity

Ms. Kim: Minjae, can I _____ _____ _____ _____ you? It _____ _____ _____ _____.

Minjae: _____ _____, Ms. Kim.

Ms. Kim: I saw that you are not _____ and _____ _____ _____ _____.

Minjae: Oh, I'm _____.

Ms. Kim: What's _____ _____?

Minjae: I just can't _____ _____ _____ _____. I _____ _____ _____ _____ _____ early but _____. I don't know _____ _____ _____ a good night's sleep.

Ms. Kim: _____ you _____ _____ to go to bed _____, not _____.

Minjae: Oh, then I _____ _____ _____ that.

1. G: 내 휴대폰 보았니?
   B: 아니, 못 봤어. 내 것으로 네 휴대폰에 전화해 봐.
   G: 내 전화는 울리지 않을 거야. 난 내 전화를 찾는 법을 모르겠어.
   B: 걱정 마. 내가 도와줄게. 우리는 그걸 곧 찾을 거야.

2. G: 오, 이 꽃은 내가 찾던 거에요. 제가 살게요.
   M: 여기 있어요. 잘 돌보세요.
   G: 저는 어떻게 돌보아야 하는지 몰라요.
   M: 물을 너무 자주 주지 마세요. 그리고 충분한 햇빛을 받게 하세요.

Ms Kim: 민재야, 나하고 얘기 좀 할까? 길게 걸리지는 않을 거야.
Minjae: 물론이지요. 김 선생님.
Ms Kim: 나는 네가 수업 시간에 집중하지 않고 잠든 것을 보았어.
Minjae: 아, 죄송해요.
Ms Kim: 무슨 일 있니?
Minjae: 단지 쉽게 잠이 들지 못해요. 일찍 잠자리에 들려고 노력하지만 실패해요. 잠을 잘 자는 법을 모르겠어요.
Ms Kim: 아마 규칙적으로 잠자리에 들려고 노력해야 할 거야. 일찍 자려고 하는 것이 아니라.
Minjae: 아, 그러면 그렇게 노력해 볼게요.

Everyday English 2 A. Function Practice

1. **G:** My _____ and leg _____.

   B: I think it's because you always _____ _____ _____.

   G: Oh, do you think so? I didn't know I have _____ _____.

   B: _____ _____ _____ _____ _____ your legs when _____ _____ in a chair.

2. **G:** Your hands are _____. Are you _____?

   B: It may be _____ _____ the _____ _____. I _____ three cans for _____ _____.

   G: That's _____ _____! _____ _____ you _____ _____ that much next time.

   B: Okay, _____ _____.

Everyday English 2 B. Listening Activity

M: Today, I'd like to talk about your _____. The eyes are really _____ _____ of our body, but _____ and _____ students are having eye problems. Some students cannot see without _____ or have _____ eyes. _____ you do not want these problems, _____ _____ take some time to _____ your eyes. When you study, try to _____ _____ for a while. _____ _____ _____ you don't look at _____ or _____ _____ for too long.

In Real Life

Olivia: You're _____ _____ _____, again!

Junho: You know I'm _____ _____ _____ _____ for _____, _____ _____?

Olivia: Of _____. But I don't think that _____ _____ will be very _____.

Junho: _____ do you _____?

Olivia: Your body needs a _____ _____ _____ _____.

Junho: But people said that I _____ _____ _____ meat.

Olivia: That's not right. They mean eating too much meat will be _____.

Junho: I don't know _____ _____ _____ _____ _____ _____ diet! It's _____!

Olivia: Make sure you have _____ _____ some _____ or _____. Oh, and _____ to eat some _____ too.

1. G: 등과 다리가 아파.
   B: 내 생각에 그건 네가 항상 다리를 꼬아서 앉기 때문이야.
   G: 어머, 너 그렇게 생각하니? 나는 내가 자세가 좋지 않은지 몰랐어.
   B: 의자에 앉을 때 다리를 꼬지 않도록 명심해.

2. G: 네 손들이 떨리고 있어. 괜찮니?
   B: 아마도 에너지 음료 때문일 거야. 내가 오늘 시험을 위해 세 캔을 마셨거든.
   G: 그건 너무 많아! 너는 다음에는 그렇게 많이 마시지 말아야 한다는 것을 명심해.
   B: 알았어. 안 그럴게.

M: 오늘, 저는 여러분의 눈에 대해 이야기하려 합니다. 눈은 정말로 중요한 우리 신체의 일부분입니다. 그러나 점점 더 많은 학생들이 안구 문제들을 겪고 있습니다. 몇몇 학생들은 안경이 없이는 볼 수 없거나 안구 건조증을 겪습니다. 만약 여러분이 이러한 문제를 겪는 것을 원하지 않는다면 여러분의 눈이 쉴 수 있는 시간을 가지도록 노력해 보세요. 여러분이 공부를 할 때, 잠시 동안이라도 바깥을 보려고 노력하세요. 컴퓨터나 휴대폰 화면을 너무 오래 보지 않도록 명심하세요.

Olivia: 너 또 밥만 먹고 있구나!
Junho: 내가 건강상의 이유로 다이어트 중인 것 알지, 그렇지 않니?
Olivia: 물론이지. 그런데 나는 밥만 먹는 것이 매우 건강하다고 생각하지 않아.
Junho: 무슨 의미야?
Olivia: 너의 몸은 특정한 양의 고기를 필요로 해.
Junho: 그런데 사람들은 내가 고기를 피해야 할 필요가 있다고 말해.
Olivia: 그건 옳지 않아. 그들이 의미하는 건 고기를 너무 많이 먹는 것이 해롭다는 거야.
Junho: 나는 좋은 다이어트를 하는 법을 모르겠어. 너무 어려워!
Olivia: 최소한 콩이나 계란을 먹어야 하는 것을 명심해. 아, 그리고 채소를 먹는 것도 잊지 마.

※ 다음 우리말에 맞도록 대화를 영어로 쓰시오.

Everyday English 1 A. Function Practice (1)

1. G: _____
   B: _____
   G: _____
   B: _____

2. G: _____
   M: _____
   G: _____
   M: _____

1. G: 내 휴대폰 보았니?
   B: 아니, 못 봤어. 내 것으로 네 휴대폰에 전화해 봐.
   G: 내 전화는 울리지 않을 거야. 난 내 전화를 찾는 법을 모르겠어.
   B: 걱정 마. 내가 도와줄게. 우리는 그걸 곧 찾을 거야.

2. G: 오, 이 꽃은 내가 찾던 거에요. 제가 살게요.
   M: 여기 있어요. 잘 돌보세요.
   G: 저는 어떻게 돌보아야 하는지 몰라요.
   M: 물을 너무 자주 주지 마세요. 그리고 충분한 햇빛을 받게 하세요.

Everyday English 1 B. Listening Activity

Ms. Kim: _____

Minjae: _____

Ms. Kim: _____

Minjae: _____

Ms. Kim: _____

Minjae: _____

Ms. Kim: _____

Minjae: _____

Ms Kim: 민재야, 나하고 얘기 좀 할까? 길게 걸리지는 않을 거야.
Minjae: 물론이지요. 김 선생님.
Ms Kim: 나는 네가 수업 시간에 집중하지 않고 잠든 것을 보았어.
Minjae: 아, 죄송해요.
Ms Kim: 무슨 일 있니?
Minjae: 단지 쉽게 잠이 들지 못해요. 일찍 잠자리에 들려고 노력하지만 실패해요. 잠을 잘 자는 법을 모르겠어요.
Ms Kim: 아마 규칙적으로 잠자리에 들려고 노력해야 할 거야. 일찍 자려고 하는 것이 아니라.
Minjae: 아, 그러면 그렇게 노력해 볼게요.

Everyday English 2 A. Function Practice

1. G: _____

   B: _____

   G: _____

   B: _____

2. G: _____

   B: _____

   G: _____

   B: _____

Everyday English 2 B. Listening Activity

M: _____

_____

_____

_____

_____

In Real Life

Olivia: _____

Junho: _____

Olivia: _____

Junho: _____

Olivia: _____

Junho: _____

Olivia: _____

Junho: _____

Olivia: _____

---

1. G: 등과 다리가 아파.
   B: 내 생각에 그건 네가 항상 다리를 꼬아서 앉기 때문이야.
   G: 어머, 너 그렇게 생각하니? 나는 내가 자세가 좋지 않은지 몰랐어.
   B: 의자에 앉을 때 다리를 꼬지 않도록 명심해.

2. G: 네 손들이 떨리고 있어. 괜찮니?
   B: 아마도 에너지 음료 때문일 거야. 내가 오늘 시험을 위해 세 캔을 마셨거든.
   G: 그건 너무 많아! 너는 다음에는 그렇게 많이 마시지 말아야 한다는 것을 명심해.
   B: 알았어. 안 그럴게.

M: 오늘, 저는 여러분의 눈에 대해 이야기하려 합니다. 눈은 정말로 중요한 우리 신체의 일부분입니다. 그러나 점점 더 많은 학생들이 안구 문제들을 겪고 있습니다. 몇몇 학생들은 안경이 없이는 볼 수 없거나 안구 건조증을 겪습니다. 만약 여러분이 이러한 문제를 겪는 것을 원하지 않는다면 여러분의 눈이 쉴 수 있는 시간을 가지도록 노력해 보세요. 여러분이 공부를 할 때, 잠시 동안이라도 바깥을 보려고 노력하세요. 컴퓨터나 휴대폰 화면을 너무 오래 보지 않도록 명심하세요.

Olivia: 너 또 밥만 먹고 있구나!
Junho: 내가 건강상의 이유로 다이어트 중인 것 알지, 그렇지 않니?
Olivia: 물론이지. 그런데 나는 밥만 먹는 것이 매우 건강하다고 생각하지 않아.
Junho: 무슨 의미야?
Olivia: 너의 몸은 특정한 양의 고기를 필요로 해.
Junho: 그런데 사람들은 내가 고기를 피해야 할 필요가 있다고 말해.
Olivia: 그건 옳지 않아. 그들이 의미하는 건 고기를 너무 많이 먹는 것이 해롭다는 거야.
Junho: 나는 좋은 다이어트를 하는 법을 모르겠어. 너무 어려워!
Olivia: 최소한 콩이나 계란을 먹어야 하는 것을 명심해. 아, 그리고 채소를 먹는 것도 잊지 마.

※ 다음 우리말과 일치하도록 빈칸에 알맞은 것을 골라 쓰시오.

The Cat Just Couldn't Help It

Scene #1.

1 *An old and _____ mouse _____.*
　A. enters　　　　B. tired

2 Mouse: *(He is _____ of _____.)* I'm _____ of _____
　from Cat.
　A. breath　　　B. running　　　C. out　　　D. tired

3 I am _____ old to run. If I _____ free, I _____ be so
　happy. *(He thinks _____ a while.)* Oh, I have an idea!
　A. were　　　B. for　　　C. would　　　D. too

Scene #2.

4 *Mouse goes and _____ something _____ the _____
　of the stage.*
　A. back　　　B. gets　　　C. from

5 Cat _____ and _____ Mouse.
　A. catches　　　B. enters

6 Mouse: *(He _____ to beg.)* I'm too smelly _____ you
　to eat! _____, have this, please. *(He gives a box of sugar
　_____ Cat.)*
　A. instead　　　B. pretends　　　C. for　　　D. to

7 Cat: *(He _____ it. His eyes get _____.)* What is it? Give
　me _____!
　A. bigger　　　B. tastes　　　C. more

8 Mouse: It's sugar. If you _____ me _____, I'll _____
　you some _____ day.
　A. let　　　B. every　　　C. bring　　　D. go

Scene #3.

9 *It is at Cat's house. Cat, now _____, is eating sugar. He has
　only _____ _____ teeth. Dog is _____ him.*
　A. few　　　B. fat　　　C. watching　　　D. a

10 Dog: *(He is _____.)* Cat, my friend, be _____. The sugar
　will _____ _____.
　A. careful　　　B. worried　　　C. bitter　　　D. get

11 Cat: What do you _____ _____ _____?
　A. mean　　　B. by　　　C. that

12 Dog: Look at _____! You are too _____ to run, and your
　teeth are too _____ to _____!
　A. fat　　　B. chew　　　C. yourself　　　D. weak

장면 1

1 한 마리의 늙고 지친 쥐가 들어
　온다.

2 Mouse: *(그는 숨이 차다.)* 나는
　고양이로부터 달아나는
　것에 질렸어.

3 나는 나이가 너무 들어서 달릴
　수 없어. 내가 만약 자유로워진
　다면, 행복할 텐데. *(그는 잠깐
　동안 생각한다.)* 오, 내게 좋은
　생각이 났어.

장면 2

4 쥐가 무대 뒤에서 무언가를 가
　져온다.

5 고양이가 들어와 쥐를 잡는다.

6 Mouse: *(그는 비는 척한다.)* 저는
　너무 냄새가 나서 당신이
　잡아먹을 수 없어요. 대신,
　이걸 드세요. *(그는 설탕 상
　자를 고양이에게 건넨다.)*

7 Cat: *(그는 그것을 맛본다. 그의
　눈이 커진다.)* 이게 뭐야?
　더 줘!

8 Mouse: 그것은 설탕이에요. 만
　약에 당신이 저를 가게
　해주면, 제가 매일 가지
　고 올게요.

장면 3

9 고양이의 집이다. 지금은 뚱뚱해
　진 고양이가 설탕을 먹고 있다.
　그는 오직 몇 개의 이빨만 가지
　고 있다. 개가 그를 바라보고 있
　다.

10 Dog: *(그는 걱정된다.)* 내 친구
　고양이야. 조심해. 그 설탕
　은 써질 거야.

11 Cat: 무슨 말이야?

12 Dog: 너 스스로를 봐! 너는 너
　무 뚱뚱해서 달릴 수 없고,
　너의 이빨은 너무 약해서
　씹을 수 없잖아!

13 Cat: *(He eats more.)* Why should I _____ or _____?
Sugar is the only thing I _____. I can't live _____ it.
A. run   B. without   C. need   D. chew

14 *Dog _____ _____ _____.*
A. out   B. sadly   C. out

Scene #4.

15 *Cat has _____ _____ the box of sugar. Mouse _____.*
A. enters   B. emptied   C. almost

16 Mouse: *(He _____.)* I think my plan _____ _____.
A. worked   B. smiles   C. has

17 Cat: *(He is _____.)* It's almost _____! Mouse, tell me _____ you get it.
A. empty   B. where   C. angry

18 Mouse: I have a friend who _____ sugar. But he's _____ _____ your claws. If you get _____ of them, you can meet him soon.
A. scared   B. rid   C. makes   D. of

19 _____: _____!
A. okay   B. Cat

Scene #5.

20 *Mouse _____ Cat a _____ of scissors and Cat cuts his _____.*
A. pair   B. claws   C. hands

21 Cat: I'm _____! Now _____ me _____ your friend!
A. take   B. ready   C. to

22 Mouse: *(He _____ _____ Cat.)* You _____ cat!
A. at   B. stupid   C. laughs

23 If you _____ fast, and had your _____ teeth and claws, I'd _____ to you. But you no _____ have them now!
A. longer   B. sharp   C. were   D. listen

24 You have _____ your _____ _____!
A. weapons   B. lost   C. biggest

25 Why _____ I listen to _____ you say now? *(He runs _____.)*
A. away   B. what   C. should

26 Cat: What! *(He _____ to run _____ Mouse, but _____.)*
Oh! I'm too _____ to run after him!
A. after   B. fat   C. failes   D. tries

※ 다음 우리말과 일치하도록 빈칸에 알맞은 말을 쓰시오.

The Cat Just Couldn't Help It

Scene #1.

1 *An _____ and _____ mouse _____.*

2 Mouse: *(He is _____ _____ _____.)* I'm _____ _____ _____ Cat.

3 I am _____ _____ _____ run. If I _____ free, I _____ _____ so happy. *(He thinks _____ _____ _____.)* Oh, I _____ _____ _____!

Scene #2.

4 *Mouse goes and _____ something _____ the _____ of _____ _____.*

5 Cat _____ and _____ Mouse.

6 Mouse: *(He _____ _____ _____.)* I'm _____ _____ _____ _____ to eat! _____, have this, please. *(He _____ a box of sugar _____ Cat.)*

7 Cat: *(He _____ _____. His eyes get _____.)* What is it? Give me _____!

8 Mouse: It's sugar. If you _____ _____ _____, I'll _____ you some _____ _____.

Scene #3.

9 *It is at Cat's _____. Cat, now _____, is eating sugar. He has only _____ _____ _____. Dog is _____ him.*

10 Dog: *(He is _____.)* Cat, my friend, _____ _____. The sugar will _____ _____.

11 Cat: What do you _____ _____ _____?

12 Dog: _____ _____ _____! You are _____ _____ _____ _____, and your teeth are _____ _____ _____ _____!

고양이는 정말 어떻게 할 수 없었다

장면 1

1 한 마리의 늙고 지친 쥐가 들어온다.

2 Mouse: *(그는 숨이 차다.)* 나는 고양이로부터 달아나는 것에 질렸어.

3 나는 나이가 너무 들어서 달릴 수 없어. 내가 만약 자유로워진다면, 행복할 텐데. *(그는 잠깐 동안 생각한다.)* 오, 내게 좋은 생각이 났어.

장면 2

4 쥐가 무대 뒤에서 무언가를 가져온다.

5 고양이가 들어와 쥐를 잡는다.

6 Mouse: *(그는 비는 척한다.)* 저는 너무 냄새가 나서 당신이 잡아먹을 수 없어요. 대신, 이걸 드세요. *(그는 설탕 상자를 고양이에게 건넨다.)*

7 Cat: *(그는 그것을 맛본다. 그의 눈이 커진다.)* 이게 뭐야? 더 줘!

8 Mouse: 그것은 설탕이에요. 만약에 당신이 저를 가게 해주면, 제가 매일 가지고 올게요.

장면 3

9 고양이의 집이다. 지금은 뚱뚱해진 고양이가 설탕을 먹고 있다. 그는 오직 몇 개의 이빨만 가지고 있다. 개가 그를 바라보고 있다.

10 Dog: *(그는 걱정된다.)* 내 친구 고양이야, 조심해, 그 설탕은 써질 거야.

11 Cat: 무슨 말이야?

12 Dog: 너 스스로를 봐! 너는 너무 뚱뚱해서 달릴 수 없고, 너의 이빨은 너무 약해서 씹을 수 없잖아!

13 Cat: *(He eats more.)* _____ should I _____ or _____?
Sugar is the only thing _____ _____. I can't live _____ it.

14 *Dog _____ _____ _____.*

Scene #4.

15 *Cat has almost _____ the box of sugar. Mouse _____.*

16 Mouse: *(He smiles.)* I think my plan _____ _____.

17 Cat: *(He is _____.)* It's _____ _____! Mouse, tell me
_____ _____ _____ it.

18 Mouse: I have a friend _____ _____ sugar. But he's
_____ _____ _____ _____. If you _____ _____
_____ _____, you can meet him soon.

19 Cat: _____!

Scene #5.

20 *Mouse _____ Cat _____ _____ _____ scissors and
_____ _____ _____ claws.*

21 Cat: I'm _____! Now _____ me _____ your friend!

22 Mouse: *(He _____ _____ Cat.)* You _____ cat!

23 If you _____ _____, and _____ your sharp teeth and
claws, _____ _____ _____ you. But you _____
_____ have _____ now!

24 You _____ _____ your _____ _____!

25 Why should I _____ _____ _____ _____ _____
now? *(He _____ _____.)*

26 Cat: What! *(He tries _____ _____ _____ Mouse, but
fails.)* Oh! I'm too _____ _____ _____ _____ him!

13 Cat: *(그는 더 먹는다.)* 왜 내가 뛰거나 씹어야 해? 나에게 필요한 건 설탕 한 가지야. 나는 그것 없이는 살 수 없어.

14 *개가 슬프게 나간다.*

장면 4

15 고양이는 설탕 상자를 거의 비웠다. 쥐가 들어온다.

16 Mouse: *(그가 미소 짓는다.)* 내 계획이 효과가 있는 것 같아.

17 Cat: *(그는 화가 났다.)* 거의 비었잖아! 쥐야, 네가 어디서 이걸 가져오는지 말해!

18 Mouse: 나에게 설탕을 만드는 친구가 하나 있어요. 하지만 그는 당신의 발톱을 무서워한답니다. 만약 당신이 그것들을 없애버리면, 당신은 곧 그를 만날 수 있을 거예요.

19 Cat: 좋아!

장면 5

20 쥐가 고양이에게 가위를 건네고, 고양이는 자신의 발톱을 자른다.

21 Cat: 나는 준비가 됐어! 이제 나를 너의 친구에게 데려다줘!

22 Mouse: *(그는 고양이를 비웃는다.)* 멍청한 고양이!

23 만약 당신이 빠르고 당신의 뾰족한 이빨과 발톱을 가지고 있다면, 나는 당신의 말을 들었겠죠! 하지만 당신은 지금은 그것들을 더 이상 가지고 있지 않아요!

24 당신은 당신의 가장 큰 무기들을 잃었어요!

25 내가 왜 당신이 지금 말하는 것을 들어야 하죠? *(그는 도망간다.)*

26 Cat: 뭐? *(고양이가 쥐를 쫓아가려고 하지만 실패한다.)* 오! 나는 너무 뚱뚱해서 그를 쫓아갈 수가 없구나!

※ 다음 문장을 우리말로 쓰시오.

The Cat Just Couldn't Help It

Scene #1.

1 An old and tired mouse enters.

➡ _____

2 Mouse: (*He is out of breath.*) I'm tired of running from Cat.

➡ _____

3 I am too old to run. If I were free, I would be so happy. (*He thinks for a while.*) Oh, I have an idea!

➡ _____

_____

Scene #2.

4 Mouse goes and gets something from the back of the stage.

➡ _____

5 Cat enters and catches Mouse.

➡ _____

6 Mouse: (*He pretends to beg.*) I'm too smelly for you to eat! Instead, have this, please. (*He gives a box of sugar to Cat.*)

➡ _____

_____

7 Cat: (*He tastes it. His eyes get bigger.*) What is it? Give me more!

➡ _____

8 Mouse: It's sugar. If you let me go, I'll bring you some every day.

➡ _____

Scene #3.

9 It is at Cat's house. Cat, now fat, is eating sugar. He has only a few teeth. Dog is watching him.

➡ _____

_____

10 Dog: (*He is worried.*) Cat, my friend, be careful. The sugar will get bitter.

➡ _____

11 Cat: What do you mean by that?

➡ _____

12 Dog: Look at yourself! You are too fat to run, and your teeth are too weak to chew!

➡ _____

13 Cat: (*He eats more.*) Why should I run or chew? Sugar is the only thing I need. I can't live without it.

➡ _____

14 Dog goes out sadly.

➡ _____

Scene #4.

15 Cat has almost emptied the box of sugar. Mouse enters.

➡ _____

16 Mouse: (*He smiles.*) I think my plan has worked.

➡ _____

17 Cat: (*He is angry.*) It's almost empty! Mouse, tell me where you get it.

➡ _____

18 Mouse: I have a friend who makes sugar. But he's scared of your claws. If you get rid of them, you can meet him soon.

➡ _____

_____

19 Cat: Okay!

➡ _____

Scene #5.

20 Mouse hands Cat a pair of scissors and Cat cuts his claws.

➡ _____

21 Cat: I'm ready! Now take me to your friend!

➡ _____

22 Mouse: (*He laughs at Cat.*) You stupid cat!

➡ _____

23 If you were fast, and had your sharp teeth and claws, I'd listen to you. But you no longer have them now!

➡ _____

_____

24 You have lost your biggest weapons!

➡ _____

25 Why should I listen to what you say now? (*He runs away.*)

➡ _____

26 Cat: What! (*He tries to run after Mouse, but fails.*) Oh! I'm too fat to run after him!

➡ _____

※ 다음 괄호 안의 단어들을 우리말에 맞도록 바르게 배열하시오.

The Cat Just Couldn't Help It

Scene #1.

1 (old / an / and / mouse / tired / enters.)
➡ _____

2 (Mouse: / is / he / of / breath.) / out // tired / I'm / running / of / Cat. / from)
➡ _____

3 (am / I / to / old / too / run. // I / if / free, / were / I / be / would / happy. / so // (he / for / thinks / a / while.) // oh, / have / I / idea! / an)
➡ _____
_____

Scene #2.

4 (goes / Mouse / and / something / gets / from / back / the / of / stage. / the)
➡ _____

5 (enters / Cat / and / Mouse. / catches)
➡ _____

6 (Mouse: / (he / to / pretends / beg.) // too / I'm / for / smelly / you / eat! / to // instead, / this, / have / please. // (he / a / gives / of / box / Cat. / to / sugar)
➡ _____
_____

7 (Cat: / (he / it. / tastes // eyes / his / bigger.) / get // is / it? / what // me / give / more!)
➡ _____

8 (Mouse: / sugar. / it's // you / let / if / go, / me / I'll / you / bring / every / some / day.)
➡ _____

Scene #3.

9 (is / it / Cat's / at / house. // now / Cat, / fat, / eating / is / sugar. // has / he / a / only / teeth. / few // is / Dog / him. / watching)
➡ _____
_____

10 (Dog: / (he / worried.) / is // my / Cat, / friend, / careful. / be // sugar / the / get / bitter. / will)
➡ _____

11 (Cat: / do / what / mean / you / that? / mean)
➡ _____

12 (Dog: / at / look / yourself! // are / you / fat / too / run, / to / and / teeth / your / are / to / weak / too / chew!)
➡ _____
_____

고양이는 정말 어떻게 할 수 없었다

장면 1

1 한 마리의 늙고 지친 쥐가 들어온다.

2 Mouse: *(그는 숨이 차다.)* 나는 고양이로부터 달아나는 것에 질렸어.

3 나는 나이가 너무 들어서 달릴 수 없어. 내가 만약 자유로워진다면, 행복할 텐데. *(그는 잠깐 동안 생각한다.)* 오, 내게 좋은 생각이 났어.

장면 2

4 쥐가 무대 뒤에서 무언가를 가져온다.

5 고양이가 들어와 쥐를 잡는다.

6 Mouse: *(그는 비는 척한다.)* 저는 너무 냄새가 나서 당신이 잡아먹을 수 없어요. 대신, 이걸 드세요. *(그는 설탕 상자를 고양이에게 건넨다.)*

7 Cat: *(그는 그것을 맛본다. 그의 눈이 커진다.)* 이게 뭐야? 더 줘!

8 Mouse: 그것은 설탕이에요. 만약에 당신이 저를 가게 해주면, 제가 매일 가지고 올게요.

장면 3

9 고양이의 집이다. 지금은 뚱뚱해진 고양이가 설탕을 먹고 있다. 그는 오직 몇 개의 이빨만 가지고 있다. 개가 그를 바라보고 있다.

10 Dog: *(그는 걱정된다.)* 내 친구 고양이야, 조심해. 그 설탕은 써질 거야.

11 Cat: 무슨 말이야?

12 Dog: 너 스스로를 봐! 너는 너무 뚱뚱해서 달릴 수 없고, 너의 이빨은 너무 약해서 씹을 수 없잖아!

13 (Cat: / (he / more.) / eats // should / why / run / I / chew? / or // is / sugar / only / the / thing / need. / I // can't / I / without / it. / live)

➡ _____

_____

14 (goes / dog / sadly. / out)

➡ _____

Scene #4.

15 (has / cat / emptied / almost / box / the / sugar. / of // enters. / Mouse)

➡ _____

16 (Mouse: / smiles.) / (he // think / I / plan / my / worked. / has)

➡ _____

17 (Cat: / is / angry.) / (he // almost / it's / empty! // tell / Mouse, / me / you / where / it. / get)

➡ _____

18 (Mouse: / have / I / friend / a / makes / who / sugar. // but / scared / he's / your / of / claws. // you / if / rid / get / them, / of / can / you / him / soon. / meet)

➡ _____

19 (okay! / Cat:)

➡ _____

Scene #5.

20 (hands / Mouse / a / Cat / pair / scissors / of / and / cuts / Cat / claws. / his)

➡ _____

21 (Cat: / ready! / I'm // take / now / to / me / friend! / your)

➡ _____

22 (Mouse: / (he / at / laughs / Cat.) // stupid / you / cat!)

➡ _____

23 (you / if / fast, / were / and / your / had / teeth / sharp / clasws. / and // I'd / to / listen / you. // you / but / longer / no / them / have / now!)

➡ _____

24 (have / you / lost / biggest / your / weapons!)

➡ _____

25 (should / why / listen / I / what / to / you / now? / say // away.) / (he / runs)

➡ _____

26 (Cat: / what! // tries / (he / run / to / after / but / Mouse, / fails.) // oh! / too / I'm / to / fat / him! / after / run)

➡ _____

_____

13 Cat: *(그는 더 먹는다.)* 왜 내가 뛰거나 씹어야 해? 나에게 필요한 건 설탕 한 가지야. 나는 그것 없이는 살 수 없어.

14 *개가 슬프게 나간다.*

장면 4

15 *고양이는 설탕 상자를 거의 비웠다. 쥐가 들어온다.*

16 Mouse: *(그가 미소 짓는다.)* 내 계획이 효과가 있는 것 같아.

17 Cat: *(그는 화가 났다.)* 거의 비었잖아! 쥐야, 네가 어디서 이걸 가져오는지 말해!

18 Mouse: 나에게 설탕을 만드는 친구가 하나 있어요. 하지만 그는 당신의 발톱을 무서워한답니다. 만약 당신이 그것들을 없애버리면, 당신은 곧 그를 만날 수 있을 거예요.

19 Cat: 좋아!

장면 5

20 *쥐가 고양이에게 가위를 건네고, 고양이는 자신의 발톱을 자른다.*

21 Cat: 나는 준비가 됐어! 이제 나를 너의 친구에게 데려다줘!

22 Mouse: *(그는 고양이를 비웃는다.)* 멍청한 고양이!

23 만약 당신이 빠르고 당신의 뾰족한 이빨과 발톱을 가지고 있다면, 나는 당신의 말을 들었겠죠! 하지만 당신은 지금은 그것들을 더 이상 가지고 있지 않아요!

24 당신은 당신의 가장 큰 무기들을 잃었어요!

25 내가 왜 당신이 지금 말하는 것을 들어야 하죠? *(그는 도망간다.)*

26 Cat: 뭐? *(고양이가 쥐를 쫓아가려고 하지만 실패한다.)* 오! 나는 너무 뚱뚱해서 그를 쫓아갈 수가 없구나!

※ 다음 우리말을 영어로 쓰시오.

The Cat Just Couldn't Help It

Scene #1.

1 한 마리의 늙고 지친 쥐가 들어온다.

➡ _____

2 Mouse: *(그는 숨이 차다.)* 나는 고양이로부터 달아나는 것에 질렸어.

➡ _____

3 나는 나이가 너무 들어서 달릴 수 없어. 내가 만약 자유로워진다면, 행복할 텐데.
(그는 잠깐 동안 생각한다.) 오, 내게 좋은 생각이 났어.

➡ _____

Scene #2.

4 쥐가 무대 뒤에서 무언가를 가져온다.

➡ _____

5 고양이가 들어와 쥐를 잡는다.

➡ _____

6 Mouse: *(그는 비는 척한다.)* 저는 너무 냄새가 나서 당신이 잡아먹을 수 없어요. 대신, 이걸 드세요.
(그는 설탕 상자를 고양이에게 건넨다.)

➡ _____

➡ _____

7 Cat: *(그는 그것을 맛본다. 그의 눈이 커진다.)* 이게 뭐야? 더 줘!

➡ _____

8 Mouse: 그것은 설탕이에요. 만약에 당신이 저를 가게 해주면, 제가 매일 가지고 올게요.

➡ _____

Scene #3

9 고양이의 집이다. 지금은 뚱뚱해진 고양이가 설탕을 먹고 있다. 그는 오직 몇 개의 이빨만 가지고 있다.
개가 그를 바라보고 있다.

➡ _____

10 Dog: *(그는 걱정된다.)* 내 친구 고양이야, 조심해, 그 설탕은 써질 거야.

➡ _____

11 Cat: 무슨 말이야?

➡ _____

12 Dog: 너 스스로를 봐! 너는 너무 뚱뚱해서 달릴 수 없고, 너의 이빨은 너무 약해서 씹을 수 없잖아!

➡ _____

13 Cat: *(그는 더 먹는다.)* 왜 내가 뛰거나 씹어야 해? 나에게 필요한 건 설탕 한 가지야. 나는 그것 없이는 살 수 없어.

➡ _____

14 개가 슬프게 나간다.

➡ _____

Scene #4.

15 고양이는 설탕 상자를 거의 비웠다. 쥐가 들어온다.

➡ _____

16 Mouse: *(그가 미소 짓는다.)* 내 계획이 효과가 있는 것 같아.

➡ _____

17 Cat: *(그는 화가 났다.)* 거의 비었잖아! 쥐야, 네가 어디서 이걸 가져오는지 말해!

➡ _____

18 Mouse: 나에게 설탕을 만드는 친구가 하나 있어요. 하지만 그는 당신의 발톱을 무서워한답니다. 만약 당신이 그것들을 없애버리면, 당신은 곧 그를 만날 수 있을 거예요.

➡ _____

_____

19 Cat: 좋아!

➡ _____

Scene #5.

20 쥐가 고양이에게 가위를 건네고, 고양이는 자신의 발톱을 자른다.

➡ _____

21 Cat: 나는 준비가 됐어! 이제 나를 너의 친구에게 데려다 줘!

➡ _____

22 Mouse: *(그는 고양이를 비웃는다.)* 멍청한 고양이!

➡ _____

23 만약 당신이 빠르고 당신의 뾰족한 이빨과 발톱을 가지고 있다면, 나는 당신의 말을 들었겠죠! 하지만 당신은 지금은 그것들을 더 이상 가지고 있지 않아요!

➡ _____

24 당신은 당신의 가장 큰 무기들을 잃었어요!

➡ _____

25 내가 왜 당신이 지금 말하는 것을 들어야 하죠? *(그는 도망 간다.)*

➡ _____

26 Cat: 뭐? *(고양이가 쥐를 쫓아가려고 하지만 실패한다.)* 오! 나는 너무 뚱뚱해서 그를 쫓아갈 수가 없구나!

➡ _____

※ 다음 우리말과 일치하도록 빈칸에 알맞은 말을 쓰시오.

Think and Write B

1. I am not _____ and I _____ things _____.
2. I cannot _____ _____ _____ in the morning.
3. I _____ _____, "In _____ _____ _____ …"
4. _____ I _____ more diligent, I _____ _____ breakfast and would _____ _____ my classes.
5. Of _____, I would not _____ _____ _____ school.
6. I would not _____ _____ my homework and _____ _____ it.
7. I know my habits are _____ _____ _____.
8. I think I _____ _____ _____ make a plan to be _____ _____ and _____ _____ a good student.
9. _____ _____ _____, I will make a list of _____ _____ _____.
10. I _____ also _____ _____ _____ _____ 30 minutes _____ every morning.

1. 나는 부지런하지 않고 일들을 미룬다.
2. 나는 아침에 일찍 일어날 수 없다.
3. 나는 항상 '10분만 더 …'라고 말한다.
4. 내가 만약 부지런하다면, 나는 아침을 먹을 것이고 수업에 집중할 수 있을 것이다.
5. 물론, 나는 학교에 늦지도 않을 것이다.
6. 나는 내 숙제를 미루지 않고 다 마칠 수 있을 것이다.
7. 나는 이 습관이 전혀 좋지 않다는 것을 잘 안다.
8. 나는 내가 더 부지런해지고 좋은 학생이 될 수 있는 계획을 세워야 한다고 생각한다.
9. 지금부터, 나는 해야 할 일의 목록을 만들 것이다.
10. 또한, 나는 매일 아침 30분 일찍 일어날 것이다.

Check Your Progress

1. G: What's _____? You _____ _____.
2. B: Oh, I think I _____ _____ 50 thousand won.
3. G: What? Did you _____ _____?
4. B: Of _____, I had it in my bag, _____ my pencil case! I've _____ it _____ _____ _____ _____!
5. G: Why _____ you _____ it there? _____ _____ you _____ that _____ _____ to school?
6. B: That money was for my new soccer ball. I don't know _____ _____ _____ my money _____.
7. G: First you _____ _____ talk to your teacher. Then _____ _____ you don't bring _____ _____ _____ _____ to school again.

1. G: 무슨 일이야? 걱정스러워 보여.
2. B: 오, 나 5만 원을 잃어버린 것 같아.
3. G: 뭐? 주의 깊게 찾아보았니?
4. B: 물론이지, 나는 가방에 있는 필통에 돈이 있었어. 나는 오랫동안 돈을 모았었어.
5. G: 왜 돈을 거기에 놓았니? 왜 그렇게 많은 돈을 학교에 가져왔니?
6. B: 그 돈은 내 새 축구공을 위한 거였어. 나는 어떻게 내 돈을 돌려받을지 모르겠어.
7. G: 우선, 네 선생님께 말씀드려야 해. 그리고 학교에 다시는 많은 돈을 가져오지 말 것을 명심해.

※ 다음 우리말을 영어로 쓰시오.

Think and Write B

1. 나는 부지런하지 않고 일들을 미룬다.
➡ _____

2. 나는 아침에 일찍 일어날 수 없다.
➡ _____

3. 나는 항상 '10분만 더 …'라고 말한다.
➡ _____

4. 내가 만약 부지런하다면, 나는 아침을 먹을 것이고 수업에 집중할 수 있을 것이다.
➡ _____

5. 물론, 나는 학교에 늦지도 않을 것이다.
➡ _____

6. 나는 내 숙제를 미루지 않고 다 마칠 수 있을 것이다.
➡ _____

7. 나는 이 습관이 전혀 좋지 않다는 것을 잘 안다.
➡ _____

8. 나는 내가 더 부지런해지고 좋은 학생이 될 수 있는 계획을 세워야 한다고 생각한다.
➡ _____

9. 지금부터, 나는 해야 할 일의 목록을 만들 것이다.
➡ _____

10. 또한, 나는 매일 아침 30분 일찍 일어날 것이다.
➡ _____

Check Your Progress

1. G: 무슨 일이야? 걱정스러워 보여.
➡ _____

2. B: 오, 나 5만 원을 잃어버린 것 같아.
➡ _____

3. G: 뭐? 주의 깊게 찾아보았니?
➡ _____

4. B: 물론이지, 나는 가방에 있는 필통에 돈이 있었어. 나는 오랫동안 돈을 모았었어.
➡ _____

5. G: 왜 돈을 거기에 놓았니? 왜 그렇게 많은 돈을 학교에 가져왔니?
➡ _____

6. B: 그 돈은 내 새 축구공을 위한 거였어. 나는 어떻게 내 돈을 돌려받을지 모르겠어.
➡ _____

7. G: 우선, 네 선생님께 말씀드려야 해. 그리고 학교에 다시는 많은 돈을 가져오지 말 것을 명심해.
➡ _____
_____

MEMO

영어 기출 문제집

적중 100

2학기

정답 및 해설

금성 | 최인철

중 2

적중 100

영어 기출 문제집

적중 100

2학기

정답 및 해설

금성 | 최인철

중 **2**

Lesson 7

Understanding Differences Makes a Difference

시험대비 실력평가   p.08

01 host   02 ②   03 ④
04 (1) (r)espect   (2) (s)et   (3) (s)tuck
05 (1) languages   (2) manners   (3) Kenyan
     (4) perfect   (5) recommend   06 ⑤
07 You should arrive at school on time.

01 주어진 관계는 반의어 관계를 나타낸다. host: 주인, 주최자, guest: 손님

02 '당신이 누군가나 무언가에 화나거나 언짢거나 만족하지 못하다고 말하다'를 나타내는 말은 complain(불평하다)이다.

03 rude: 무례한

04 respect: 존중하다, set: 정하다, stick: 붙이다

05 Kenyan: 케냐의 manners: 예의, 예절, language: 언어, perfect: 완벽한, recommend: 추천하다

06 주어진 문장에서 wave는 '흔들다'를 뜻하며 이와 같은 의미로 쓰인 것은 ⑤번이다. 나머지는 모두 '파도'를 가리킨다.

07 on time: 정시에

서술형 시험대비   p.09

01 rude
02 (1) traditional   (2) unbelievable   (3) upset
     (4) waved   (5) invite
03 (1) greeted   (2) host   (3) nodded
04 (1) Seoul is the capital city of Korea.
     (2) Tom carved his name on the tree.
     (3) She is a great dress designer.
     (4) He looks younger than his age.
05 (1) Koreans often shake hands bowing their head.
     (2) The villagers called upon him to solve the town's problem.
     (3) I have trouble walking because of my backache.
     (4) Would you introduce the traditional stone towers in Korea?

01 주어진 관계는 반의어 관계를 나타낸다. polite: 예의 바른, rude: 무례한

02 unbelievable: 믿을 수 없는, traditional: 전통적인, invite: 초대하다, upset: 속상한, 화난, wave: 흔들다

03 greet: 인사하다, host: 주인, 주최자, nod: 고개를 끄덕이다

04 capital city: 수도, carve: 새기다, 조각하다, dress: 옷, 의복, age: 나이

05 shake hands: 악수하다, call upon: ~을 요청하다, 부탁하다, have trouble ~ing: ~하는데 어려움을 겪다

교과서
Conversation

핵심 Check   p.10~11

1 heard
2 told / know
3 tell you something / What
4 me tell you

교과서 대화문 익히기

Check(√) True or False   p.12

1 T   2 F   3 T   4 F

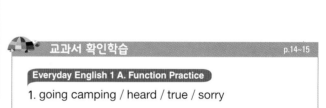

교과서 확인학습   p.14~15

Everyday English 1 A. Function Practice

1. going camping / heard / true / sorry
2. heard that, science contest / interested in / sign up, prize, winner / Thanks for
3. carve pumpkins, What else / scary costumes / sounds

Everyday English 1 B

some time / what / I heard that / went on / more about your trip, thinking of / see, to visit, interesting places / recommend, go / visiting, one of the most famous museums / Thanks for

Everyday English 2 A. Function Practice

1. something about love / the most important, respect / agree, Respecting
2. Look at / tall, pretty / something about, at first / the most popular places

travel writer, important lesson, while traveling, rude, age, found out, culture, differently, older, experience, learning, understanding

In Real Life

speaking / up / social studies, cultural differences, having trouble finding / called, other cultures / perfect / welcome, Good

---

시험대비 기본평가 p.16

01 I heard that it will rain tomorrow.　　02 ①

03 I heard that there is a science contest next week.

04 ⑤

02 내일 캠핑을 갈 계획에 신이 나 있다가 비가 온다는 소식을 들었으므로 ①번이 적절하다. disappointed: 실망한, nervous: 긴장한

04 Somi의 참가 신청 여부는 대화를 통해 알 수 없다.

시험대비 실력평가 p.17~18

01 (B) → (D) → (C) → (A)　　02 ③　　　03 ②, ④

04 ②　　　　05 ⑤　　　06 ④　　　07 ③, ④

08 ⓔ → visiting　　　09 ⑤

10 I'd like to tell you something about love.

11 They agree that the most important thing in love is respect.

01 (B) 계획 설명 → (D) 날씨에 관해 언급 → (C) 놀람 표현 → (A) 유감 표현

02 (A) carve: 조각하다, curve: 구부리다, (B) starry: 별이 많은, scary: 무서운, (C) sweat: 땀, sweets: 사탕

04 (A) 목적어 역할을 하는 명사절을 이끄는 that, (B) be interested in: ~에 관심을 갖다, (C) sign up: 가입하다, 신청하다

05 대화를 통해 Brian이 언제 과학 대회에 신청을 해야 하는지는 알 수 없다.

06 유감 및 사실을 표현하는 ④번이 적절하다.

07 (A)는 '그럴 리 없어.'라는 놀람을 표현하고 있으므로 ③, ④번으로 바꾸어 쓸 수 있다.

08 recommend는 to부정사를 목적어로 취하지 않고 동명사 또는 명사절을 목적어로 취한다.

09 스페인에서 가장 흥미로운 장소가 어디인지는 대화를 통해 알 수 없다.

---

11 소녀와 소년은 사랑에 있어서 가장 중요한 것은 존중이라는 것에 동의한다.

서술형 시험대비 p.19

01 (A) a family trip　(B) Spain

　(C) a really nice country to visit

　(D) many interesting places.

　(E) visit the Prado Museum in Madrid

02 ⓒ → because of

03 It was because many people asked her age.

04 When I asked him if he would help me, he nodded.

01 오늘 나는 이번 여름에 스페인으로 가족 여행을 다녀온, Alex를 만나서 유용한 정보를 얻었다. 나는 이번 겨울 스페인을 방문할 계획을 세워서 이에 대한 정보가 필요했다. Alex는 스페인은 정말로 방문하기 좋은 나라이며 많은 흥미로운 곳들이 있다고 말했다. 그 가운데, 그는 내게 마드리드에 있는 Prado 박물관을 방문할 것을 조언하였다. 그곳은 세계의 가장 유명한 박물관들 중 하나이다. 나는 그곳을 방문하기로 결정했다. 나는 이번 겨울 스페인 방문을 기대한다.

02 because of+명사구, because+절

03 많은 사람들이 그녀에게 나이를 물었기 때문에 한국인들은 무례하다고 생각했었다.

04 nod: 고개를 끄덕이다

교과서
Grammar

핵심 Check p.20~21

1 (1) who[whom/that]　(2) which[that]　(3) about whom

　(4) which

2 (1) which[that] / what　(2) that[which] / what

　(3) that[which] / what

시험대비 기본평가 p.22

01 (1) There were many children at the zoo which[that] Tom and Jane visited.

3

(2) Those boys who[whom/that] the woman is looking after look very cute. 또는 Those boys after whom the woman is looking look very cute.

(3) I want to wear the dress that[which] Elizabeth made.

(4) I have the book that[which] Molly really liked.

02 (1) what　(2) who[whom/that]　(3) which[that]

　(4) for whom　(5) which[that]

03 (1) which[that] / in which　(2) which[that] / what

　(3) which[that] / What

01 (1), (3), (4) 사물을 선행사로 취하는 목적격 관계대명사가 쓰여야 하므로 which 혹은 that을 쓴다. (2) 사람을 선행사로 취하는 목적격 관계대명사이므로 who나 whom 혹은 that을 쓴다. 이때 who(m)은 전치사 after의 목적어로 쓰이고 있다.

02 선행사가 사람이면서 관계사절에 동사나 전치사의 목적어가 빠져 있다면 who, whom을 쓸 수 있고, 이를 대신하여 that을 써도 무방하다. 선행사가 사물인 경우에는 which 혹은 that을 쓴다.

03 관계절이 이끄는 문장에서 동사나 전치사의 목적어가 빠져 있을 경우 쓰이는 관계대명사는 목적격 관계대명사이다. 선행사가 사람이면 who, whom, 선행사가 사물이면 which를 쓸 수 있으며 that으로 모두 대체 가능하나, 전치사가 관계대명사 앞에 쓰인 경우 that을 쓸 수 없다. what은 선행사를 포함하고 있는 관계대명사이다.

시험대비 실력평가

p.23~25

01 ①, ④　　02 ⑤　　　03 ④

04 (1) I know the thing which you did last summer.

　(2) I know what you did last summer.

05 ③　　　06 ①　　　07 what　　08 ④

09 ③　　　10 ⑤

11 She is looking for the man who[whom/that] she saw in her dream.

12 ⑤　　　13 ②　　　14 ①　　　15 you

16 ④, ⑤

17 (who/whom/that) we depend on when we are in danger

18 ④, ⑤　　　19 What I wrote　　　20 ⑤

21 ④　　　22 ③　　　23 ③

01 lost의 목적어였던 the jacket 대신에 목적격 관계대명사가 쓰인 것이다. 따라서 사물을 선행사로 취하는 which가 적절하며 이를 대신하여 that을 써도 무방하다.

02 주격 관계대명사는 생략이 불가능하다.

03 주어진 문장의 밑줄 친 that은 불완전한 문장을 이끄는 관계대명사 that이다. 따라서 ④번이 정답이다.

04 두 문장 'I know the thing. You did it last summer.'를 하나로 만든 것이다. 사물이 선행사이므로 which 혹은 that을 쓰고 이를 선행사와 묶어서 what으로 표현할 수 있다.

05 'play tennis with David'라는 의미이므로 with whom이 적절하며, 선행사를 포함하여 쓰이는 관계대명사는 what이다.

06 전치사의 목적어로 쓰인 목적격 관계대명사의 자리이다. 전치사가 관계대명사 앞에 쓰인 경우 that을 쓸 수 없다.

07 the thing which를 what으로 쓴 문장이다.

08 관계대명사가 이끄는 문장은 불완전하다. which는 목적격 관계대명사로 쓰이고 있으므로 it을 없애고 which you picked up 이라고 쓰는 것이 적절하다.

09 관계대명사 that은 전치사 다음에 쓸 수 없다.

10 'Focus on the thing that you have to do now.'에서 the thing that을 what으로 쓴 것이다.

11 'She is looking for the man. She saw him in her dream.'을 하나로 합친 문장이다.

12 whom I spoke to라고 쓰는 것이 적절하다.

13 주어진 문장의 빈칸에 들어갈 말은 what이다. 모두 앞의 명사를 수식하는 관계대명사 that, which가 쓰이지만 ②번은 명사절을 이끄는 what이 들어간다.

14 ⓐ it 삭제 ⓑ are → is ⓒ that → which ⓔ which → what

15 Where is the coffee that[which] you brought?

16 전치사 for의 목적어로 쓰인 whom이다. 전치사가 문장 맨 뒤에 있을 때에는 that을 써도 무방하나, 전치사가 관계대명사 앞으로 올 경우 반드시 for whom으로 써야 한다.

17 who(m)를 대신하여 that을 써도 좋으며, 목적격 관계대명사이므로 생략해도 무방하다.

18 'I'll give you the thing that you want.'에서 목적격 관계대명사 that을 생략할 수 있고, the thing that을 what으로 쓸 수 있다.

19 관계대명사 what은 '~하는 것'이라고 해석된다.

20 불완전한 절을 이끌며 주절 내에서 명사 역할을 하는 것은 관계대명사 what이다.

21 관계대명사 that은 전치사 다음에 쓸 수 없다.

22 두 개의 빈칸 모두 사물을 선행사로 취하며 불완전한 절을 이끌고 있으므로 관계대명사 which 또는 that을 쓰는 것이 적절하다.

23 Seeing의 목적어 역할을 하면서 동시에 불완전한 절을 이끌고 있으므로 what을 쓰는 것이 적절하다.

01 Tell me about the cats that you take care of on the streets.

02 whom[who/that] I told you / about whom I told

03 (1) The woman whom[who/that] I met last week was very kind.

(2) Shrek is the movie which[that] I liked the most when I was young.

(3) I will return the money which[that] I borrowed from my friends yesterday.

(4) Is this the camera which[that] you have been looking for?

04 the thing that he gave me / what he gave me

05 Show me what you have in your pocket.

06 with that → with whom

07 What I want to eat[have]

08 that[which] you saw yesterday

09 (1) which(또는 that) / on which

(2) who[whom/that] / with whom

(3) which[that] / in which

(4) What

10 (1) He is the singer. I have wanted to meet him in person.

(2) Paul is my friend. I can rely on him.

(3) Is this the rabbit? You are taking care of it.

(4) The museum was closed. I wanted to visit the museum.

(5) This is the thing. John gave it to me on my birthday.

11 I know the girl with whom Tom danced.

12 You should accept what he offered.

13 whom you met / you met

14 what I want to read

15 The boy whom I saw on Wednesday is American.

---

01 해석: 네가 길에서 돌보는 그 고양이들에 대해서 말해줘.

02 전치사 about이 문장 끝에 있을 때에는 whom을 대신하여 who 또는 that을 써도 좋지만 전치사가 관계대명사 앞으로 올 경우 about whom이 적절하다.

03 (1), (2), (3) whom, which를 대신하여 관계대명사 that을 써도 무방하다. (4) 'Is this the camera for which you have been looking?'이라고 써도 좋다.

04 'This is the thing. He gave me the thing.'을 하나로 만든 문장이다.

05 '네 호주머니에 가지고 있는 것'이라고 하였으므로 관계대명사 what이 you have in your pocket을 이끌도록 문장을 만든다.

06 관계대명사 that은 전치사 뒤에 쓰일 수 없다.

07 '저녁으로 내가 먹고 싶은 것'이라고 하였으므로 관계대명사 what을 사용하여 문장을 만들 수 있다. 혹은 The thing which I want to eat[have]이라고 써도 좋다.

08 saw를 대신하여 watched를, that을 대신하여 which를 써도 좋다.

09 불완전한 문장을 이끌면서 앞서 나온 명사를 수식하는 것은 관계대명사 who(m), which이며 이를 대신하여 that을 써도 좋다. 그러나 관계대명사 that은 전치사 다음에 쓸 수 없음에 유의한다. 반면 what은 불완전한 문장을 이끌면서 명사 역할을 한다.

10 관계대명사 what은 the thing which 혹은 the thing that으로 풀어쓸 수 있다.

11 I know the girl who(m)(또는 that) Tom danced with.'라고 써도 무방하다.

12 '그가 제안한 것'이라고 하였으므로 what he offered라고 쓰는 것이 적절하다.

13 목적격 관계대명사 whom을 대신하여 who 또는 that을 써도 좋다. 목적격 관계대명사는 생략 가능하다.

14 '내가 읽고 싶은 것'이라는 의미이다.

15 whom을 대신하여 who 또는 that을 써도 좋다.

확인문제   p.28

1 T   2 F   3 T   4 T   5 F

확인문제   p.29

1 F   2 F   3 T   4 T   5 T   6 F

교과서 확인학습 A   p.30~31

01 Welcome to   02 are interested in, that

03 about other cultures, a look

04 upset   05 from Greece

06 her to be friends, shook

07 rude   08 down, what, meant was

09 countries, nodding, means, shaking

10 who has been invited

11 anything about

12 manners I need to know, me some advice

13 that, are invited, leave, on

14 that, enough food

15 However, finish, has prepared

16 If, leave, that   17 anyone speak

18 minutes late for

19 When, looked, angry

20 that, try to keep, does, mean

21 appointment, in German

22 that, to be on time   23 is set, be kept

24 be punctual

25 the information you needed

26 what you have, was

27 Understanding cultural differences

28 visit

with my German friend.

19 When I finally met him, he looked very angry.

20 He said that I must try to keep my "Termin" better. What does it mean?

21 Smile: "Termin" means "appointment" in German.

22 Germans think that it's important to be on time.

23 In Germany, there is a saying, "What is set should be kept."

24 So, please be punctual with Germans.

25 Did you find the information you needed?

26 We hope that what you have read was helpful and interesting.

27 Understanding cultural differences can make a difference in your life.

28 Please visit our website again!

1 Welcome to "Culture Shock"!

2 If you are interested in cultures around the world, this is the website that you are looking for!

3 You can ask and answer any questions you may have about other cultures. Let's take a look!

4 Suji: I'm very upset.

5 There is a new student from Greece in my school.

6 I asked her to be friends with me but she shook her head.

7 How rude!

8 Ocean: Calm down. I'm sure what she really meant was "yes."

9 In some countries like Greece, Turkey, and Iran, nodding your head means "no" and shaking your head means "yes."

10 Shao: Help! I'm a Chinese boy who has been invited to a Kenyan friend's house.

11 But I don't know anything about Kenya.

12 Are there any manners I need to know? Please give me some advice!

13 Clever: I heard that when Chinese people are invited to someone's house, they leave some food on their plate.

14 It shows that there was enough food for the guest.

15 However, with Kenyan people, please finish all the food the host has prepared.

16 If you leave food, it means that you didn't like it.

17 Diego: Does anyone speak German?

18 Today, I was 5 minutes late for an appointment

01 ③   02 She felt upset.   03 ④

04 ④   05 nod   06 which, that

07 It is polite to leave some food on our plate.

08 ⑤   09 ②   10 interesting

11 It was because Diego didn't keep his appointment.

12 ⑤   13 ⑤   14 ③

15 She shook her head.   16 ③   17 ⑤

18 Shao has been invited to a Kenyan friend's house.

19 ④   20 is set

21 that you need, helpful and interesting   22 ③

23 ④   24 ②

01 친구가 되자는 요청에 그리스인 친구가 고개를 저은 것을 보고 무례하다고 느끼는 것이 가장 적절하다.

02 글을 게시할 당시 수지는 화가 나 있었다.

03 새로운 학생은 그리스에서 왔다고 하였다.

04 숙제를 도와주었다고 하였으므로 도움을 요청한 것에 대한 승낙의 표현이 들어가는 것이 옳다. 터키에서는 고개를 흔드는 것이 좋다는 의미라고 하였으므로 ④번이 적절하다.

05 머리를 아래위로 움직이면서 어떠한 질문에 '네'라고 대답함을 표시하는 것은 '끄덕이다(nod)'이다. approval: 승인

06 빈칸 ⓐ에는 목적격 관계대명사가 들어간다. 사물이 선행사이므로 which 혹은 that을 쓸 수 있다.

07 중국 사람들이 누군가의 집에 초대되었을 때 음식을 남긴다고 하였으므로, 중국인 친구의 집에 초대되면 접시에 음식을 남기는 것이 예의바르다고 할 수 있다.

08 케냐 사람들과 함께 식사를 할 경우 주인이 준비한 음식을 모두

먹는 것이 좋다고 하였다. 그렇지 않으면 당신이 음식을 좋아하지 않았다는 것을 의미하기 때문이다.

09 대답에서 Termin이라는 단어의 설명을 하고 있으므로 ②번이 가장 적절하다.

10 흥미를 유발한다는 의미이므로 현재분사로 쓰는 것이 적절하다.

11 Diego가 약속 시간에 늦었기 때문이다

12 Diego는 5분 늦게 도착하여 친구를 만났다고 하였으므로 ⑤번은 글의 내용과 일치하지 않는다.

13 밑줄 친 ⓐ는 불완전한 문장을 이끌면서 앞선 명사를 수식하는 관계대명사 that이다. 모두 완전한 문장을 이끄는 명사절 접속사이지만 ⑤번은 관계대명사이다.

14 수지는 그리스에서 온 새로운 학생 때문에 화가 났다.

15 수지가 친구가 되고 싶다고 했을 때 그리스에서 온 학생은 고개를 저었다고 하였다.

16 '때'를 의미하는 when이 가장 적절하다.

17 중국인들이 음식을 남기는 이유는 (C) 손님을 위한 충분한 음식이 있었음을 보여주는 것임 - (B) 그러나 케냐 사람들은 음식을 모두 먹음 - (A) 음식을 남기면 음식을 좋아하지 않았다는 의미가 됨.

18 Shao는 케냐인 친구의 집으로 초대받았다고 하였다.

19 Shao가 케냐인 친구 집에 초대를 받은 것이다.

20 '정해진'이라는 의미가 되어야 하므로 수동태로 쓰는 것이 적절하다.

21 목적격 관계대명사 that을 대신하여 which를 써도 좋다.

22 Diego의 친구가 화가 난 이유는 Diego가 약속에 늦어서이다.

23 advice는 셀 수 없는 명사이다.

24 미라가 David에게 해준 조언은 식사예절이다.

---

01 글의 내용에 따르면 고개를 끄덕이는 것은 '싫다'는 의미이고 고개를 흔드는 것은 '좋다'는 의미이다.

02 "Culture Shock"은 서로 다른 문화에 관한 질문과 대답이 있는 웹 사이트이다.

03 수지는 그리스 학생이 자신과 친구가 되기를 원치 않는다고 생각하여 화가 난 것이다.

04 목적격 관계대명사이므로 that은 생략해도 무방하다. '~을 찾다'는 look for로 쓴다. 따라서 전치사 for를 쓰는 것이 적절하다.

05 Shao는 케냐 문화에 관해 잘 모르기 때문에 조언을 구하는 글을 올렸으며, 방문하는 곳은 케냐인 친구의 집이다.

06 중국 사람들은 누군가의 집에 초대되었을 때, 접시에 음식을 남겨두는데, 이러한 행동은 손님에게 충분한 음식이 제공되었음을 보여주는 것이라고 하였다.

07 케냐인의 집에서 음식을 남기면, 그 음식을 좋아하지 않아서 남겼음을 의미한다.

08 독일어 Termin을 가리키는 말이다.

09 '정해진 것'이라고 하였으므로 관계대명사 what이 수동태 is set을 이끌도록 문장을 만드는 것이 적절하다. 도덕적 의무를 나타내며 '~해야만 한다'는 의미의 조동사는 should이다.

10 punctual은 '시간을 엄수하는'이라는 의미로 위 글의 on time과 같은 의미이다. on time: 시간을 어기지 않고

11 문화적 차이를 이해하는 것은 삶을 변화시킨다고 하였다.

12 You needed the information.이라고 써도 좋다.

13 David는 이번 겨울에 한국을 방문할 예정이다.

14 한국 문화에 대해 잘 모르는 외국인이라면 가장 나이가 많은 어른이 식사를 시작하기 전에 자신이 먼저 먹을지도 모른다.

서술형 시험대비

01 (A) yes   (B) yes

02 It is a website with questions and answers about different cultures.

03 It's because she thought the Greek student didn't want to be her friend.

04 this is the website (that) you are looking for

05 knew → didn't know / Chinese house → Kenyan house

06 접시에 음식을 남겨두는 것

07 It means we didn't like the food.

08 Termin

09 What is set should be kept

10 on time

11 cultural differences

12 Did you find the information? You needed it.

13 He will visit Korea this winter.

14 start eating, the oldest person

영역별 핵심문제
p.41~45

01 unbelievable   02 ②   03 ②

04 (1) calm   (2) complaining   (3) confuse

05 (1) on time   (2) sign up   (3) take a look
   (4) make a difference   (5) get rid of

06 ②

07 I heard that people carve pumpkins on Halloween.

08 They wear scary costumes and visit houses to get sweets.

09 ②   10 ②   11 ⑤   12 ②

13 Let me tell you an important lesson that I learned while traveling.   14 ⑤

15 ③   16 ④, ⑤   17 what I bought

18 ④

19 Math is the subject which I studied hard.

20 ④   21 ③   22 ④   23 ③

24 What is the most important

25 ③

26 My dad is angry because of what I did.

27 ④　　　　28 ③　　　　29 shaking　30 ④

31 People of Greece, Turkey, and Iran express "no" by nodding their head.

32 ②　　　　33 ⑤　　　　34 ③

01 주어진 관계는 반의어 관계를 나타낸다. believable 믿을 수 있는, unbelievable 믿을 수 없는

02 당신이 당신의 집이나 당신이 돈을 지불하는 특정한 행사에 초대하는 사람을 가리키는 말은 guest(손님)이다.

03 punctual: 시간을 지키는

04 calm: 진정시키다, complain: 불평하다, confuse: 혼동하다

05 sign up: 참가하다, 신청하다, take a look: ~을 보다, get rid of: ~을 제거하다, ~을 없애다, on time: 정시에, make a difference: 변화를 일으키다

06 주어진 문장에서 capital은 '수도'를 뜻하며 이와 같은 의미로 쓰인 것은 ②번이다. ①, ③, ④번은 '자본', ⑤번은 '대문자'의 뜻이다.

08 아이들은 할로윈에 무서운 의상을 차려 입고 사탕을 얻기 위해 여러 집들을 방문한다.

09 (A)는 말할 시간을 가리키므로 to talk, (B)는 have trouble ~ing: ~하는 데 어려움을 겪다, (C) '~라고 불리는'을 뜻하므로 called

10 Diego는 사회 숙제 때문에 걱정하였지만 수지의 도움을 받아 기뻐함을 알 수 있다

11 Diego는 수지에게 문화 차이에 관한 질문을 하지 않았다.

12 대화의 흐름상 '그러나'가 적절하므로 ②번이 알맞다. on the other hand: 반면에

14 Tina는 다른 문화를 배우고 이해하는 것의 중요성에 대해 알게 되었다.

15 전치사가 관계대명사 앞에 있을 경우 관계대명사를 생략할 수 없다.

16 '내가 할 수 있는 것'이라는 의미이므로 what이 들어가고 이를 풀어서 쓰면 the thing which이다. 이때 which는 목적격 관계대명사이므로 생략하여 the thing만 쓸 수 있다.

17 '내가 가게에서 산 것'이라는 의미를 완성하는 것이 적절하다. 관계대명사 what은 '~하는 것'이라고 해석되는 것이 일반적이다.

18 관계대명사 that은 전치사 다음에 쓸 수 없다.

19 which를 대신하여 that을 쓰거나 생략해도 무방하다.

20 ① 관계대명사 that은 전치사 다음에 쓸 수 없으므로 at which ② 주어가 단수이므로 is ③ 사물이 선행사이므로 which ⑤ the thing which 혹은 what만 쓰는 것이 옳다. ④ 목적격 관계대명사가 생략되어 있다.

21 This is the shop that I bought these pants at.

22 주어진 문장의 that은 불완전한 절을 이끄는 관계대명사 that이

다. 모두 완전한 절을 이끄는 접속사이지만 ④번은 불완전한 절을 이끄는 관계대명사 that이다.

23 첫 번째 빈칸에는 tell의 직접목적어를 이끌 수 있는 관계대명사 what, 두 번째 빈칸에는 전치사의 목적어로 관계대명사 that이 쓰일 수 없으며, 세 번째 빈칸에는 사물을 선행사로 받아주는 관계대명사 which 혹은 that이 오는 것이 적절하다.

24 질문에 대한 답으로 '내 삶에서 가장 중요한 것은 가족이야.'라는 말을 하고 있다. 'The thing which is the most important'를 'What is the most important'로 만든 것이다.

25 관계대명사 that은 전치사 다음에 쓸 수 없다.

26 '아빠는 내가 한 것 때문에 화가 나셨다'는 의미이다. 따라서 what을 쓰는 것이 적절하다.

27 be interested in: ~에 흥미를 느끼다

28 위 글은 웹 사이트의 특징에 관하여 말하고 있다

29 고개를 흔드는 것이 "좋다"는 의미라는 것을 유추할 수 있다.

30 불완전한 문장을 이끌고 있으며, '그녀가 정말로 의미한 것'이라는 의미를 갖도록 관계대명사 what을 쓰는 것이 적절하다.

31 그리스, 터키, 이란 사람들이 머리를 끄덕이며 '싫다'는 표현을 한다.

32 결론짓는 문장이 이어지고 있으므로 So가 가장 적절하다.

33 독일인들과 함께 할 때는 시간을 잘 지키라는 조언이 적절하다. 따라서 punctual이라고 쓰는 것이 옳다.

34 Diego는 약속 시간에 5분 늦었다고 하였다.

단원별 예상문제　　　　p.46~49

01 ④　　　02 ③　　　03 ⑤　　　04 ③

05 ⑤　　　06 ⑤

07 He is having trouble finding the right information.

08 She advises him to visit a website called "Culture Shock."

09 They ask and answer questions about other cultures on the website.

10 (D) → (B) → (E) → (A) → (C)　　　11 ②

12 ②, ③　　　13 ③

14 which I borrowed at the library are

15 the thing that I heard / what I heard

16 (1) This is the thing which makes you beautiful.
(2) This is what makes you beautiful.

17 ④　　　18 ③　　　19 ③

20 there was enough food for the guest　21 ②

22 ①　　　23 He feels excited about the trip.

24 The oldest person starts to eat first in Korea.

25 ④

01 왜 처음에 사람들이 에펠탑을 싫어했는지 대화를 통해 알 수 없다.

02 주어진 문장에 이어 한국인들의 문화를 설명하는 내용이 나오는 (C)가 적절하다.

03 한국인들이 다른 문화들을 이해하기 위해 무엇을 하는지는 대화를 통해 알 수 없다.

04 이어지는 대화에서 여행에 대한 정보를 제공하고 있으므로 주어진 문장이 들어가기에 (C)가 알맞다.

05 ⓐ는 추천하는 표현이지만 ⓑ번은 의구심을 나타낸다.

07 Diego는 올바른 정보를 찾는 데 어려움을 겪고 있다.

08 수지는 "Culture Shock"이라고 불리는 웹 사이트를 방문할 것을 조언하였다.

09 사람들은 "Culture Shock"이라고 불리는 웹 사이트에서 다른 문화들에 대해 질문하고 답한다.

10 (D) 사실 확인 → (B) 정보 요청 → (E) 스페인에 대한 의견 표현 → (A) 방문지 추천 요청 → (C) 방문지 추천 및 이유 설명

11 the thing which는 what을 풀어 쓴 것이다.

12 관계대명사 that은 전치사 다음에 쓸 수 없다. 또한 관계대명사 앞에 전치사가 올 경우 관계대명사는 whom을 써 주어야 한다.
look up to: 존경하다

13 두 문장 The man was kind. We met him with the children.을 하나로 합친 것이다.

14 which를 대신하여 that을 쓰거나 생략해도 좋다. 핵심 주어가 The books이므로 수의 일치는 복수동사 are로 한다.

15 the thing which라고 써도 좋다. 관계대명사 what은 선행사를 포함하는 관계대명사이다. 따라서 the thing that을 what으로 표현할 수 있다.

16 which를 대신하여 that을 써도 좋다.

17 the thing which[that]로 쓰거나 혹은 what만 쓰는 것이 적절하다.

18 두 문화의 반대되는 차이를 보여주고 있으므로 However를 쓰는 것이 적절하다.

19 목적격 관계대명사는 생략할 수 있다.

20 중국 사람들은 손님을 위한 충분한 음식이 있었음을 보여주기 위하여 음식을 남긴다고 하였다.

21 Shao의 케냐인 친구가 저녁을 먹기 위해 초대한 것인지는 나와 있지 않다.

22 사물을 선행사로 받고 있으므로 which가 쓰일 수 있다.

23 David는 한국 여행에 신이 나 있다고 하였다.

24 한국에서는 나이가 가장 많은 사람이 식사를 먼저 시작한다고 하였다.

25 for a while: 잠시 for a long time: 오랫동안

서술형 실전문제   p.50~51

01 He visited Spain this summer.

02 It's because she is thinking of visiting Spain this winter.

03 He recommends visiting the Prado Museum in Madrid.

04 who / what

05 (1) which Mindy was sitting
    (2) on which Mindy was

06 what I drew

07 which I like the most

08 What I want to buy today is a new computer.

09 [B]-[A]-[C]

10 Understanding cultural differences can make a difference in your life.

11 be punctual

12 what the host prepared

13 table manner, finish, that is prepared

---

01 Alex는 이번 여름에 스페인을 방문했다.

02 Mina는 이번 겨울 스페인을 방문할 생각이기 때문에 스페인에 대한 정보를 요청한다.

03 Alex는 마드리드에 있는 Prado 박물관을 방문할 것을 추천한다.

04 who를 대신하여 whom이나 that을 써도 좋다.

05 (1)번의 관계대명사 which를 대신하여 that을 쓰거나 생략해도 무방하다. 하지만 전치사가 관계대명사 앞에 쓰인 (2)번의 경우 which를 대신하여 that을 쓸 수 없으며 생략하는 것도 불가능하다.

06 '내가 그린 것'이므로 관계대명사 what을 써서 문장을 완성할 수 있다. the thing (which 또는 that) I drew라고 써도 좋다.

07 목적격 관계대명사 which를 대신하여 that을 써도 좋다.

08 the thing which(또는 that)는 관계대명사 what으로 바꿀 수 있다.

09 [B] 오늘 독일인 친구와의 약속에 늦음 - [A] 마침내 친구를 만났을 때 친구가 화가 나 보임 - [C] 그는 내가 "Termin"을 더 잘 지켜야 한다고 말함.

10 '문화 차이를 이해하는 것'이라고 하였으므로 Understanding cultural differences 혹은 To understand cultural differences라고 쓰는 것이 적절하다.

11 독일인 친구와 약속을 할 때에는 시간을 엄수하는 것이 중요하다.

12 주인이 준비한 것이 충분해서 배부르게 만들었다는 것을 보여주기 위해서 음식을 남기는 것이 예의라고 하였다.

13 케냐에서는 준비된 음식을 모두 먹어야만 한다는 식사 예절이 있다.

|모범답안|

01 (A) science   (B) be held next week   (C) sign up
    (D) a big prize

02 (1) What I want to eat is ice cream.

   (2) Sleeping is what I need now.

   (3) Forget about what you heard about me. / Tell
    me what you will see tomorrow.

03 traditional Japanese clothes, a flower pattern,
   very colorful, at a festival

01 나는 과학에 많은 관심을 갖고 있다. 나는 소미로부터 좋은 소식을 들었다. 그녀는 내게 과학 대회가 다음 주에 열릴 것이라고 이야기해 주었다. 그녀는 내게 참가하라고 격려하였다. 그녀는 우승자에게 큰 상이 있다고 말했다. 나는 시도해 보기로 결정했다. 나는 그녀가 그것에 대해 내게 이야기해 주어 고마웠다.

01 ①

02 (1) country   (2) difference   (3) German

03 ①

04 (1) What time is our appointment this Friday?

   (2) In Asia, people usually bow when they meet.

05 (C) → (B) → (D) → (A)

06 ⑤

07 It has become one of the most popular places.

08 respect   09 ⑤

10 He has an interest in science.

11 A big prize is prepared for the winner.

12 ②   13 ③, ④

14 What he said an hour ago is not true.

15 ③

16 What I want to become

17 ⑤   18 ②   19 ③   20 ④

21 ⑤   22 saying

23 what she really meant   24 ③

25 She asked the new student from Greece to be
   friends with her.

01 보통 중앙 정부가 운영되는 한 국가의 가장 중요한 마을이나 도시를 가리키는 말은 capital(수도)이다.

02 country: 나라, 국가, difference: 차이, 다름, German: 독일의

03 plate: 접시, 요리

04 appointment: 약속, bow: (고개를) 숙이다

05 (C) 주제 소개하기 → (B) 무엇인지 질문 → (D) 주제 설명하기
   → (A) 동의 및 의견 표현

06 (A)와 ①~④는 모두 주제를 소개하는 표현이다.

07 에펠탑은 요즘 파리에서 가장 인기 있는 장소 중의 하나가 되었다.

09 (A)와 나머지는 모두 동의를 표현하지만 ⑤번은 오해를 지적하는 표현이다.

10 Brian은 과학에 관심을 갖고 있다.

11 과학 대회 우승자를 위해 큰 상이 준비되어 있다.

12 '내일 비가 온다'고 들었다는 말에 '뭐?'라고 하는 것으로 보아 It can't be true.가 적절하다.

13 빈칸에는 happened의 주어이자 주절의 주어가 필요하다. 따라서 The thing which[that] 혹은 이를 하나로 합친 What이 적절하다.

14 The thing that은 What으로 표현할 수 있다.

15 ⓑ 선행사가 the story이므로 관계대명사로 which 혹은 that을, ⓒ 관계대명사 that은 전치사 다음에 쓸 수 없으므로 in which를 쓰는 것이 적절하다.

16 '내가 미래에 되고 싶은 것'이라고 하였으므로 '~하는 것'이라고 해석되는 관계대명사 what을 활용하여 문장을 만든다.

17 '알라딘이 원하는 것'이라는 의미이므로 관계대명사 what, 선행사가 the mice이므로 관계대명사 which, 'I spoke to the woman'이므로 to whom을 쓰는 것이 적절하다.

18 (A)는 중국인들을 가리키는 말이며, (B)는 음식을 남기는 것을 의미한다.

19 중국에서 예의바른 식사 예절은 음식을 남기는 것이라고 하였다.

20 이어지는 글의 내용으로 보아 시간을 지키는 것이 중요하다는 말이 들어가는 것이 적절하다.

21 독일어 Termin이 무슨 의미인지를 묻기 위하여 글을 올렸다.

22 사람들이 종종 사용하는 문장으로 인간의 삶과 경험에 관한 정보 혹은 조언을 제공하는 것은 '속담, 격언'이다.

23 관계대명사 what은 '~하는 것'이라는 의미로 쓰인다.

24 (A) the website를 선행사로 하는 목적격 관계대명사 that, (B) 복수 명사가 이어지고 있으므로 other, (C) '머리를 흔드는 것'을 의미하므로 주어 역할을 하는 동명사 shaking이 쓰이는 것이 적절하다.

25 수지는 그리스에서 온 친구에게 친구가 되기를 요청하였다.

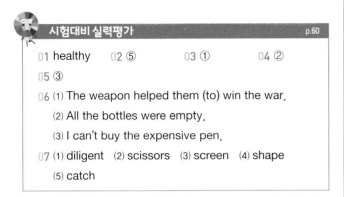

Take Control of Your Life

시험대비 실력평가 p.60

01 healthy 02 ⑤ 03 ① 04 ②
05 ③
06 (1) The weapon helped them (to) win the war.
  (2) All the bottles were empty.
  (3) I can't buy the expensive pen.
07 (1) diligent (2) scissors (3) screen (4) shape
  (5) catch

01 주어진 관계는 반의어 관계를 나타낸다. sick: 아픈, healthy: 건강한
02 '누군가가 특정한 상황에서 해야 하는 것에 대한 의견이나 제안'을 나타내는 말은 advice(조언, 충고)이다.
03 catch: 잡다
04 주어진 문장에서 shape은 '체형, 몸매'를 가리킨다. 이와 같은 의미로 쓰인 것은 ②번이다. ①, ③: (어떤) 모양으로 만들다[빚다], ④, ⑤: 모양, 형태
05 out of breath 숨이 가쁜, get rid of 제거하다, 없애다, be tired of ~에 싫증이 나다
06 weapon: 무기, empty: 텅 빈, expensive: 비싼
07 shape: 모양, catch: 잡다, diligent: 부지런한, scissors: 가위, screen: 화면

서술형 시험대비 p.61

01 empty
02 (1) used to (2) be in good shape (3) out of breath
  (4) Make sure (5) get rid of
03 (1) panting (2) pretended (3) regularly
04 (1) The cookies are so hard that I cannot chew them.
  (2) Tigers and lions have sharp claws.
  (3) I can't concentrate during the class.
  (4) It is not easy to get rid of a bad habit.
05 (1) I don't know how to open this bottle.
  (2) I'm on a diet to lose weight.
  (3) Make sure you should not put off.
  (4) I hate these vegetables because they taste bitter.

01 주어진 관계는 반의어 관계를 나타낸다. empty: 텅 빈, full: 가득 찬
02 make sure: 반드시 ~하다, out of breath: 숨이 가쁜, be used to -ing: ~하는 데 익숙하다, get rid of: ~을 없애다, 제거하다 be in good shape: 건강하다, 몸매가 좋다
03 pant: 헐떡거리다, pretend: ~인 척하다, regularly: 규칙적으로
04 chew: 씹다, claw: (동물의) 발톱, concentrate: 집중하다 get rid of: ~을 제거하다, 없애다
05 bottle: 병, put off: 미루다, be on a diet: 다이어트 중이다, bitter: (맛이) 쓴

Conversation

핵심 Check p.62~63

1 (1) don't know how to choose / Why don't you
  (2) good / You'd better
2 (1) sight, easy / Make sure (2) You should

교과서 대화문 익히기

Check(√) True or False p.64

1 T 2 F 3 T 4 T

교과서 확인학습 p.66~67

Everyday English 1 A. Function Practice (1)

1. Call, mine / ring, know how to / Don't worry, help, find it
2. looking for, take it / Here, Take, care / how to care / water, enough light

Everyday English 1 B. Listening Activity

have a word, take long / course / concentrating, falling asleep / sorry / the matter / fall asleep easily, tried / failed, how to get / should try, early, try doing

Everyday English 2 A. Function Practice

1. hurt / cross your legs / poor posture / Make sure, you sit
2. shaking, okay / energy drink, drank, today's test / too much, Make sure / I won't

Everyday English 2 B. Listening Activity

eyes, important, more, more, glasses, dry, If, try to, rest, look outside, Make sure, computer, phone screens

In Real Life

rice / on a diet, health reasons / only eating rice, healthy / mean, certain amount, meat / needed, avoid / harmful / be on a good, too difficult / at least, beans, eggs, don't forget, vegetables

시험대비 기본평가 p.68

01 ⓒ → how 02 ⑤ 03 ② 04 ⑤

01 이어지는 대화에서 꽃을 관리하는 방법을 설명하고 있으므로 how가 적절하다.

03 이어지는 대화에서 주어진 문장에서 언급한 문제들을 막기 위한 방법이 제시되고 있으므로 (B)가 알맞다.

04 학생들이 컴퓨터나 휴대폰 화면을 본 후에 얼마나 오랫동안 휴식을 취해야 하는지는 알 수 없다.

시험대비 실력평가 p.69~70

01 나와 잠시 이야기를 할 수 있을까? 02 ④
03 ⑤ 04 I don't know how to find my phone.
05 ③ 06 ⑤ 07 ⑤
08 because of → because
09 It's because she always crosses her legs.
10 ⑤ 11 ⑤ 12 ④

02 (A) 뒤에 명사가 이어지므로 전치사 during, (B)는 동사의 병렬 구조이므로 failed, (C)는 잠을 잘 잘 수 있는 방법을 가리키므로 how가 적절하다.

03 김 선생님은 민재에게 규칙적으로 잠자리에 들 것을 권하였다.

05 소녀는 전화기를 찾을 수 없어 걱정하고 있음을 알 수 있다.

06 ⓐ와 나머지 표현은 모두 '울리다'를 의미하지만 ⑤번은 '반지'를 뜻한다.

07 ⑤번을 제외한 나머지는 모두 다리를 꼬지 말 것을 충고하는 표현이다.

08 because 뒤에는 주어 동사를 동반한 절이 이어진다.

09 Brian에 따르면 Sue는 항상 다리를 꼬기 때문에 등과 다리에 통증이 있다.

10 나머지는 모두 많이 마시지 말 것을 충고하지만 ⑤번은 많이 마실 것을 권유하는 표현이다.

11 민수가 손이 떨리는 것은 에너지 드링크 때문이므로 공부를 못 하고 있는지는 알 수 없다.

12 왜 늦게까지 깨어 있었는지 묻는 질문에 또 늦으면 안 된다는 대

답은 어색하다.

서술형 시험대비 p.71

01 It's because he couldn't fall asleep easily.
02 She advised him to go to bed regularly, not early.
03 (A) concentrate (B) fell asleep (C) I couldn't fall asleep (D) how to get a good night's sleep (E) trying to go to bed regularly
04 It's because he drank three cans of energy drink for today's test.
05 She advises him not to drink the energy drink that much next time.
06 (C) → (B) → (D) → (A)

01 민재는 쉽게 잠들 수 없었기 때문에 수업에 집중할 수 없었다.

02 김 선생님은 민재에게 일찍이 아니라 규칙적으로 잠자리에 들도록 노력할 것을 충고하였다.

03 오늘 나는 김 선생님께 미안함을 느꼈다. 나는 그녀의 수업에 집중할 수 없었고 수업 중에 잠이 들었다. 그녀는 내게 무엇이 문제인지 물어보셨다. 나는 왜 내가 그녀의 수업에 집중할 수 없었는지 설명했다. 이유는 내가 일찍 잠자리에 들려할지라도 쉽게 잠이 들 수 없었다는 것이다. 나는 내가 어떻게 잠을 잘 잘 수 있는지 모르기 때문에 혼란스러웠다. 그 때, 그녀는 일찍 자려는 것이 아니라 규칙적으로 잠자리에 들도록 노력할 것을 추천하셨다. 나는 내가 오늘밤에는 쉽게 잠을 잘 수 있기를 바란다.

04 민수는 오늘 시험을 위해 에너지 음료 3캔을 마셨기 때문에 손을 떨고 있다.

05 수지는 민수에게 다음에는 그토록 많은 에너지 음료를 마시지 말 것을 조언한다.

06 (C) 전화기를 보았는지 질문 → (B) 대답 및 찾을 방법 설명 → (D) 대답 및 문제 해결 못함을 설명 → (A) 안심시키기

교과서
Grammar

핵심 Check p.72~73

1 (1) too tired to talk / so tired that he can't talk
  (2) easy enough, to / easy that we
2 (1) didn't have to, would be / have to, won't be
  (2) had, could buy / don't have, can't buy

01 (1) saving → save   (2) too → so   (3) can → could

    (4) go → went

02 (1) had   (2) made   (3) arrived   (4) were[was]

    (5) took

03 (1) Kevin is so lazy that he can't exercise

    regularly.

    (2) The room is so big that it can hold twenty

    people.

    (3) Molly is so lazy that she can't take the job.

    (4) This ladder is so long that it can reach there.

    (5) The machine is so old that I can't operate it

    well.

01 (1), (2) too ~ to V로 '너무 ~해서 V할 수 없는'이란 의미를 나타내며, 이는 'so ~ that 주어 can't 동사원형'으로 쓸 수 있다. (3), (4) 가정법과거는 현재 사실과 반대되는 상황을 가정하는 것으로 'If 주어 were[과거 동사] ~, 주어 would[should/could/might] 동사원형'으로 나타낼 수 있다.

02 가정법과거는 현재 사실과 반대되는 가정을 할 때 쓰이며 'If+주어+과거동사, 주어+조동사의 과거+동사원형'의 형태로 쓰인다. (4) be동사는 가정법과거에서 인칭에 관계없이 were을 쓰지만 주어가 1, 3인칭 단수일 때는 was를 쓰기도 한다.

03 '~하기에 너무 …한'이란 의미로 쓰이는 'too ~ to V'는 'so ~ that 주어 can't 동사원형'과 같고, '~하기에 충분히 …한'이란 의미로 쓰이는 '~enough to V'는 'so ~ that 주어 can 동사원형'으로 쓰일 수 있다.

01 ③   02 ③   03 ⑤

04 If I remembered her phone number, I could call her.

05 ②, ④   06 ④   07 ④

08 He was so upset that he couldn't think clearly.

09 ③   10 ④   11 ③   12 ④

13 ④

14 As I don't travel more often, I can't tell you many

    interesting things.

15 ④   16 ③

17 too bright to go to bed

18 You look so tired that you can't work with us right

    now.

19 ⑤

20 were you, I would ask your parents for some help

21 ③   22 If you helped me, I would help you.

23 It's too cold to go outside.

01 '~할 만큼 충분히 …한'이란 의미의 'so ~ that 주어 can 동사원형'은 '~ enough to V'와 같다.

02 현재 돈이 많지 않기 때문에 집을 살 수 없다고 하였으므로 가정법 과거를 사용하여 '내가 돈이 많다면 집을 살 수 있을 텐데.'라는 문장을 완성할 수 있다.

03 '너를 데리러 가기에 충분히 운전을 잘한다.'는 의미가 들어가는 것이 적절하다.

04 현재와 반대되는 상황을 가정하고 있으므로 가정법과거를 써서 나타낼 수 있다.

05 '~할 만큼 충분히 …한'이란 의미의 'so ~ that 주어 can 동사원형'은 '~ enough to V'와 같다.

06 너무 피곤해서 산을 오를 수 없는 것이 유감이라고 하였으므로 '내가 피곤하지 않다면 산을 오를 텐데.'라는 가정법과거 문장이 적절하다.

07 가정법 과거를 나타내는 문장이므로 I would study라고 쓰는 것이 적절하다.

08 '너무 ~해서 …할 수 없는'이란 의미로 쓰이는 too ~ to V는 'so ~ that 주어 can't와 같다 주절의 시제가 과거이므로 couldn't를 쓰는 것에 유의한다.

09 'too ~ to V'는 '너무 ~해서 …할 수 없는'이라는 의미이다.

10 현재와 반대되는 가정을 하고 있으므로 가정법과거를 쓰는 것이 적절하며, 가정법 과거는 'If+주어+were[과거 동사], 주어 would[could/might/should]+동사원형'으로 표현한다.

11 소파를 옮기기에 너무 약해서 소파를 옮길 수 없다는 의미를 완성하는 것이 적절하다.

12 현재 아프지 않기 때문에 의사에게 진찰을 받으러 가지 않을 것이라는 의미이므로 '내가 아프다면, 의사에게 진찰을 받으러 갈 텐데.'라는 의미의 ④번이 적절하다.

13 그는 너무 친절해서 '싫어'라는 말을 할 수 없다.는 의미이므로 'too ~ to V'를 써서 나타내는 것이 적절하다.

14 가정법과거 문장을 사용하여 현재 여행을 더 자주 할 수 없기 때문에 너에게 많은 흥미로운 이야기를 해 줄 수 없다는 말을 하고 있다.

15 주어진 문장을 영어로 쓰면 'These roses are beautiful enough to attract many people.'이다.

16 가까이 산다면 더 자주 볼 수 있을 것이라는 가정법 과거 문장이 쓰이는 것이 적절하다. 가정법과거는 'If+주어+과거동사, 주어+would(could/should/might)+동사원형'으로 쓴다.

17 '너무 ~해서 …할 수 없는'은 'too ~ to V'로 표현할 수 있다.

18 '너무 ~해서 …할 수 없는'이란 의미로 쓰이는 'too ~ to V'는 'so ~ that 주어 can't'와 같다.

19 가정법 과거 문장이므로 could를 쓰는 것이 적절하다.

20 '내가 너라면 너의 부모님에게 도움을 요청할 텐데.'라는 말을 쓸 수 있다.

21 ① too hot to drink ② too lazy to do ④ would feel

happy ⑤ not to tell

22 '네가 나를 돕지 않기 때문에 나도 너를 돕지 않겠다'고 말하고 있다. 따라서 '네가 나를 돕는다면, 나도 너를 도울 텐데.'라는 가정법 과거 문장을 쓸 수 있다.

22 '너무 ~해서 …할 수 없는'은 'too ~ to V'으로 표현할 수 있다.

서술형 시험대비
p.78~79

01 As I don't have a car, I can't go there to see you.

02 (1) famous enough to
   (2) too shy to
   (3) too dark to

03 had nice shoes, go to the party

04 (1) He is rich enough to buy an expensive car.
   (2) He is so rich that he can an expensive car.

05 If I lived alone, I wouldn't clean my room.

06 honest enough to / so honest that he can

07 The girl's feet are so small that she can't wear the shoes.

08 If the little mermaid had two legs, she could go and meet the prince.

09 (1) If I knew your e-mail address, I could send you an e-mail.
   (2) As I am busy, I won't help you.
   (3) If the socks were not too expensive, I would buy them.
   (4) As we are not close friends, I will not tell you the secret.
   (5) If they didn't visit the museum, I would not follow them.

10 too big[large] to wear

11 We are so young that we can't drive.

12 If Jane liked him, she would invite him.

13 too big to ride

14 arrived at the station, could catch

15 It is too high to reach. It will be too sour to eat.

01 현재 차가 없기 때문에 너를 보러 그곳에 갈 수 없다는 의미이다.

02 (1) 그녀는 많은 사람들이 알아볼 만큼 충분히 유명해. (2) James는 많은 사람들 앞에서 이야기하기엔 너무 수줍어. (3) 너무 어두워서 책을 읽을 수 없어. 불 좀 켜 줄래?

03 멋진 신발이 없어서 파티를 갈 수 없는 상황이므로 이에 반대되는 가정은 가정법과거를 써서 할 수 있다. would를 대신하여 could를 써도 좋다.

04 '~할 만큼 충분히 …한'은 '… enough to V' 혹은 'so ... that 주어 can 동사원형'으로 나타낼 수 있다.

05 이어지는 문장으로 보아 '내가 혼자 산다면, 내 방을 청소하지 않을 텐데.'라는 의미의 말을 했음을 알 수 있다.

06 '~할 만큼 충분히 …한'은 '... enough to V' 혹은 'so ... that 주어 can 동사원형'으로 나타낼 수 있다.

07 소녀의 발이 너무 작아서 신발을 신을 수 없다고 하였으므로 '너무 ~해서 …할 수 없는'이라는 의미의 'so ~ that 주어 can't 동사원형'으로 표현할 수 있다.

08 두 다리가 없어서 왕자님을 만나러 가지 못한다고 하였으므로 '두 다리가 있다면, 왕자님을 만나러 갈 수 있을 텐데.'라는 문장으로 쓸 수 있다.

09 가정법과거는 현재 사실과 반대되는 것을 가정하는 것이다. (1) 내가 너의 이메일 주소를 안다면, 나는 너에게 이메일을 보낼 수 있을 텐데. (2) 내가 바쁘지 않다면, 나는 너를 도울 텐데. (3) 그 양말이 너무 비싸지 않다면, 나는 그것을 살 텐데. (4) 우리가 가까운 친구라면, 나는 너에게 그 비밀을 말할 텐데. (5) 그들이 박물관을 방문하지 않으면, 나는 그들을 따라가지 않을 텐데.

10 옷이 너무 커서 입을 수 없어서 더 작은 사이즈가 있는지를 물었다고 볼 수 있다.

11 '너무 ~해서 …할 수 없는'은 'too ~ to V'로 표현할 수 있으며, 이는 'so ~ that 주어 can't 동사원형'과 같다.

12 Jane은 David를 좋아하지 않아서 파티에 초대하지 않았다. '만약 그녀가 David를 좋아한다면 파티에 초대할 것이다'라는 가정법과거 문장으로 바꿔 쓴다.

13 열 살인 자신이 일곱 살들을 위한 자전거를 타기에는 덩치가 너무 크다는 말이 들어가는 것이 적절하다.

14 arrive: 도착하다

15 '너무 ~해서 …할 수 없는'은 'too ~ to V'를 써서 나타낼 수 있다.

교과서
Reading

확인문제
p.80

1 T 2 T 3 T 4 F 5 F

확인문제
p.81

1 T 2 T 3 T 4 F 5 T 6 F

교과서 확인학습 A
p.82~83

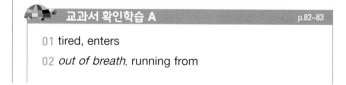

01 tired, enters

02 *out of breath*, running from

03 too old to, were, would be, *for*, have an idea

04 *gets, from*   05 enters, catches

06 *pretends to*, too smelly for you, Instead, *gives, to*

07 *tastes it, bigger*, more

08 let, go, bring

09 *house, fat, a few, watching*

10 *worried*, be careful, bitter

11 mean by that

12 yourself, too fat to run, too weak to chew

13 Why, run, chew, I need, without

14 *goes out*   15 *emptied, enters*

16 has worked

17 *angry*, empty, where you get

18 who makes, scared of, them

19 Okay

20 *hands, Cat cuts his*   21 take, to

22 *laughs at*, stupid

23 were fast, had, I'd listen to, them

24 have lost   25 what you say, *away*

26 *to run after*, fat to run

1 *An old and tired mouse enters.*

2 Mouse: (*He is out of breath.*) I'm tired of running from Cat.

3 I am too old to run. If I were free, I would be so happy. (*He thinks for a while.*) Oh, I have an idea!

4 *Mouse goes and gets something from the back of the stage.*

5 Cat enters and catches Mouse.

6 Mouse: (*He pretends to beg.*) I'm too smelly for you to eat! Instead, have this, please.
   (*He gives a box of sugar to Cat.*)

7 Cat: (*He tastes it. His eyes get bigger.*) What is it? Give me more!

8 Mouse: It's sugar. If you let me go, I'll bring you some every day.

9 *It is at Cat's house. Cat, now fat, is eating sugar. He has only a few teeth. Dog is watching him.*

10 Dog: (*He is worried.*) Cat, my friend, be careful. The sugar will get bitter.

11 Cat: What do you mean by that?

12 Dog: Look at yourself! You are too fat to run, and your teeth are too weak to chew!

13 Cat: (*He eats more.*) Why should I run or chew? Sugar is the only thing I need. I can't live without it.

14 *Dog goes out sadly.*

15 *Cat has almost emptied the box of sugar. Mouse enters.*

16 Mouse: (*He smiles.*) I think my plan has worked.

17 Cat: (*He is angry.*) It's almost empty! Mouse, tell me where you get it.

18 Mouse: I have a friend who makes sugar. But he's scared of your claws. If you get rid of them, you can meet him soon.

19 Cat: Okay!

20 *Mouse hands Cat a pair of scissors and Cat cuts his claws.*

21 Cat: I'm ready! Now take me to your friend!

22 Mouse: (*He laughs at Cat.*) You stupid cat!

23 If you were fast, and had your sharp teeth and claws, I'd listen to you. But you no longer have them now!

24 You have lost your biggest weapons!

25 Why should I listen to what you say now? (*He runs away.*)

26 Cat: What! (*He tries to run after Mouse, but fails.*) Oh! I'm too fat to run after him!

01 ②   02 ④

03 He looks old and tired.   04 ③   05 ③

06 were no sugar   07 ②   08 ③

09 Because he wants more sugar.

10 get rid of his claws   11 (B)–(C)–(A)

12 If I were[was] free, I would be happy.

13 ③

14 It's because he is too old.

15 ④   16 ⑤   17 ⑤   18 ③

19 ③   20 ⑤

21 He or she is not diligent and puts things off.

22 ③   23 ⑤

01 위 글은 희곡이다.

02 쥐는 고양이에게 설탕 상자를 주었고 고양이는 이것을 맛보고는 더 달라고 하였으므로 ④번이 정답이다.

03 그는 늙고 피곤한 쥐라고 하였다.

04 설탕을 먹는 고양이가 뚱뚱해져서 달릴 수도 없을 지경이 되었음에도 계속해서 설탕을 먹고 있으므로 주의를 주는 말이 들어가는 것이 적절하다.

05 고양이는 지금 달릴 수 없을 만큼 뚱뚱하다고 하였다.

06 '설탕이 없다면, 나는 살 수 없을 텐데.'라는 말이다. 현재 사실에 반대되는 가정을 하는 가정법과거를 써서 나타낼 수 있다.

07 내용으로 미루어 보아 설탕을 어디에서 가지고 오는지 말해 달라는 것이 가장 적절하다.

08 고양이가 가위를 가지고 온 것이 아니라, 쥐가 고양이에게 가위를 건넨 것이다.

09 고양이는 더 많은 설탕을 먹고 싶으므로 쥐의 친구를 만나기를 원한다.

10 쥐는 고양이가 자기의 발톱을 자르기를 원한다.

11 (B) 커피 우유와 에너지 음료가 처음에는 집중하는 데 도움을 주는 것처럼 보였지만 시간이 지날수록 의존도가 높아지자 - (C) 주변에서 걱정을 하며 사과를 먹거나 녹차를 마실 것을 권함 - (A) 이러한 것들이 도움이 되긴 했지만 커피 우유나 에너지 음료만큼은 아니라고 생각함.

12 가정법과거는 현재 사실과 반대되는 가정을 할 때 쓰인다. 따라서 '내가 만약 자유로워진다면, 나는 행복할 텐데.'라는 문장으로 쓸 수 있다.

13 빈칸 (A)에는 to부정사의 의미상의 주어인 'for+목적격'이 쓰인다. 따라서 전치사 for를 쓰는 것이 적절하다.

14 쥐는 너무 나이가 들어서 달릴 수 없다고 하였다.

15 이빨이 너무 약해서 씹을 수 없다는 것이 적절하다.

16 글의 내용에 따르면 개와 고양이는 서로 친구이다.

17 laugh at: ~을 비웃다 ① be interested in: ~에 흥미가 있다 ② take care of: ~을 돌보다 ③ look up to: ~을 존경하다 ④ care about: ~에 마음을 쓰다 ⑤ be surprised at: ~에 놀라다

18 ③번 다음 문장의 대명사 them이 가리키는 것은 your claws이다.

19 고양이가 후회하고 있다는 것을 알 수 있다.

20 쥐의 친구가 어디에 사는지는 알 수 없다.

21 필자의 문제는 부지런하지 못하고 일들을 미루는 것이다.

22 밑줄 친 (A)는 things를 수식하는 형용사로 쓰인 to부정사이다. ① 진주어 ② 부사적 용법 중 목적 ③ idea를 수식하는 형용사적 용법 ④ 부사적 용법 중 감정의 원인 ⑤ 목적어

23 글쓴이는 30분 일찍 일어날 것이라고 하였다.

서술형 시험대비   p.90~91

01 He gave a box of sugar to Cat.

02 I am so old that I can't run.

03 He promises to bring Cat sugar every day.

04 He feels worried.

05 careful, sugar, what

06 It's because he is too[so] fat.

07 sugar

08 fail

09 Cat's claws, a pair of scissors

10 I think my plan has worked.

11 **빨리 달리는 것, 뾰족한 이빨과 발톱**

12 He was in the brown bottle.

13 Because the place was so good that he couldn't leave it.

01 쥐가 고양이에게 준 것은 설탕 상자이다.

02 '너무 ~해서 …할 수 없다'는 의미의 'too ~ to V'는 'so ~ that 주어 can't 동사원형'과 같다.

03 쥐는 고양이에게 매일 설탕을 갖다 주겠다고 약속한다.

04 고양이 친구를 만난 개는 고양이를 걱정하였다.

05 개는 고양이에게 그가 너무 많은 설탕을 먹지 않도록 주의하라고 했다. 하지만 고양이는 개가 말하는 것을 듣지 않았다.

06 고양이가 달릴 수 없는 이유는 너무 뚱뚱해서이다.

07 설탕을 가리키는 대명사이다.

08 만약 당신이 하려고 애쓰던 어떤 것을 실패하게 된다면, 당신은 그것을 할 수 없거나 혹은 그것을 성공하지 못한 것이다.

09 쥐가 말한 것에 따르면, 그의 친구는 고양이의 발톱을 두려워한다. 그래서 쥐는 고양이에게 가위를 가져다주었다.

10 work: 효과가 있다

11 만약 고양이가 빠르고 뾰족한 이빨과 발톱을 가지고 있다면 쥐는 고양이의 말을 들었을 것이라고 말하며 이 큰 무기들을 잃었다고 하였다.

12 봄이 왔을 때도 Bob은 여전히 갈색 병 안에 있었다고 하였다.

13 병 속이 너무 좋아서 그곳을 떠날 수 없었다고 하였다.

영역별 핵심문제   p.93~97

01 diligent   02 ①   03 ①

04 (1) running after   (2) running away   (3) as well

05 (1) stupid   (2) weak   (3) harmful   (4) meat   (5) rest

06 ①   07 ①

08 (1) I'm tired of studying every day.

   (2) He is no longer living here. / He is not living here any longer.

09 ②   10 ⓔ → to eat   11 ⑤

12 Make sure you don't cross your legs

13 ⑤   14 (E) → (B) → (A) → (D) → (C)

15 ③   16 ④

17 It is too late to play a computer game.

18 ③

19 (1) Your room is too messy for us to use.

   (2) Your room is so messy that we can't use it.

20 If I were[was] not too anxious, I could watch the

game.

21 ④ 　　　　22 ③ 　　　　23 ②

24 If I went to bed early, I would get up early in the morning.

25 can't swim, will take swimming lessons

26 wise enough to make

27 ② 　　　28 ③ 　　　29 ④ 　　　30 ②

31 What do you mean by that? 　　　32 ④

33 funny videos on the Internet

34 He stays up late at night to watch videos.

---

01 주어진 관계는 반의어 관계를 나타낸다. diligent: 부지런한, lazy: 게으른

02 '길고 가는 몸과 보통 밝은 색의 4개의 큰 날개를 가진 나는 곤충'을 나타내는 말은 butterfly(나비)이다.

03 salty: 짠

04 run after: 쫓다, run away: 달아나다 as well: 또한

05 harmful: 해로운, meat: 고기, weak: 약한, stupid: 어리석은, rest: 휴식을 취하다

06 주어진 문장에서 fat은 '뚱뚱한'을 가리키며 이와 같은 의미를 나타내는 것은 ①번이다. 나머지는 모두 '지방'을 가리킨다.

07 take a rest: 휴식을 취하다, rest: 휴식, 나머지

08 no longer= not ~any longer 더 이상 ~ 아니다

09 빈칸 (A)에 이어지는 말에서 상대방의 의견에 대한 반대 의견을 나타내고 있으므로 ②번이 적절하다.

10 forget to ~할 것을 잊다, forget ~ing: ~한 것을 잊다

11 Olivia는 Junho에게 최소한 콩이나 계란을 먹고 채소도 먹을 것을 조언하였다.

13 Brian은 Sue가 다리를 꼬는 좋지 않은 자세를 갖고 있다는 것을 지적하였다.

14 (E) 죄송함 표현 → (B) 문제가 무엇인지 질문 → (A) 문제 설명 → (D) 조언 → (C) 반응

15 가정법과거이므로 조동사의 과거형을 쓰는 것이 적절하다.

16 가정법과거가 쓰이는 것이 옳으므로 (A)는 went, that절이 이어지고 있으므로 (B)는 so tall, 가정법과거이므로 (C)는 could가 적절하다.

17 '너무 ~해서 …할 수 없는'은 'too ~ to V'로 나타낼 수 있다.

18 영화가 보기에 너무 무섭다는 의미가 적절하므로 too scary to watch를 쓰는 것이 자연스럽다.

19 방이 너무 지저분해서 우리가 사용할 수 없다는 하나의 문장으로 만들 수 있다.

20 '내가 너무 초조하지 않다면, 나는 그 게임을 볼 수 있을 텐데.'라는 문장으로 쓸 수 있다. 가정법과거는 'If+주어+과거동사, 주어+조동사의 과거+동사원형'이다.

21 현재 15세 미만이라면 혼자 나갈 수 없다는 의미이므로, 가정법과거를 사용하여 '15세 미만이 아니라면, 혼자 나갈 수 있다'는

22 '너무 ~해서 …할 수 없는'이라는 의미의 'too ~ to V'는 'so ~ that 주어 can't 동사원형'과 같다.

23 코트를 사고 싶지만 충분한 돈이 없는 현재 상황을 말하고 있으므로, 가정법 과거를 사용하여 '내게 충분한 돈이 있다면, 나는 코트를 하나 살 텐데.'라는 문장으로 쓸 수 있다.

24 현재 상황과 반대하여 가정하고 있으므로 가정법과거를 써서 문장을 완성하는 것이 적절하다.

25 '내가 수영을 할 수 있다면, 나는 수영 수업을 듣지 않을 텐데.'라는 의미이므로 '내가 수영을 할 수 없기 때문에 나는 수영 수업을 들을 것이다.'는 말로 쓸 수 있다.

26 '~할 만큼 충분히 …한'은 '… enough to V'로 표현할 수 있다.

27 고양이에게 더 이상 쫓기지 않고 행복하기를 원하던 쥐가 좋은 생각이 났다고 하였으므로 이어질 내용으로는 ②번이 가장 적절하다. trick: 계략

28 out of breath: 숨이 찬

29 개의 말로 미루어 보아 개는 고양이를 걱정하고 있음을 알 수 있다.

30 (A) 고양이가 쥐를 잡았기 때문에 이어지는 글에서 쥐가 비는 척하였다. (B) 설탕을 먹은 고양이는 더 달라고 했기 때문에 쥐가 자신을 놓아주면 매일 설탕을 가져다주겠다고 하였으며, (C) 설탕을 계속 먹은 고양이는 뚱뚱해졌다.

31 mean: ~을 의미하다

32 고양이가 매일 얼마만큼의 설탕을 먹었는지는 알 수 없다.

33 인터넷에 있는 재미있는 동영상을 가리키는 말이다.

34 Tom이 늦게까지 깨어 있는 이유는 동영상을 보기 위해서이다.

단원별 예상문제 　　　　　　　p.98~101

01 ① 　　　　02 ⓒ → failed 　　　　03 ⑤

04 He wants to talk about students' eyes.

05 They have eye problems.

06 They should try to take some time to rest their eyes.

07 don't you? 　　　　08 ③ 　　　　09 ⑤

10 ④ 　　　11 ③ 　　　12 ④ 　　　13 ③

14 ⑤

15 The table was so heavy that she could not move it.

16 If I danced well, I could win the school dance contest.

17 As he is not with us, he won't tell many interesting stories.

18 ④ 　　　19 ③ 　　　20 ④

21 As you are not fast, and don't have your sharp teeth and claws, I will not listen to you.

22 ② 　　　　23 ⓐ were[was] ⓑ would enjoy

01 have a word with: ~와 잠깐 이야기하다

02 tried와 병렬 관계로 과거 시제로 쓰여야 하므로 failed가 알맞다.

03 김 선생님이 무슨 과목을 가르치는지는 알 수 없다.

04 Mr. Kim은 학생들의 눈에 관에 이야기하고 싶어 한다.

05 점점 더 많은 학생들이 안구 문제를 갖고 있다.

06 학생들은 눈을 보호하기 위해 눈이 쉴 시간을 갖기 위해 노력해야 한다.

07 부가의문문으로 앞 문장이 긍정문이며 일반동사가 나오므로 do 동사를 이용하여 부가의문문을 만든다.

08 (B) 너무 많은 고기를 먹는 것은 해롭다는 의미가 되어야 하므로 harmful, (C) 준호는 건강한 다이어트 하는 법을 모르겠다고 하였으므로 이는 어렵다는 difficult가 자연스럽다. (D) 잊지 말 것을 당부하고 있으므로 forget이 적절하다.

09 (A)와 나머지 표현들은 모두 주제를 소개하는 표현이다.

10 안구 건조와 같은 문제를 겪지 않기 위해 눈이 쉴 수 있는 시간을 갖도록 해야 한다.

11 위 글을 영어로 옮기면, 'If I had many pencils, I would draw many things.'이다.

12 '너무 ~해서 …할 수 없는'이라는 의미의 'too ~ to V'는 'so ~ that 주어 can't 동사원형'과 같다.

13 현재 바쁘다는 문장이 이어지므로, 가정법과거를 써서 '내게 한 주의 휴가가 주어진다면, 나는 일본으로 여행을 갈 텐데.'라는 문장을 쓸 수 있다.

14 주절의 시제가 과거이므로 couldn't walk라고 쓰는 것이 적절하다.

15 탁자가 너무 무거워서 그녀는 그것을 옮길 수 없었다는 말로 쓸 수 있다.

16 가정법과거는 현재 사실과 반대되는 것을 가정할 때 쓴다. 따라서 현재 내가 춤을 잘 추지 못하므로 '내가 춤을 잘 춘다면'이라는 가정으로 문장을 만들 수 있다.

17 가정법과거는 현재 사실을 반대하여 가정하는 것이므로 직설법으로 전환할 때 현재 시제를 쓰는 것에 유의한다.

18 쥐의 대사로 보아 고양이를 비웃는 것을 알 수 있다.

19 설탕을 너무 많이 먹은 고양이는 결국 너무 뚱뚱해져서 쥐를 쫓아가지 못한 것을 유추할 수 있다.

20 설탕을 만드는 친구이다.

21 가정법과거이므로 현재와 반대되는 사실을 가정하는 것이다.

22 설탕을 거의 다 먹은 고양이는 쥐가 어디에서 설탕을 구하는지 말해달라고 하였다.

23 가정법과거 문장으로, 현재 Bob가 나비가 되지 못한 사실을 반대로 가정한 것이다. 가정법과거는 'If+주어+과거동사, 주어+조동사의 과거형+동사원형'으로 표현할 수 있다.

24 [D] 어느 날 Bob는 갈색 병을 발견함 - [B] 그곳에서 며칠 동안 머물자 친구들이 나오라고 함 - [A] Bob는 친구들의 말을 듣지 않고 병 안에 머묾 - [C] 봄이 되자 친구들은 따뜻한 공기 안에서 여기저기 날아다녔지만 Bob만이 갈색 병 안에 남아 있음

25 Bob이 병 안에 머물면서 무엇을 먹었는지는 알 수 없다.

서술형 실전문제 p.102~103

01 The problem is that he is eating only rice.

02 It's because people said that he needed to avoid meat.

03 Her advice is to have at least some beans or eggs and not to forget to eat some vegetables too.

04 The problems were too difficult to be solved in one day.

05 (1) As today is not Friday, school will not be over earlier.

(2) If today were Friday, school would be over earlier.

06 If I were[was] not embarrassed, I could go out.

07 If I watered it enough,

08 It is so weak that it can't grow tall.

09 It's because he ate too much sugar.

10 run or chew

11 ⓔ → earlier

12 From now on

13 smelly that Cat couldn't eat him, a box of sugar

01 준호의 식단의 문제는 오직 밥만 먹는다는 것이다.

02 사람들이 그가 고기를 피해야 할 필요가 있다고 이야기했기 때문이다.

03 그녀의 조언은 최소한의 콩이나 계란을 먹고 약간의 채소를 먹는 것도 또한 잊지 않는 것이다.

04 '너무 ~해서 …할 수 없는'이라는 의미의 'so ~ that 주어 can't 동사원형'은 'too ~ to V'과 같다.

05 오늘이 '금요일이라면'이라는 말로 가정하고 있으므로 가정법과거를 써서 나타낼 수 있다. 직설법으로 쓸 경우 '오늘은 금요일이 아니기 때문에 수업이 더 일찍 끝나지 않을 것이다'라는 말로 쓸 수 있다.

06 '나는 너무 창피해서 나갈 수 없다'는 문장인데 현재의 반대 상황을 가정법과거를 활용하여 '내가 창피하지 않다면, 나갈 수 있을 텐데.'라는 말로 쓸 수 있다.

07 '충분히 물을 주면 더 크게 자랄 텐데'라는 말로 쓰는 것이 적절하다.

08 '너무 ~해서 …할 수 없는'이라는 의미는 'so ~ that 주어 can't 동사원형'으로 쓸 수 있다.

09 고양이는 개의 조언에도 불구하고 자신에게 필요한 것은 설탕 한 가지라고 말하며 그것이 없이는 살 수 없다고 하였다. 따라서 고양이가 뚱뚱해진 이유는 설탕을 너무 많이 먹어서라고 유추할 수 있다.

10 고양이는 자신이 달리거나 씹을 이유가 없다고 하였으므로 '자신이 뛰거나 씹을 수 없는 것에 개의치 않았다'라고 말할 수 있다.

11 부지런한 학생이 되기 위해서 30분 더 일찍 일어나겠다는 것이 적절하다.

12 from now on: 지금부터

13 쥐가 고양이에게 잡혔을 때, 쥐는 자신이 너무 냄새가 나서 고양이가 자신을 먹을 수 없다고 말하였다. 그리고 고양이에게 설탕 상자를 건넸다.

창의사고력 서술형 문제   p.104

|모범답안|

01 (A) rice (B) on a diet (C) a certain amount of meat (D) meat (E) eating too much meat (F) beans or eggs (G) vegetables

02 (1) had her own room
   (2) came to see me
   (3) were[was] thirsty

03 I don't clean my room, I can't easily find where I put my things, will clean my room once a week.

01 Olivia는 준호가 또 오직 밥만 먹고 있는 것을 본다. 그는 건강상의 이유로 다이어트 중이다. Olivia는 그것이 건강하지 않을 것이라고 생각한다, 왜냐하면 그의 몸은 특정한 양의 고기를 필요로 하기 때문이다. 그러나 준호는 그가 고기를 피해야 할 필요가 있다고 들었다. Olivia는 그것이 옳지 않다고 말한다. 그녀는 너무 많은 고기를 먹는 것은 해로울 것이라고 말한다. 준호는 어떻게 올바른 다이어트를 하는지 모른다. 이것은 그에게 매우 어렵다. Olivia의 조언은 약간의 콩이나 계란 또한 먹는 것이다. 그녀는 그가 또한 약간의 채소들을 먹어야 하는 것을 잊지 말아야 한다고 덧붙였다.

단원별 모의고사   p.105~108

01 ②   02 ③   03 ②

04 (1) What diet do you recommend for me?
   (2) Cut the paper with the scissors.

05 (D) → (A) → (B) → (C)

06 Make sure you have at least some beans or eggs.

07 ⑤   08 ④   09 ②   10 ④

11 (1) I can't fall asleep easily at night.

---

(2) The farmer planted beans on the field.
(3) Butterflies fly here and there in spring.

12 (B) → (D) → (A) → (C)

13 ②   14 ③

15 If the necklace were[was] not too expensive, I could buy it.

16 If I didn't have many things to do, I could watch the movie with you.

17 I am so forgetful that I can't remember what I have to do.

18 ④   19 ③   20 ③   21 what

22 run   23 ③   24 ④

25 becoming a butterfly

01 '삼키기에 더 쉽게 만들기 위해 입속에서 치아로 음식을 작은 조각으로 물어뜯다'를 가리키는 말은 chew(씹다)이다.

02 (A)는 안구 문제로써 눈이 건조함을 나타내야 하므로 dry, (B)는 잠시 바깥을 바라보아야 하므로 outside, (C)는 너무 오랫동안을 뜻하는 'long'이 적합하다.

04 recommend: 추천하다, scissors: 가위

05 (D) 물건 구매 결정 → (A) 물건 건네주기 → (B) 능력 부인하기 → (C) 꽃을 키우는 법 설명

07 오직 밥만 먹는 것의 좋은 효과가 무엇인지는 알 수 없다.

08 주어진 문장은 쉽게 잠이 들 수 없는 문제를 이야기하고 있으므로 무슨 문제가 있느냐고 묻는 대답으로 적절하다. 그러므로 (D)에 위치하는 것이 알맞다.

09 두 사람의 관계는 학생과 교사라는 것을 알 수 있다.

10 김 선생님은 민재에게 규칙적으로 잠자리에 들 것을 조언한다.

11 fall asleep: 잠들다, plant: 심다, bean: 콩, butterfly: 나비

12 (B) 문제 확인 및 괜찮은지 질문 → (D) 원인 설명 →(A) 충고하기 → (C) 반응

13 너무 빨리 달려서 우리는 그 차를 세울 수 없었다는 의미가 가장 적절하다.

14 가정법과거이므로 would be라고 쓰는 것이 적절하다.

15 목걸이가 너무 비싸서 살 수 없다고 하였으므로 '목걸이가 너무 비싸지 않다면, 나는 그것을 살 수 있을 텐데.'라는 말로 쓸 수 있다.

16 해석: 내게 할 일이 많이 없다면, 나는 너와 함께 영화를 볼 수 있을 텐데.

17 '너무 ~해서 …할 수 없는'이라는 의미의 'too ~ to V'는 'so ~ that 주어 can't 동사원형'과 같다.

18 배경은 고양이의 집이고, 고양이에게 이빨이 몇 개만 남아 있었다. 개는 고양이를 걱정하고 있지만 고양이는 개의 말을 귀담아 듣지 않았다.

19 개는 고양이에게 (A)와 같이 말하며 설탕을 지나치게 많이 먹는 것이 고양이에게 위험하다는 것을 말하고 싶어 한다.

20 be scared of: ~을 두려워하다 get rid of: ~을 제거하다

21 '당신이 지금 말하는 것'이란 의미이며 관계대명사 what이 적절하다.

22 run after: ~을 쫓다

23 쥐는 고양이를 친구에게 데려가지 않았다.

24 셀 수 있는 명사를 수식하는 것은 a few이다.

25 Bob의 친구들이 Bob에게 나오라고 한 이유는 나비가 될 준비를 하기 위해서이다.

교과서 파헤치기

Lesson **7**

단어 TEST Step 1   p.02

01 언어	02 (고개를) 숙이다, 인사하다
03 수도	04 파도; 손을 흔들다 05 예의, 예절
06 고개를 끄덕이다	07 나라, 국가, 시골 08 약속
09 추천하다	10 혼동하다
11 감사하는, 고마워하는	12 존중하다; 존중
13 약속하다; 약속	14 침착한; 진정시키다
15 자신감 있는	16 무례한, 예의 없는 17 무서운
18 마른, 얇은	19 차이, 다름 20 새기다, 조각하다
21 전통의	22 인사하다 23 손님, 하객
24 믿기 어려운	25 주인, 주최자 26 완벽한, 완전한
27 접시	28 옷, 의복 29 준비하다
30 시간을 지키는	31 속상한, 화난 32 의상
33 상	34 붙이다 35 무료로
36 ~을 제거하다, ~을 없애다	37 ~에 참가하다
38 변화를 일으키다	39 등록하다, 신청하다
40 ~하는 데 어려움을 겪다	41 정시에
42 ~을 요청하다, ~을 부탁하다	43 악수하다

단어 TEST Step 2   p.03

01 thin	02 recommend	03 bow
04 unbelievable	05 rude	06 calm
07 prepare	08 respect	09 advice
10 appointment	11 upset	12 stick
13 carve	14 greet	15 costume
16 traditional	17 country	18 difference
19 language	20 manner	21 clothing
22 nod	23 guest	24 host
25 punctual	26 complain	27 scary
28 promise	29 plate	30 confident
31 thankful	32 perfect	33 confuse
34 wave	35 for free	36 have trouble -ing
37 call upon	38 get rid of	39 sign up
40 take part in	41 make a difference	
42 shake hands	43 be interested in	

단어 TEST Step 3   p.04

1 punctual, 시간을 지키는   2 rude, 예의 없는
3 carve, 조각하다   4 advice, 조언, 충고   5 wave, 파도
6 bow, 고개를 숙이다   7 capital, 수도
8 complain, 불평하다   9 host, 주인, 주최자

10 respect, 존중   11 guest, 손님   12 prize, 상
13 recommend, 추천하다   14 traditional, 전통적인
15 appointment, 약속   16 shock, 충격

대화문 TEST Step 1   p.05~06

Everyday English 1 A. Function Practice

1. going camping with / heard, will rain / can't be true / on the news
2. heard that, science contest / interested in / sign up, prize, winner / Thanks for telling
3. will be / heard, carve pumpkins. What else / scary costumes, to get / sounds

Everyday English 1 B

do, have, time / what / I heard that, went to Spain / went to / more about your trip, thinking of visiting / to visit, many interesting places / recommend, go / recommend visiting, one of the most famous museums / Thanks for

Everyday English 2 A. Function Practice

1. like to, something about love / the most important, respect / agree with, Respecting, other's differences
2. Look at / tall, pretty / something about, at first / the most popular places, these days

Everyday English 2 B

travel writer, important lesson, while traveling, rude, age, found out, because of, culture, differently, older, need to, experience, learning, understanding other cultures

In Real Life

speaking / time to talk / up / social studies, cultural differences, having trouble finding, right information / like to tell, called, other cultures / sounds perfect, Thank, for / welcome, Good

대화문 TEST Step 2   p.07~08

Everyday English 1 A. Function Practice

1. G: I'm going camping with my family tomorrow!
   B: Hmm.... I heard that it will rain tomorrow.
   G: What? It can't be true.
   B: I'm sorry, but it was on the news.
2. G: I heard that there is a science contest next week.
   B: Really? I'm interested in science.
   G: Then you should sign up. There is a big prize for the winner.

B: Great! Thanks for telling me.

3. G: It will be Halloween soon!

B: I heard that people carve pumpkins on Halloween. What else do people do?

G: Children wear scary costumes and visit houses to get sweets.

B: That sounds interesting.

Everyday English 1 B

Mina: Alex, do you have some time?

Alex: Yes, Mina, what is it?

Mina: I heard that you went to Spain this summer!

Alex: Yes, I went on a family trip.

Mina: Can you tell me more about your trip? I'm thinking of visiting Spain this winter.

Alex: I see. I think Spain is a really nice country to visit. There are many interesting places.

Mina: Where do you recommend that I go?

Alex: I recommend visiting the Prado Museum in Madrid. It's one of the most famous museums in the world.

Mina: Thanks for the help!

Everyday English 2 A. Function Practice

1. G: I'd like to tell you something about love.

B: What is it?

G: I think the most important thing in love is respect.

B: I agree with you. Respecting each other's differences is very important.

2. B: Look at the Eiffel Tower.

G: It's really tall and pretty!

B: I'd like to tell you something about the Eiffel Tower. People didn't like it at first.

G: Really? But it has become one of the most popular places in Paris these days!

Everyday English 2 B

Tina: Hello, everyone. My name is Tina and I'm a travel writer. Today, I'd like to tell you an important lesson that I learned while traveling. When I first visited Korea, I thought Koreans were rude because many people asked me my age. However, I later found out that this was because of their culture. Koreans use language differently to people who are older than them, so they need to know the other person's age. This experience has taught me the importance of learning and understanding other cultures.

In Real Life

Suji: Hello, Suji speaking.

Diego: Hi, it's me, Diego. Do you have time to talk?

Suji: Yes, what's up?

Diego: I'm doing my social studies homework on cultural differences, but I'm trouble finding the right information.

Suji: I'd like to tell you about a website called "Culture Shock." I heard that people ask and answer questions about other cultures on that website.

Diego: That sounds perfect. Thank you for your help.

Suji: You're welcome. Good luck with the homework.

본문 TEST Step 1   p.09~10

01 Welcome to   02 interested, around, looking for

03 answer, may, other, take   04 very upset

05 There, new, from

06 be, with, shook   07 How rude

08 down, what, meant

09 countries, nodding, means, shaking

10 been invited, friend's

11 anything about

12 there, need to, advice

13 that, invited, leave, on

14 that, enough food

15 However, finish, has prepared

16 If, leave, that   17 anyone speak

18 minutes late, appointment with

19 finally met, looked, angry

20 that, keep, better, mean

21 means, appointment, German

22 that, to, on time

23 saying, set, kept

24 be punctual with

25 find, information, needed

26 what, have, helpful

27 Understanding, difference, life   28 visit, website

본문 TEST Step 2   p.11~12

01 Welcome to

02 are interested in, around, that, looking for

03 about other cultures, take a look

04 upset   05 There, from Greece

06 her to be friends, shook, head   07 rude

08 Calm down, sure what, meant was

09 countries like, nodding, means, shaking

10 Chinese, who has been invited to

11 anything about

12 there, manners I need to know, me some advice

13 heard that, are invited, leave, on, plate

14 that, enough food

15 However, finish, has prepared

16 If, leave, means that, didn't

17 anyone speak German

18 minutes late for, appointment with

19 When, finally met, looked, angry

20 that, must try to keep, does, mean

21 appointment, in German

22 that, to be on time   23 is set, be kept

24 be punctual with Germans

25 the information you needed

26 what you have, was

27 Understanding cultural differences, make a difference

28 visit our website

18 오늘, 저는 독일 친구와의 약속에 5분 늦었어요.

19 마침내 그를 만났을 때, 그는 매우 화가 나 보였어요.

20 그는 내가 "Termin"을 더 잘 지키도록 노력해야 한다고 말했어요. 그것은 무엇을 뜻하나요?

21 Smile: "Termin"은 독일어로 약속을 의미합니다.

22 독일인들은 제시간에 오는 것이 중요하다고 생각해요.

23 독일에서는 "정해진 것은 지켜져야 한다."는 말이 있어요.

24 그러니, 독일인들과 함께 할 때는 시간을 잘 지키세요.

25 당신에게 필요했던 정보를 찾았나요?

26 우리는 당신이 읽은 것이 도움이 되고 재미있기를 바랍니다.

27 문화 차이를 이해하는 것은 당신의 삶을 변화시킬 겁니다.

28 저희 웹 사이트를 또 방문해 주세요!

1 "Culture Shock"에 오신 것을 환영합니다!

2 만약 당신이 세계 각국의 문화에 관심이 있다면, 이곳이 바로 당신이 찾던 웹 사이트입니다.

3 당신은 다른 문화에 대해 가지고 있는 질문을 묻고 답할 수 있습니다. 함께 살펴봅시다!

4 Suji: 나는 굉장히 속상해요.

5 우리 학교에는 그리스에서 새로 온 학생이 있어요.

6 나는 그녀에게 나와 친구가 되자고 했지만, 그녀는 고개를 저었어요.

7 정말 무례해요!

8 Ocean: 진정해요. 나는 그녀가 진짜 의미했던 것은 "응"이었다고 확신해요.

9 그리스, 터키, 이란과 같은 몇몇 나라에서는 고개를 끄덕이는 것이 "싫다"는 의미이고 고개를 흔드는 것이 "좋다"를 의미해요.

10 Shao: 도와주세요! 나는 케냐인 친구 집에 초대된 중국 소년이에요.

11 하지만 저는 케냐에 대해서 아무것도 몰라요.

12 제가 알아야 할 예의가 있나요? 저에게 조언을 해 주세요!

13 Clever: 제가 알기로는, 중국 사람들이 누군가의 집에 초대되었을 때, 접시에 음식을 남긴다고 들었어요.

14 그것은 손님에게 충분한 음식이 제공되었음을 보여줘요.

15 하지만, 케냐 사람들과 함께 하는 경우, 주인이 준비한 음식을 모두 드세요.

16 만약에 음식을 남기면, 그것은 당신이 그 음식을 좋아하지 않았다는 것을 의미해요.

17 Diego: 혹시 여기 독일어 하는 사람이 있나요?

1 Welcome to "Culture Shock"!

2 If you are interested in cultures around the world, this is the website that you are looking for!

3 You can ask and answer any questions you may have about other cultures. Let's take a look!

4 Suji: I'm very upset.

5 There is a new student from Greece in my school.

6 I asked her to be friends with me but she shook her head.

7 How rude!

8 Ocean: Calm down. I'm sure what she really meant was "yes."

9 In some countries like Greece, Turkey, and Iran, nodding your head means "no" and shaking your head means "yes."

10 Shao: Help! I'm a Chinese boy who has been invited to a Kenyan friend's house.

11 But I don't know anything about Kenya.

12 Are there any manners I need to know? Please give me some advice!

13 Clever: I heard that when Chinese people are invited to someone's house, they leave some food on their plate.

14 It shows that there was enough food for the guest.

15 However, with Kenyan people, please finish all the food the host has prepared.

16 If you leave food, it means that you didn't like it.

17 Diego: Does anyone speak German?

18 Today, I was 5 minutes late for an appointment with my German friend.

19 When I finally met him, he looked very angry.

20 He said that I must try to keep my "Termin" better. What does it mean?

21 Smile: "Termin" means "appointment" in German.

22 Germans think that it's important to be on time.

23 In Germany, there is a saying, "What is set should be kept."

24 So, please be punctual with Germans.

25 Did you find the information you needed?

26 We hope that what you have read was helpful and interesting.

27 Understanding cultural differences can make a difference in your life.

28 Please visit our website again!

구석구석지문 TEST Step 1   p.19

Project Work Step 1

1. would like to tell
2. is celebrated on, fourth
3. eat, pumpkin pie
4. Before eating, thankful for

Check Your Progress 1

1. everyone
2. I'd like to tell, myself
3. As, thin, weak
4. Because of, when I was young
5. was always, when I met
6. give up on myself
7. tried my best, more confident
8. around the world, give hope
9. real beauty inside, like, did

Check Your Progress 4~6

1. Dear
2. visiting, am, excited about
3. worries, cultural differences
4. to get some advice
5. Love

구석구석지문 TEST Step 2   p.20

Project Work Step 1

1. Hello. Our group would like to tell you about Thanksgiving Day in the United States of America.
2. It is celebrated on the fourth Thursday of November.
3. People eat turkey and pumpkin pie.
4. Before eating dinner, families share things that they are thankful for.

Check Your Progress 1

1. W: Hello, everyone.
2. Today, I'd like to tell you a story about myself.
3. As you can see, I'm very thin and weak.
4. Because of my looks, I didn't have any friends when I was young.
5. I was always very nervous when I met new people.
6. However, I didn't give up on myself.
7. I tried my best to be more confident.
8. Now, I travel around the world and give hope to many people.
9. I hope more people will find the real beauty inside themselves like I did.

Check Your Progress 4~6

1. Dear Mira,
2. Hello, Mira. I'm visiting Korea this winter and I am very excited about the trip.
3. But what worries me are the cultural differences.
4. So, I was hoping to get some advice from you.
5. Love, David

13 beg, 간청하다, 구걸하다   14 harmful, 해로운
15 butterfly, 나비   16 advice, 조언, 충고

단어 TEST Step 1   p.21

01 양, 총액	02 쓴	03 직업, 경력
04 던지다	05 약한	06 모양, 형태
07 애벌레	08 (동물의) 발톱	
09 구걸하다, 간청하다		10 편안한
11 규칙적으로	12 부지런한, 근면한	13 잠이 든
14 텅 빈; 비우다	15 집중하다	16 건강한
17 자세	18 용감한	19 씹다
20 뚱뚱한, 살찐	21 욕심 많은, 탐욕스러운	
22 해로운	23 추천하다	24 대신에
25 어리석은, 멍청한	26 호기심 많은	27 비싼
28 무례한	29 휴식; 쉬다	30 ~인 척하다
31 짠	32 무기	33 똑똑한, 영리한
34 콩	35 ~을 제거하다, ~을 없애다	

36 건강하다, 몸매가 좋다
37 ~하는 데 익숙하다   38 ~을 미루다
39 다이어트(식이요법) 중이다   40 달아나다
41 합산하다   42 ~에 싫증이 나다   43 숨이 가쁜

단어 TEST Step 2   p.22

01 bean	02 asleep	03 press
04 add	05 caterpillar	06 posture
07 claw	08 clever	09 regularly
10 weapon	11 stage	12 diligent
13 empty	14 brave	15 expensive
16 shape	17 stupid	18 greedy
19 concentrate	20 harmful	21 amount
22 instead	23 chew	24 bitter
25 comfortable	26 pretend	27 recommend
28 healthy	29 curious	30 career
31 rude	32 throw	33 weak
34 screen	35 be tired of	36 run away
37 add up	38 out of breath	39 get rid of
40 be used to -ing		41 no longer
42 put off	43 run after	

단어 TEST Step 3   p.23

1 weak, 약한   2 bitter, 쓴   3 healthy, 건강한
4 empty, 텅 빈   5 catch, 잡다   6 comfortable, 편안한
7 greedy, 탐욕스러운   8 rude, 무례한   9 claw, 발톱
10 chew, 씹다   11 scissors, 가위   12 weapon, 무기

대화문 TEST Step 1   p.24~25

Everyday English 1 A. Function Practice (1)

1. Did, see / Call, with mine / ring, know how to find / Don't worry, help, find it
2. looking for, take it / Here, Take good care of / how to care / Don't water, should get enough light

Everyday English 1 B. Listening Activity

have a word with, won't take long / Of course / concentrating, falling asleep during classes / sorry / the matter / fall asleep easliy, tried to go to bed, failed, how to get / Maybe, should try, regularly, early / will try doing

Everyday English 2 A. Function Practice

1. back, hurt / cross your legs / poor posture / Make sure you don't cross , you sit
2. shaking, okay / because of, energy drink, drank, today's test / too much, Make sure, don't drink / I won't

Everyday English 2 B. Listening Activity

eyes, important parts, more, more, glasses, dry, If, try to, rest, look outside, Make sure, computer, phone screens

In Real Life

eating only rice / on a diet, health reasons don't you / course, only eating rice, healthy / What, mean / certain amount of meat / needed to avoid / harmful / how to be on a good, too difficult / at least, beans, eggs, don't forget, vegetables

대화문 TEST Step 2   p.26~27

Everyday English 1 A. Function Practice (1)

1. G: Did you see my phone?
   B: No, I didn't. Call your phone with mine.
   G: My phone will not ring. I don't know how to find my phone.
   B: Don't worry. I'll help you. We will find it soon.
2. G: Oh, this flower is the one I'm looking for. I'll take it.
   M: Here it is. Take good care of it.
   G: I don't know how to care.
   M: Don't water it too often. And it should get enough light.

Ms. Kim: Minjae, can I have a word with you? It won't take long.

Minjae: Of course, Ms. Kim.

Ms. Kim: I saw that you are not concentrating and falling asleep during classes.

Minjae: Oh, I'm sorry.

Ms. Kim: What's the matter?

Minjae: I just can't fall asleep easily. I tried to go to bed early but failed. I don't know how to get a good night's sleep.

Ms. Kim: Maybe you should try to go to bed regularly, not early.

Minjae: Oh, then I will try doing that.

Everyday English 2 A. Function Practice

1. G: My back and leg hurt.

   B: I think it's because you always cross your legs.

   G: Oh, do you think so? I didn't know I have poor posture.

   B: Make sure you don't cross your legs when you sit in a chair.

2. G: Your hands are shaking. Are you okay?

   B: It may be because of the energy drink. I drank three cans for today's test.

   G: That's too much! Make sure you don't drink that much next time.

   B: Okay, I won't.

Everyday English 2 B. Listening Activity

M: Today, I'd like to talk about your eyes. The eyes are really important parts of our body, but more and more students are having eye problems. Some students cannot see without glasses or have dry eyes. If you do not want these problems, try to take some time to rest your eyes. When you study, try to look outside for a while. Make sure you don't look at computer or phone screens for too long.

In Real Life

Olivia: You're eating only rice, again!

Junho: You know I'm on a diet for health reasons, don't you?

Olivia: Of course. But I don't think that only eating rice will be very healthy.

Junho: What do you mean?

Olivia: Your body needs a certain amount of meat.

Junho: But people said that I needed to avoid meat.

Olivia: That's not right. They mean eating too much meat will be harmful.

Junho: I don't know how to be on a good diet! It's too difficult!

Olivia: Make sure you have at least some beans or eggs. Oh, and don't forget to eat some vegetables too.

본문 TEST Step 1 p.28~29

01 tired, enters
02 *out, breath*, tired, running
03 too, were, would, *for*
04 *gets, from, back*   05 *enters*, catches
06 *pretends*, for, Instead, *to*
07 *tastes, bigger*, more
08 let, go, bring, every
09 *fat, a few, watching*
10 *worried*, careful, get better   11 mean by that
12 yourself, fat, weak, chew
13 run, chew, need, without   14 *goes out sadly*
15 *almost emptied, enters*
16 *smiles*, has worked
17 *angry*, empty, where
18 makes, scared of, rid   19 Cat, Okay
20 *hands, pair, claws*   21 ready, take, to
22 *laughs at*, stupid
23 were, sharp, listen, longer
24 lost, biggest weapons
25 should, what, *away*
26 *tries, after, failes*, fat

본문 TEST Step 2 p.30~31

01 old, tired, enters
02 *out of breath*, tired of running from
03 too old to, were, would be, *for a while*, have an idea
04 *gets, from, back, the stage*   05 *enters*, catches
06 *pretends to beg*, too smelly for you, Instead, *gives*, to
07 *tastes it, bigger*, more
08 let me go, bring, every day
09 *house, fat, a few teeth, watching*
10 *worried*, be careful, get bitter   11 mean by that
12 Look at yourself, too fat to run, two weak to chew
13 Why, run, chew, I need, without 14 *goes out sadly*
15 *emptied, enters*   16 has worked

17 *angry*, almost empty, where you get

18 who makes, scared of your claws, get rid of them

19 Okay 20 *hands*, a *pair of, Cat cuts his*

21 ready, take, to

22 *laughs at*, stupid

23 were fast, had, I'd listen to, no longer, them

24 have lost, biggest weapons

25 listen to what you say, runs *away*

26 *to run after*, fat to run after

22 Mouse: (그는 고양이를 비웃는다.) 멍청한 고양이!

23 만약 당신이 빠르고 당신의 뾰족한 이빨과 발톱을 가지고 있다면, 나는 당신의 말을 들었겠죠! 하지만 당신은 지금은 그것들을 더 이상 가지고 있지 않아요!

24 당신은 당신의 가장 큰 무기들을 잃었어요!

25 내가 왜 당신이 지금 말하는 것을 들어야 하죠? (그는 도망 간다.)

26 Cat: 뭐? (고양이가 쥐를 쫓아가려고 하지만 실패한다.) 오! 나는 너무 뚱뚱해서 그를 쫓아갈 수가 없구나!

---

1 한 마리의 늙고 지친 쥐가 들어온다.

2 Mouse: (그는 숨이 차다.) 나는 고양이로부터 달아나는 것에 질렸어.

3 나는 나이가 너무 들어서 달릴 수 없어. 내가 만약 자유로워진다면, 행복할 텐데. (그는 잠깐 동안 생각한다.) 오, 내게 좋은 생각이 났어.

4 쥐가 무대 뒤에서 무언가를 가져온다.

5 고양이가 들어와 쥐를 잡는다

6 Mouse: (그는 비는 척한다.) 저는 너무 냄새가 나서 당신이 잡아먹을 수 없어요. 대신, 이걸 드세요. (그는 설탕 상자를 고양이에게 건넨다.)

7 Cat: (그는 그것을 맛본다. 그의 눈이 커진다.) 이게 뭐야? 더 줘!

8 Mouse: 그것은 설탕이에요. 만약에 당신이 저를 가게 해주면, 제가 매일 가지고 올게요.

9 고양이의 집이다. 지금은 뚱뚱해진 고양이가 설탕을 먹고 있다. 그는 오직 몇 개의 이빨만 가지고 있다. 개가 그를 바라보고 있다.

10 Dog: (그는 걱정된다.) 내 친구 고양이야, 조심해, 그 설탕은 써질 거야.

11 Cat: 무슨 말이야?

12 Dog: 너 스스로를 봐! 너는 너무 뚱뚱해서 달릴 수 없고, 너의 이빨은 너무 약해서 씹을 수 없잖아!

13 Cat: (그는 더 먹는다.) 왜 내가 뛰거나 씹어야 해? 나에게 필요한 건 설탕 한 가지야. 나는 그것 없이는 살 수 없어.

14 개가 슬프게 나간다.

15 고양이는 설탕 상자를 거의 비웠다. 쥐가 들어온다

16 Mouse: (그가 미소 짓는다.) 내 계획이 효과가 있는 것 같아.

17 Cat: (그는 화가 났다.) 거의 비었잖아! 쥐야, 네가 어디서 이걸 가져오는지 말해!

18 Mouse: 나에게 설탕을 만드는 친구가 하나 있어요. 하지만 그는 당신의 발톱을 무서워한답니다. 만약 당신이 그것들을 없애버리면, 당신은 곧 그를 만날 수 있을 거예요.

19 Cat: 좋아!

20 쥐가 고양이에게 가위를 건네고, 고양이는 자신의 발톱을 자른다

21 Cat: 나는 준비가 됐어! 이제 나를 너의 친구에게 데려다 줘!

1 An old and tired mouse enters.

2 Mouse: (*He is out of breath.*) I'm tired of running from Cat.

3 I am too old to run. If I were free, I would be so happy. (*He thinks for a while.*) Oh, I have an idea!

4 Mouse goes and gets something from the back of the stage.

5 Cat enters and catches Mouse.

6 Mouse: (*He pretends to beg.*) I'm too smelly for you to eat! Instead, have this, please. (*He gives a box of sugar to Cat.*)

7 Cat: (*He tastes it. His eyes get bigger.*) What is it? Give me more!

8 Mouse: It's sugar. If you let me go, I'll bring you some every day.

9 It is at Cat's house. Cat, now fat, is eating sugar. He has only a few teeth. Dog is watching him.

10 Dog: (*He is worried.*) Cat, my friend, be careful. The sugar will get bitter.

11 Cat: What do you mean by that?

12 Dog: Look at yourself! You are too fat to run, and your teeth are too weak to chew!

13 Cat: (*He eats more.*) Why should I run or chew? Sugar is the only thing I need. I can't live without it.

14 Dog goes out sadly.

15 Cat has almost emptied the box of sugar. Mouse enters.

16 Mouse: (*He smiles.*) I think my plan has worked.

17 Cat: (*He is angry.*) It's almost empty! Mouse, tell me where you get it.

18 Mouse: I have a friend who makes sugar. But he's scared of your claws. If you get rid of them, you can meet him soon.

19 Cat: Okay!

20 Mouse hands Cat a pair of scissors and Cat cuts his claws.

21 Cat: I'm ready! Now take me to your friend!

22 Mouse: (*He laughs at Cat.*) You stupid cat!

23 If you were fast, and had your sharp teeth and claws, I'd listen to you. But you no longer have them now!

24 You have lost your biggest weapons!

25 Why should I listen to what you say now? (*He runs away.*)

26 Cat: What! (*He tries to run after Mouse, but fails.*) Oh! I'm too fat to run after him!

구석구석지문 TEST Step 1   p.38

Think and Write B

1. diligent, put, off
2. get up early
3. always say, 10 more minutes
4. If, were, would have, focus of
5. course, be late for
6. put off, would finish
7. not good ones
8. will have to, more diligent, to be
9. From now on, things to do
10. am, going to get up, earlier

Check Your Progress

1. wrong, look worried
2. have lost
3. search carefully
4. course, inside, saved, for a long time
5. did, put, Why did, bring, much money
6. how to get, back
7. have to, make sure, a lot of money

구석구석지문 TEST Step 2   p.39

Think and Write B

1. I am not diligent and I put things off.
2. I cannot get up early in the morning.
3. I always say, "In 10 more minutes..."
4. If I were more diligent, I would have breakfast and would focus on my classes.
5. Of course, I would not be late for school.
6. I would not put off my homework and would finish it.
7. I know my habits are not good ones.

---

8. I think I will have to make a plan to be more diligent and to be a good student.

9. From now on, I will make a list of things to do.

10. I am also going to get up 30 minutes earlier every morning.

Check Your Progress

1. G: What's wrong? You look worried.

2. B: Oh, I think I have lost 50 thousand won.

3. G: What? Did you search carefully?

4. B: Of course, I had it in my bag, inside my pencil case! I've saved it for a long time!

5. G: Why did you put it there? Why did you bring that much money to school?

6. B: That money was for my new soccer ball. I don't know how to get my money back.

7. G: First you have to talk to your teacher. Then make sure you don't bring a lot of money to school again.